The Dow Jones-Irwin Guide To
Using IRAs

The Dow Jones-Irwin Guide To
Using IRAs

James Michael Ullman
and
Norman Bercoon, CPA

DOW JONES–IRWIN
Homewood, Illinois 60430

This publication is designed to provide accurate and authoritative information in regard to the subject matter covered. It is sold with the understanding that the publisher is not engaged in rendering legal, accounting, or other professional service. If legal advice or other expert assistance is required, the services of a competent professional person should be sought.

From a Declaration of Principles jointly adopted by a Committee of the American Bar Association and a Committee of Publishers.

ISBN 0-87094-689-7
ISBN 0-87094-774-5 (paperback)

Library of Congress Catalog Card No. 85-61900

Printed in the United States of America

2 3 4 5 6 7 8 9 0 K 3 2 1 0 9 8 7 6

Preface

Individual Retirement Arrangements (IRAs) are one of the most powerful personal finance tools ever made available to Americans who work for a living.

They can benefit people in all income brackets, and they are the first and only tax shelter millions of Americans of relatively modest means will ever enjoy. As *Chicago Sun–Times* financial columnist Edwin Darby observed, "The IRA device is without doubt the greatest tax benefit accorded the middle class since the Constitution was amended in 1913 to permit federal taxation of incomes."

Learning to use the IRA program is like learning to use any other tool. The more you understand IRAs—their limitations, the rules and regulations surrounding them, and your obligations with an IRA as well as the many investment opportunities they offer—the more effectively you can use them.

Although the IRA program has been simplified over the years, there's nothing simple about it. IRAs are creatures of the U.S. Tax Code, and learning about them takes time and effort. But by understanding how IRAs work and the kinds of investments you can make with them, you can fully harness the power of this everyman's tax shelter.

When you open an IRA, you're making a long-term commitment and assuming serious obligations. There are tax penalties if you break the rules, whether through ignorance or design. Consequently, it's in your own best interest to have a working knowledge of the laws, rules, and regulations covering IRAs, especially those covering your own circumstances.

Congress intended IRAs to be a simple form of retirement plan for the unsophisticated taxpayer. Since IRAs were authorized in 1974, however, the technical literature about them has expanded continuously. As with almost all sections of the Internal Revenue Code, the questions, explanations, and controversies over the IRA section, together with regulations, pronouncements, and decisions, proliferate endlessly.

The Commerce Clearing House takes more than 150 pages in its widely used tax services to describe this "simple" retirement program. The Research Institute of America describes IRAs in about 77 pages (including the regulations) of rather fine print. The Bureau of National Affairs in its "Tax Management" portfolio on IRAs, used mostly by tax lawyers and accountants, devotes more than 150 pages, many in small print, to this subject. Prentice-Hall and other widely known services have also published extensively on IRAs.

Despite all this analysis by professional technical writers, there are so many gray areas in the rules and regulations on IRAs that individual problems and cases continually find their way into the upper levels of the IRS and even the courts for interpretation and guidelines.

Nobody knows the answer to every question related to IRAs, and new questions are being asked every day. There are always areas of tax law where no clear understanding of what the law means exists until definitive decisions or rulings are made. Moreover, tax laws themselves are constantly being revised by Congress. Each time a new law is passed, many old questions are no longer of concern, while new questions are raised.

For these reasons, this book won't attempt to clear up every tax question related to IRAs. However, it will give everyone who has an IRA or is thinking of setting one up a good working understanding of the basic rules covering IRAs. It will also be a good general working reference to some of the more complicated points of tax law that bear on IRAs.

For most readers, this will be enough. But if you venture into areas of IRA law where the answers to your questions are not clearly set forth in this book (or in the IRS publications cited in this book), you should seek professional advice. We also try to point out circumstances where it would be a good idea to get professional advice before taking any action.

Even the decision as to where and what kind of an IRA you set up is important. It's true you can transfer or roll over assets from one IRA to another if you don't like the first IRA. But although you shouldn't hesitate to move IRAs for good reason, there are hazards inherent in moving them too often. If a technical error is made during a move, you could suffer inconvenience or even be required to pay costly penalties. Unless you just want a temporary "parking place," presumably when you open an IRA it's with the hope that it will meet your needs for a reasonable period of time.

And there's always the inertia factor. Once an IRA is established, you may allow it to remain with that sponsor for years no matter how poorly it is doing simply because moving it would be too much trouble. So it pays to ask the right questions before opening any IRA.

Unfortunately, there is no "perfect" IRA investment, any more than there are any "perfect" investments in general. Every investment represents a compromise of some kind. There's also the question of whether an investment is appropriate for you—and that depends on who and what you are.

The law that allows everyone who works to have IRAs has triggered a marketing battle of epic proportions. Understandably, the banks, savings institutions, mutual funds, brokerage houses, and insurance companies that want you to open IRAs with them are emphasizing the strong points of their products, while ignoring those of their competitors. Trying to weigh the merits of the many kinds of IRAs being offered is further complicated by new IRA plans constantly being introduced.

Also, the best investment option or options for you may change over the years, just as you will change. What it adds up to is that once you understand what the investment options are, only you can decide on the investments that best meet your needs.

James Michael Ullman
Norman Bercoon

Contents

Contributions. Backup Income Tax Withholding. No Withholding on IRAs—Until You Take Money Out. Have Contributions Credited to the Correct Year. Premiums for IRA Deposits a "Gray Area." Be Wary of Unusual Investment Arrangements. How Long Should You Keep IRA Records?

also Be Made within 60 Days. These Rollovers Can Be Made at Any Time. To Keep the "Roll Back" Option, Don't Mix Assets. You Needn't Roll All the Assets Over. Nondeductible Voluntary Contributions Cannot Be Rolled Over. Deductible Voluntary Contributions Can Be Rolled Over. Rollovers of Some Partial Distributions Now Allowed. Rollover of Property Received in a Distribution. Annuity-to-IRA Rollover. Keogh-to-IRA Rollover. Rollover by a Surviving Spouse. Employer Rollovers Pros and Cons if You're Still Working: *If You Have a Choice, Should You Leave the Money in the Company Plan and Allow It to Grow There Tax-Free for as Long as the Company Allows It? Should You Roll the Entire Employer Plan Distribution into an IRA? Should You Take Part of the Money, Pay Tax on It, and Roll the Remainder into an IRA? If You Roll All or Any Portion of the Employer Plan Distribution into an IRA, Should You Preserve the Option to Roll It Back to Some Other Employer Plan by Always Keeping These Assets Separate from Your Other Assets?* Employer Rollover Pros and Cons When You Retire: *Should You Take the Lump-Sum Distribution or Regular Monthly Benefits for the Rest of Your Life? If You Decide to Take the Distribution, Should You Roll All of It into an IRA or Keep It All? Should You Take Part of the Distribution and Roll the Other Part Over?* Weighing the Tax Bite from 10-Year Averaging. If in Doubt, Roll It Over. Spouse Must Now Consent to a Lump-Sum Distribution.

11 Age 59½ and After: Taking Money out of Your IRA 165

Age 59½ an "IRA Milestone." IRAs as an Income-Leveling Device. Pros and Cons of Taking It All: *First, Consider the Tax Consequences. Next, Look at Yourself.* IRA Distributions and Social Security. After You Reach Age 70: *Taking Everything Out. Buying an Insurance Annuity. Paying the IRA Out to Yourself in Regular Payments over a Permissible Period.* Using the IRS Multiples—Tables for Individuals. Multiples for Two People. You Don't Have to Stretch Out the Payments. Don't Wait until the Last Minute to Decide. Penalties for Excess Accumulations after Age 70: *Since 1985, the Minimum*

Withdrawal Penalty Apparently Applies to Each IRA You Own. Backup Withholding on IRA Distributions. Distribution Choices if You Are an IRA Beneficiary.

Investors: *Don't Invest in Anything You Don't Fully Understand. This Applies to the Simplest IRA Investments as Well as the Most Complicated. Don't Invest in Anything You Don't Feel Comfortable With. As a Rule (but not Always!) the Higher the Return on an Investment, the Greater the Risk. The Younger You Are, the More Time You Have to Correct Mistakes. The Closer You Get to Retirement, the More Cautious You Should Be. In General, Be Wary of Investment Concepts that Haven't Had Time to Establish a Track Record.* IRA Investments to Avoid. IRAs at Banks and Savings Institutions: *Savings Account Pros and Cons. Penalties not All the Same. What Are Market Rates? Which Way Will Interest Rates Go? Kinds of Savings Accounts. Money Market Deposit Accounts (MMDAs). Long-Distance Banking. How Compounding Affects IRA Growth. Comparing Rates and Yields: When Lower May Be Higher. "Simple" Interest: When More May Be Less. Multiple Rate IRAs.* Mutual Fund IRAs: *Load and No-Load Funds. Load and No-Load Distinctions Blurring. Read the Fund's Prospectus. Mutual Fund Performance. Fund Families and Types of Funds. Money Market Mutual Funds. Switching Strategies. Learning More about Mutual Funds. Self-Directed Accounts, Zeros, and Other Brokerage House IRAs. Self-Directed IRAs. Is a Self-Directed Account Right for You? When Does a Self-Directed Account Pay? Zero-Coupon Bonds. Limited Partnership IRAs. Other Self-Directed IRAs. Brokered CDs. SIPC Insurance Coverage at Brokerage Houses* Insurance Company IRAs: *Costs May Vary Greatly. Insurance IRA Pros and Cons. Rules Similar to Those for Other IRAs. Buying Retirement Income with an Annuity. Insurance in Connection with IRAs.* Individual Retirement Bonds. Collectibles.

Part One

HARNESSING YOUR IRA POWER

1

The IRA Season:
The New "Rites of Spring"

In the short time the Individual Retirement Arrangement (IRA) program has been open to all Americans who work, it has created a new American financial tradition—a clearly defined "IRA season" that is fast becoming to some IRA sponsors what Christmas is to department stores.

The season begins in January, as people seeking to maximize their tax-sheltered earnings contribute to their IRAs as early in the new year as they can. Traffic begins building to a peak in March and early April as the deadline for filing federal income tax returns for the previous year (and making IRA contributions for it) nears. The final days before April 15 are marked by an advertising and promotional blitz by IRA sponsors, and some institutions remain open nights and weekends to handle last-minute crowds.

Behind this mounting activity is a rising appreciation by IRA sponsors of the immense potential of the IRA program—not only do people in it contribute more money year after year, but many people who can afford IRAs still don't have them—as well as the public's growing understanding of the power of this personal finance tool.

WHY IRA ACTIVITY IS GROWING

Investments in IRAs rose from $32 billion in 1982 to an estimated $132 billion at the end of 1984, and sponsors reported heavy traffic during the early months of 1985.

For consumers, the first and most obvious reason for beginning to use the IRA program has been to put away more money for retirement. This is what Congress had in mind when it created the program and what sponsors usually stress in promotional materials emphasizing how regular contributions over a long period of time could bring spectacular gains.

However, as interest in the IRA program mounted, people began to perceive that IRAs can be a great tax shelter and a vehicle for alternative investments in addition to being a potential source of retirement income. In fact, many people who expect to have their retirement needs met through other sources are using IRAs primarily for these other purposes.

IRAs are also becoming recognized as especially effective financial tools for people between the ages of 59½ and 70½, when you can withdraw as much or as little as you like from an IRA without paying a tax penalty.

The older people who are still working are, the more likely they are to have an IRA or IRAs. A 1984 study by the Employee Benefit Research Institute in Washington and the U.S. Department of Health and Human Services found that the median age of IRA contributors is about 46, compared with about 36 for the population as a whole, and the highest use of IRAs is between ages 55 and 64. It also found that half the people who set up IRAs did so primarily for the tax deduction.

Another growing use for an IRA is to shelter a lump-sum distribution received from a company retirement plan. Because of the IRA program, more companies are allowing employees who retire—or are terminated after working long enough to earn retirement benefits—to take their retirement money in a lump-sum distribution instead of as a pension.

Many people have their first contact with the IRA program when given a lump-sum retirement distribution—sometimes with little warning, if they have been terminated from their jobs. Simply deciding whether to roll the money into an IRA or to pay tax on it right away and start using it can be a difficult decision, and often the sum involved is larger than the person has ever handled before.

Finally, if you are relatively young and start early enough, IRAs can be a real retirement fortune-building mechanism. Regular contributions over time can build IRAs large enough to provide a retirement income surpassing what you could enjoy through social security combined with most pension plans.

For IRA sponsors, one lure of the IRA program is that most contributors keep putting more money in. As a rule, the IRA customer is a repeat customer, adding more to the IRA each year. As every businessperson knows, this is the best kind of customer to have.

Another attraction is the many potential new customers. According to the Investment Company Institute, some 72 percent of U.S. households still don't have IRAs. And while about 43 percent of these say they lack the money and another 16 percent aren't eligible, that still leaves a sizable number of prospects who might be persuaded to open IRAs.

The IRA program also gives sponsors an opportunity for "cross-selling"—that is, ultimately selling other financial services to people whose first contact with the institution is to open an IRA.

As a result, each succeeding "IRA season" finds competition for IRA contributions more intense than before—and the more money sponsors spend to promote their investments, the greater the participation in the program.

IRA FUNDAMENTALS ARE EASY TO UNDERSTAND

One reason the IRA program has grown so rapidly is that while it is complex in many of its details, the fundamentals are easy to grasp.

No matter what kind of work you do, an IRA allows you to shelter up to $2,000 of earned income from federal taxation each year. If you have a nonworking spouse, you can set up a so-called spousal IRA, which for you and your spouse together has an annual contribution limit of $2,250. And a working couple can contribute (and deduct) up to $2,000 of earnings each, for a maximum of $4,000 a year.

More important the longer you maintain your IRA, the interest, dividends, or capital gains it earns is sheltered until you're ready to withdraw some or all of the money in it—and then you pay tax only on what you withdraw.

Congress made these economic opportunities available to all Americans who work for a living beginning in 1982. Before that, you weren't allowed to contribute to an IRA if you participated in a pension, retirement, or profit-sharing plan at work. (However, if you received a lump-sum payment from a plan at work, you were allowed to postpone your tax bill by rolling it over into an IRA.)

But since 1982, IRAs could be opened by anyone who earns income for services whether they are covered by a pension plan on the job or not. This includes self-employed people with so-called Keogh plans, which now in many respects are similar to qualified employer retirement plans. If you have a Keogh plan, you can have an IRA too.

If you're one of the more than 40 million Americans with a qualified retirement or profit-sharing plan at work, you also have the option of making your IRA contribution to your employer's plan if your employer will allow it, and then deducting the contribution on your tax return.

One important difference between money in IRAs and the money you accumulate in most other ways is that you cannot pass the bulk of it on to generations of your descendants. Sooner or later the money in your IRA must be withdrawn— either by you or by your heirs—and as it is withdrawn, it must be taxed at ordinary income rates.

But even if inflation has increased living costs over that span, you'd probably have more money for your retirement than you could have acquired in any other way. Because you paid no tax on your IRA's earnings while it was growing, if you invested well its growth should have exceeded the inflation rate. With after tax dollars you don't need for yourself after you retire, you could make investments to leave to your heirs. Even if there's nothing left for your heirs, your IRA may have saved them the expense of helping to support you.

Opening an IRA can be as simple as signing a custodial or trustee agreement with an IRA sponsor. When you file your tax return, you subtract your IRA contribution or contributions from your earnings before income taxes are calculated.

There is a special line on the first page of the return for listing the amount contributed, and you may use either the short or the long form.

You can invest your IRA contributions in a wide variety of ways, including savings accounts, mutual funds, insurance annuities, and even real estate and oil and gas partnerships—just so you invest through a sponsor with a plan that meets IRS requirements. An IRA can also be set up as a self-directed trust held by a custodian, allowing you to buy or sell stocks or make a wide variety of other investments.

Under current rules, about the only IRA investments barred by law are life insurance policies, collectibles, and certain instruments pledged for indebtedness.

What many people who already have IRAs don't realize is that you have a lot of flexibility in changing investments and moving money around (assuming a particular IRA's sponsor doesn't penalize you unduly for moving it.) You can also have as many IRAs as you wish, just so long as your total IRA contributions for any year don't exceed the limit.

And money you invest in your IRA needn't come directly from your earnings. It can come from your savings or any other source.

However, money you contribute to your IRA should be money you know you'll be able to get along without for a while. Unless you're disabled, if you withdraw money before age 59½, you must pay a tax penalty to the IRS. This penalty isn't so large that it should deter you from opening an IRA—but it wouldn't make sense to put money in an IRA if you thought there would be a good chance you'd have to take it out soon, or if doing so would work a financial hardship on you or on your family.

And while Uncle Sam gives you a big tax break with an IRA, he won't pay for your mistakes. If you make a bad investment and suffer a loss, you won't be able to deduct it from your current income. Your IRA will simply be worth that much less.

COMPOUNDED GROWTH EFFECTIVE AT ANY AGE

The power of compounding is well understood by professional money managers. Thanks to the IRA program, it is now becoming much better understood by growing numbers of middle-class Americans.

Assuming your IRA investment is profitable, it can expand your capital with ever-increasing momentum by working much as compound interest does. (And if yours is an interest-paying IRA, in most cases that's exactly what you're earning.) Periodic investments begin to grow at a surprisingly rapid pace in even a short time.

People nearing retirement can still build a fund large enough to provide a fairly substantial new source of retirement income. Middle-aged people willing and able to stick to an IRA program can easily build a six-figure retirement fund—and younger people in a position to afford the contributions can probably build a seven-figure fund.

Tables 1–1 through 1–3 illustrate how $2,000, $2,250, and $4,000 invested in an IRA at the start of each year would grow at various constant rates of return. (For tables that enable you to calculate year-by-year IRA growth for any sum at various interest rates, both with regular amounts added each year and for a lump sum, see Appendix A.)

If you could invest $2,000 at the start of each year at a constant 10 percent return, your IRA would grow to $35,062 in 10 years, $69,898 in 15 years, $126,004 in 20 years, $361,886 in 30 years, and $973,702 in 40 years. If you're married, have a nonworking spouse, and maintain a spousal IRA with a

TABLE 1–1 ■ Maximum Individual IRA Contribution (How $2,000 Invested at Start of Each Year Would Grow at Various Rates of Return)

Plan Years Completed	6 percent	8 percent	10 percent	12 percent	14 percent
5	$ 11,950	$ 12,670	$ 13,430	$ 14,230	$ 15,070
10	27,942	31,290	35,062	39,308	44,088
15	49,344	58,648	69,898	83,506	99,960
20	77,984	98,844	126,004	161,396	207,536
25	116,312	157,908	216,362	298,666	414,664
30	167,602	244,690	361,886	540,584	813,474
35	236,240	372,204	596,252	966,926	1,581,344
40	328,094	559,560	973,702	1,718,284	3,059,816

TABLE 1–2 ■ **Maximum Spousal IRA Contribution** *(How $2,250 Invested at Start of Each Year Would Grow at Various Rates of Return)*

Plan Years Completed	6 percent	8 percent	10 percent	12 percent	14 percent
5	$ 13,444	$ 14,254	$ 15,109	$ 16,009	$ 16,954
10	31,435	35,201	39,445	44,221	49,599
15	55,512	65,979	78,635	93,960	112,455
20	87,732	111,200	141,755	181,571	233,478
25	130,851	177,647	243,407	355,999	466,497
30	188,552	275,276	407,122	608,157	915,158
35	265,770	418,730	670,784	1,087,792	1,779,012
40	369,106	629,505	1,095,415	1,933,070	3,442,293

TABLE 1–3 ■ **Maximum Working Couple Contribution** *(How $4,000 Invested at Start of Each Year Would Grow at Various Rates of Return)*

Plan Years Completed	6 percent	8 percent	10 percent	12 percent	14 percent
5	$ 23,900	$ 25,340	$ 26,860	$ 28,460	$ 30,140
10	55,884	62,580	70,124	78,616	88,176
15	96,688	117,296	139,796	167,040	199,920
20	155,968	197,688	252,008	322,792	415,072
25	232,634	315,816	432,724	597,332	829,328
30	335,204	489,380	723,772	1,081,168	1,626,948
35	472,480	744,408	1,192,504	1,933,852	3,162,688
40	656,188	1,119,120	1,947,404	3,436,404	6,119,632

maximum $2,250 annual contribution, your IRA's growth will be that much greater. At a constant 10 percent return, you'd have $39,445 in 10 years, $141,755 in 20 years, $407,122 in 30 years, and $1,095,415 in 40 years.

Working couples able to contribute $2,000 each to an IRA would be able to build a six-figure fund within 15 years—and, if in a position to start early enough, would stand a good chance of building a retirement fund in the seven-figure neighborhood.

However, it's not necessary to invest the maximum each year in order to build a substantial IRA. Even a modest investment can grow to surprising size.

Contributing just $25 a month at a constant 10 percent return would build an IRA worth $19,984 in 20 years, $56,513 in 30 years, and $158,103 in 40 years. By contributing $50 a month you could accumulate $39,968 in 20 years, $113,026 in 30 years, and $316,206 in 40 years.

RETIREMENT INCOME CREATES MORE LEVERAGE

For many people, the numbers in those tables don't even tell the whole story. If you're going to use an IRA to help finance your retirement, your IRA investments are further leveraged by the retirement income your IRAs will buy.

At an average 10 percent return, a 55-year-old worker contributing $2,000 to an IRA at the start of each year for 10 years could enjoy an extra annual income for the following 20 years of $4,118, for a total payout of $82,360. If the 55-year-old's spouse also works and contributes the $2,000 maximum, their $40,000 investment would give them an annual retirement income of $8,236, for a total $164,720 payout.

A 45-year-old worker could buy a retirement income of $14,800 a year, a total payout of $296,000; a 45-year-old working couple could earn a retirement income of $29,600, a $592,000 payout.

The sooner you start, the greater the power of this leverage. A worker at age 25 investing $2,000 a year for 40 years would earn a retirement income of $114,371 for the next 20 years, a total payout of $2,287,420.

Of course, interest rates and investment returns could fall in the future. Even though interest rates in the mid-1980s were down substantially from the peak of early in the decade, they were still historically high. If they fall further, many of the investment returns in the tables in this book may not be available with reasonable safety.

But if that happened, it would probably mean the overall inflation rate is under control. That would be good news. A low, stable inflation rate would make it easier to plan for retirement without worrying about the risk of inflation eroding your retirement buying power. On the other hand, higher inflation and interest rates in the future could produce even higher returns than those in the tables.

As far as IRA investments are concerned, future return doesn't matter as much as earning a tax-sheltered return that at least matches and preferably exceeds the inflation rate. If you do that, you'll still come out ahead in terms of real purchasing power.

WHY CONGRESS WANTS IRAs FOR EVERYONE

One reason Congress made it possible for all workers to have IRAs was to encourage people to save more money. There's concern over the fact that the United States has one of the lowest personal savings rates among major industrialized nations. More savings are needed to rebuild our aging industrial plants and finance home buyers.

There's also concern over inadequacies in the private pension system. Although the system has grown substantially, many people still receive little or no help from private pensions when they retire. A government study found that of people retiring in the early 1980s, only 55.7 percent of the married couples, 41.3 percent of the unmarried men, and 43.1 percent of the unmarried women had either private or public employment pensions. Only 33 percent of married men and their wives and 15.9 percent of unmarried people had private or public pension income more than $400 a month.

But there's no doubt that Congress also viewed IRAs as a way to take some of the pressure off the social security system.

Social security isn't likely to go down the tube, but it has great financial problems. It was never intended as a full retirement system. Rather, it is seen as one of "three tiers" of retirement income; the other tiers are pension income and asset income from investments and from IRAs, Keogh plans, and similar programs.

In 1983 Congress made several changes to bolster social security. One of them now requires higher-income beneficiaries to include up to half of their social security benefits as taxable income.

However, great pressures on the system remain. There's no doubt that each Congress and administration will somehow keep social security checks arriving on schedule. But with other pressures building to curb federal budget deficits, it's likely the trend will be toward smaller cost-of-living adjustments and bigger penalties for retiring early. (By the year 2027, another change in the 1983 law will extend the age at which a retiree can receive full benefits from 65 to 67.)

For younger workers, the future looks grim. The social security tax has already risen from under 2 percent to a level of 14.1 percent in 1985, and after further increases it will reach 15.3 percent by 1990. At the same time, the wage base on which social security tax is applied has also been rising. For two reasons, the situation will get worse. One is that retired people are living much longer—and in the current system, an American worker is repaid lifetime contributions to social security in about two years. Everything paid after that must come from taxes on people still working. The other reason is our declining population rate, which means fewer people are entering the work force to pay the tax. This gives rise to what *The Wall Street Journal* called "a time bomb ticking away in the system"—the graying of the U.S. population means that fewer and fewer workers must support more and more social security recipients.

Without major changes, the time bomb will explode early in the 21st century. The bulge of today's young workers will put a tremendous burden on the system as they become retirees. The burden may be so great that their children and grandchildren may find it impossible to pay for their support through social security.

When the system began, there were about 40 Americans at work for every American receiving social security. Today, every retiree is supported by 3.2 active workers. This could drop to 3.0 by the year 2000—and, according to one Social Security Administration forecast, this ratio could plunge to just 2 by the year 2055. If that happened without major adjustments in the system, workers and employers combined would have to pay as much as 43 percent of wages subject to social security to support retirees—and it's not likely they'd be willing or able to do that.

If you are a young adult, you must make the prudent assumption that when you retire, your social security benefits when adjusted for inflation will be relatively less than those enjoyed by your parents and grandparents. On the other hand, through the IRA program, Congress is giving you an opportunity to make up the difference—and then some. Through the magic of long-term, tax-sheltered compounding, each dollar you put into an IRA today will multiply many times. If you are 22 years old, for instance, every $1 placed in an IRA earning a constant 10 percent return today would be worth more than $60 when you are age 65.

IRA CEILINGS COULD GO UP AGAIN

If history is any guide, there's a good chance the IRA contribution limits will be increased again in the future, especially if inflation rates turn back up.

Liberalizing rules and expanding benefits over the years has been the history of both the IRA program and the first personal pension plan, the Keogh program for self-employed people (doctors, lawyers, architects, writers, small-business owners, and the like).

In this country, the personal pension plan idea began in 1962 when Congress authorized Keogh plans for the self-employed in a law called H.R. 10. The goal was to give self-employed people an opportunity to build tax-sheltered pension plans similar in many respects to employer-paid retirement plans, where money also grows tax free until withdrawn.

At first there was so much red tape that hardly anyone signed up. And originally, Keogh participants were limited to sheltering $2,500 or 10 percent of their earned income, whichever was smaller. But rules were simplified, and in 1974 Keogh limits were raised to $7,500 or 15 percent of earned income in a monumental law called the Employment Retirement Income Security Act of 1974 (ERISA).

ERISA also authorized the first IRA program. It was aimed at allowing workers without pension plans on the job to build their own retirement funds, and it included rollover provisions that gave people pension portability. In part, IRAs were modeled on the Canadian Registered Retirement Program in effect since 1957.

The original IRA ceilings were the lesser of $1,500 or 15 percent of income. Later Congress created the spousal IRA, with a combined $1,750 limit. To qualify, one spouse had to be a worker not participating in a plan on the job, and the other had to be unemployed, with no earned income. Congress also simplified IRA rules and allowed employers to set up IRAs for their employees if they wished.

The Economic Recovery Tax Act of 1981 made the IRA "universal," greatly expanded the program, and thereby changed its nature. In addition to raising IRA contribution limits, it opened the program to people who already participated in plans at work.

It also increased Keogh contribution limits, which were further increased by the Tax Equity and Fiscal Responsibility Act of 1982 (TEFRA). In many respects, Keogh plans (discussed in Chapter 12) are now the same as employer-paid company plans, and IRAs are now a universal retirement plan option for everyone who works. Since 1981 several proposals have been made in Congress to raise IRA contribution limits. As IRAs become more widely held, support for these proposals is likely to increase.

The success of the IRA program has also inspired special interest groups to press for special-purpose IRAs to fund such things as home purchases or college educations.

WILL THE GOVERNMENT TAKE IT ALL AWAY?

Some critics have counseled against investing in IRAs on grounds that the government might change the rules one day and begin taxing money people thought was safely sheltered— or might begin paying lower (or no) social security benefits to people with IRAs.

This is possible but not likely. The more people who have IRAs, and the more the money in them grows and becomes an important part of their financial holdings, the stronger the political constituency for IRAs will become. This constituency also includes banks, savings institutions, life insurance companies, and the Wall Street financial establishment. It may never become as powerful as the constituency that has developed around social security, but it could develop considerable political muscle—certainly enough to keep the IRA program alive and assure that its beneficiaries are not penalized for their thrift.

WHAT IS IN THIS BOOK

This book will show you what can be accomplished with the IRA program and will suggest some new ways to use it. It also shows how to maximize the return on your IRA by following a few commonsense practices. Some of these could be as or more important in determining how large your IRAs grow than the kinds of IRA investments you make.

In the beginning, IRAs were a red tape nightmare. Rules and procedures have been simplified since IRAs were first authorized. Nevertheless, in many respects they are still quite complicated. Unfortunately, many people you consult for more information about IRAs don't know as much about how IRAs work as they should. For your own protection and to give you the confidence needed to use the IRA program to its fullest potential, you should become familiar with the basic IRA rules.

In simple language, the book explains how IRAs work. It stresses the importance of understanding your rights and obligations and of avoiding costly technical mistakes in handling your IRA or IRAs.

The first section deals with IRAs in general. It explains why IRAs are great investments, discusses ways in which IRAs can be tailored to your needs, and shows how following some consistent investment practices can maximize your IRA return.

The second section is a comprehensive discussion of technical aspects of the IRA program. Everyone who owns an IRA should become familiar with the material in Chapter 5, which summarizes the basic information about IRAs, as well as Chapter 6, which discusses how to avoid problems with the IRS. Other chapters deal with IRAs and women, rollovers and transfers, employer pension plans, and other personal retirement plans.

Chapter 10 discusses rollovers into IRAs from employer plans, for many people the most important financial decision they will ever make. If you're nearing age 70½, when you'll soon be required to start distributing your IRA to yourself, you should read Chapter 11. It explains the new and greatly liberalized IRS distribution rules and the minimum amounts that must be withdrawn each year to avoid costly penalties.

This chapter also includes a discussion of what will become a subject of growing importance—the options for people who are IRA beneficiaries.

The book's final section covers specific IRA investments, moving from setting up an IRA and where to get advice to what your IRA investment options are. These options have significantly expanded, due in part to financial deregulation and in part to the efforts of IRA marketers to create new financial products for investors with $2,000 or less to commit at one time. Deregulation has profoundly changed the kinds of IRAs offered by banks and savings institutions, and tables in this section will help you compare those IRA investments.

The appendixes contain two potentially useful sets of tables for IRA investors. One set enables you to project the growth of any sized IRA, with or without regular additions, for up to 40 years at various interest rates. The other is the set of life expectancy tables used by the IRS to calculate the minimum you must withdraw from an IRA each year after required distributions begin. The multiples on these tables are also used to calculate the minimums that IRA beneficiaries must withdraw if they elect this method of distribution.

ABOUT THE TABLES IN THIS BOOK

Many tables in this book project what would happen to an IRA at a theoretical "constant rate of return" in the future. These examples are for purposes of making general estimates and comparisons only and obviously would be difficult or impossible to attain in the real world.

As discussed in Appendix A, these examples (as well as examples in other books and in literature prepared by IRA sponsors) are based on idealized conditions, which in many cases could not be achieved in the real world. For most investments, it's unlikely that you could earn the same constant rate over a long period of time, and you may not be able to make the contributions or withdrawals on the dates the tables assume you would.

Nevertheless, these tables will help you make reasonably accurate estimates of what you can accomplish with your own IRA program under different conditions and then make realistic plans based on these estimates.

Many examples in this book are based on an assumed 10 percent return, which could be achieved with safety in even the most conservative IRA investments when this material was prepared.

Market conditions can change quickly. A surge in interest rates would make higher returns more typical, while a drop in rates would lower the return IRA investors (and all other investors) could anticipate on fixed-yielding investments, especially CDs, money market mutual funds, bond funds, and investments in all types of bonds, including zero-coupon bonds. Do *not* assume that returns available when you read this book are still typical. It is likely that, to at least some degree, they will be higher or lower.

2

Why IRAs Are
Great Investments

Although since 1982, the IRA program has been open to everyone who works, many people are still unaware of its advantages. Among these are the following:

- It cuts your tax bill each year.
- It shelters the interest, dividends, and capital gains your IRA earns until you're ready to start withdrawing money—which can be any time between ages 59½ and April 1 following the year in which you become 70½. (At that time, you *must* start withdrawing.) The longer these tax-sheltered earnings keep piling up, the bigger the fund you can build.
- It's completely under your control. You decide where to invest your money—and can count on having it when you retire or decide to use it for any other purpose. No matter how often you change jobs, your IRA is always there, making it especially useful for people who change jobs often.
- You don't have to contribute each year if you can't afford to or don't want to. As far as the IRS is concerned, you can put as much or as little in your IRA (or IRAs) as you wish so long as you don't exceed the annual contribution limits.

- You'll be better prepared for retirement if it's forced on you before you're ready. Many people don't retire because they want to. Either they must stop working for health reasons or they're put out to pasture before they wish to retire.
- You can switch investments from one IRA to another as circumstances change.
- You have great flexibility in adapting to changes in your income or financial circumstances during the crucial years between ages 59½ and 70½. If you're still earning compensation, you can continue contributing to your IRA during these years even though you're making withdrawals.
- It gives aggressive investors the same tax advantage held by mutual funds and institutional investors over individual investors. In making selling decisions, you can concentrate on timing. Because the IRA isn't subject to capital gains taxes, you don't have to worry about whether gains are short or long term.
- It can be inherited by anyone (or any number of people) you designate if you die before the money in it is exhausted. If your spouse is your designated beneficiary and you die before distributions from your IRA have begun, your spouse may delay taking distributions until the year you would have reached age 70½ if he or she wishes.
- If you own a business, you can set up an IRA for yourself without having to include your employees, which you must do with a Keogh plan.
- If used for retirement income, the IRA's payout can be structured so you'll never outlive it.
- It can be your basic private retirement program if you have no other pension or retirement plan except social security.
- It is liquid at all times. Although you may have to pay penalties for taking money out before you are age 59½, it provides easy access to funds in an emergency. If the money has been compounding tax sheltered in the IRA long enough, even with the penalty your overall return may be higher than on taxable investments of comparable safety.

- It gives you an opportunity to further diversify your investments and can complement hard-asset investments, real estate, or other investments that may not be in an advantageous market cycle when you must liquidate.

HOW INFLATION ERODES BUYING POWER

Whether used for retirement or some other purpose, for many people an IRA's main value will be to help keep up with—and hopefully beat—inflation.

Because an IRA's earnings are compounding tax sheltered, you have an opportunity to increase the real purchasing power of the assets in the IRA. During periods of high inflation, this gives the IRA a much better chance of at least maintaining purchasing power than most of your other financial assets; during periods of relatively low inflation, its purchasing power should actually grow.

It is particularly during retirement that an IRA can help offset inflation and maintain decent living standards. For most people, social security and their other pension benefits combined (if they have other benefits) may not be enough for a comfortable retirement for long—if at all. Many pension plans are of the "defined benefit" type. They spell out the benefits you're to receive. A predetermined formula specifies what your retirement income will be —usually so much per month or year, or a proportion of your past income.

The trouble is that there's often no way to adjust for inflation after you retire. A 1983 Department of Labor study found that between 1973 and 1979, postretirement increases for retirees amounted to only about two fifths of the rise in the consumer price index. Earlier studies found that between 1966 and 1977, consumer prices were rising almost three times as fast as the average annual per capita pension plan benefits.

As inflation erodes buying power, living standards fall for people who must live on fixed retirement incomes or on retirement incomes that do not rise as much as the inflation rate.

Unfortunately, people may not realize the degree to which even an apparently "low" rate of inflation can erode the purchasing power of a relatively fixed income until too late. When people in their mid- or late 70s discover that what they once thought would be an adequate retirement income is now woefully inadequate, there is little they can do to increase their income.

Table 2–1 shows how various rates of inflation can erode buying power. Even at the "low" 4 percent inflation rate achieved between 1982 and 1984, the buying power of a $10,000 retirement income would be reduced to $8,219 in five years, $6,756 in 10 years, $5,553 in 15 years, and $4,564—or about 46 cents on the dollar—in 20 years.

As measured by the consumer price index, between 1971 and 1980 the inflation rate averaged 7.8 percent. From 1976 to 1980, it averaged 8.9 percent. While it dropped to around 4 percent in 1982–84, it would be premature to conclude that the threat of another rise in inflation is over. And even at a 4 percent inflation rate, the dollar's buying power would be reduced by about one third in a decade.

IRAs CUT YOUR TAX BILLS

Many people underestimate the importance of the first great economic benefit of an IRA, which is as a tax shelter. This alone makes an IRA a useful money management tool no matter what your age or financial goals.

Basically, IRAs are much like the retirement plans millions of Americans have at work. In these, your employer contributes money into a plan (and you may be allowed to contribute some too). For all practical purposes, your employer's contribution is additional income for you unless you leave the plan before you have earned rights to any benefits. But you don't pay taxes on this money, which your employer uses to make tax-sheltered investments in a pension fund for all employees. You're not liable for taxes until your employer starts paying you benefits or you take a lump-sum distribution from the plan.

With an IRA, your most immediate benefit is to lower taxes beginning with the first year for which you make an IRA investment (see Table 2–2). Money you contribute to your IRA is deducted on your tax return for that year. If you're in a 25 percent tax bracket and contribute $2,000 to an IRA, you'll reduce your tax obligation for that year by 25 percent of $2,000, or $500. If you're in a 40 percent bracket, you'll reduce it by

TABLE 2-1 ■ How Inflation Erodes Retirement Buying Power (*Future Buying Power of $10,000 Annual Retirement Income Today at Various Inflation Rates*)

	Inflation Rate						
Years	2 percent	4 percent	6 percent	8 percent	10 percent	12 percent	15 percent
5	$9,057	$8,219	$7,473	$6,806	$6,209	$5,674	$4,972
10	8,203	6,756	5,584	4,632	3,855	3,220	2,472
15	7,430	5,553	4,173	3,152	2,394	1,827	1,229
20	6,730	4,564	3,118	2,145	1,486	1,037	611

2 WHY IRAs ARE GREAT INVESTMENTS ■ 23

TABLE 2–2 ■ How Tax Bills Are Lowered While You Build Your IRA *(Total Tax Deferred at Various Tax Brackets)*

Plan Years Completed	$2,000—Maximum Annual Individual Contribution				
	20 percent	25 percent	30 percent	40 percent	50 percent
1	$ 400	$ 500	$ 600	$ 800	$ 1,000
5	2,000	2,500	3,000	4,000	5,000
10	4,000	5,000	6,000	8,000	10,000
20	8,000	10,000	12,000	16,000	20,000
30	12,000	15,000	18,000	24,000	30,000
40	16,000	20,000	24,000	32,000	40,000
	$2,250—Maximum Annual Spousal Contribution				
1	$ 450	$ 563	$ 675	$ 900	$ 1,125
5	2,250	2,813	3,375	4,500	5,625
10	4,500	5,625	6,750	9,000	11,250
20	9,000	11,250	13,500	18,000	22,500
30	13,500	16,875	20,250	27,000	33,750
40	18,000	22,500	27,000	36,000	45,000
	$4,000—Maximum Working Couple Contribution				
1	$ 800	$ 1,000	$ 1,200	$ 1,600	$ 2,000
5	4,000	5,000	6,000	8,000	10,000
10	8,000	10,000	12,000	16,000	20,000
20	16,000	20,000	24,000	32,000	40,000
30	24,000	30,000	36,000	48,000	60,000
40	32,000	40,000	48,000	64,000	80,000

$800; if in a 50 percent bracket, by $1,000. In other words, right at the start Uncle Sam is giving you that much extra money to play with—provided you invest it in an IRA.

In time, these tax reductions alone can add up to a significant sum. The table showing this is actually conservative because it assumes you'll always be in the same tax bracket. But most people move into higher brackets as their incomes increase during their working lives. Your total tax reduction with an IRA would probably be greater than the table indicates.

Obviously the longer you continue contributing to an IRA, the greater the immediate savings on your income tax. But even if you're not in the highest tax brackets, these savings can be impressive over even a relatively short span. If you're in a 30 percent bracket and contribute $2,000 to an IRA for five years, you will have saved $3,000 in taxes; if you have a working spouse who also contributes $2,000 each year, you will have saved $6,000 in taxes.

(Note: Actual tax rates may differ from year to year. These examples are for making general estimates of how IRAs can reduce tax obligations.)

COMPARE TAX–EQUIVALENT RETURNS

Because an IRA shelters income from immediate taxation, one way to measure its value as an investment is to compare its return with the taxable-equivalent return on investments that are not sheltered.

The taxable-equivalent return will depend on your tax bracket. As Table 2–3 shows, equivalent returns on IRA investments are usually far above what you could expect to earn without a tax shelter.

If your IRA earns 10 percent and you're in a 25 percent bracket, it would be the equivalent of a 13.33 percent taxable return. If you're in a 30 percent bracket, it would be the equivalent of 14.29 percent; if in a 40 percent bracket, of 16.67 percent; and if in a 50 percent bracket, of 20 percent.

If you can manage to earn a 12 percent return on your IRA and are in a 25 percent bracket, it would be the equivalent of a taxable 16 percent; if in a 30 percent bracket, of 17.14 per-

TABLE 2–3 ■ Taxable Equivalent IRA Returns at Various Investment Yields

Tax Bracket (percent)	Investment Yields				
	6 percent	8 percent	10 percent	12 percent	14 percent
20%	7.50%	10.00%	12.50%	15.00%	17.50%
25	8.00	10.67	13.33	16.00	18.67
30	8.57	11.43	14.29	17.14	20.00
35	9.25	12.31	15.38	18.46	21.54
40	10.00	13.33	16.67	20.00	23.33
45	10.91	14.55	18.18	21.82	25.45
50	12.00	16.00	20.00	24.00	28.00

cent; if in a 40 percent bracket, of 20 percent; and if in a 50 percent bracket, of 24 percent.

THE POWER OF TAX–SHELTERED COMPOUNDING

The key to an IRA's great power as a personal finance tool is that all of its interest, dividends, and capital gains are sheltered from taxation, too. This gives IRA investments a great edge over investments that are not tax sheltered.

The longer an IRA is kept going, the more this power can work to increase the value of your investments. Assuming your IRA investment is earning a positive return, it combines the magic of compound interest with a tax shelter.

Table 2–4 shows the tax-sheltered gains you'd have with an IRA if you invested $2,000 at the beginning of each year at constant 6, 8, 10, 12, and 14 percent returns.

Nobody knows what interest rates will do in the future. But if your IRA earned a constant 10 percent return, after 10 years your total $20,000 investment would already be worth $35,062, a $15,602 gain. After 20 years your $40,000 invested would be worth $126,004. In 30 years your $60,000 investment would be worth $361,886; and in 40 years your $80,000 investment would be worth $973,702, a gain of $893,702. For each dollar invested, including money invested in the final year, you'd have $12.17.

Maximum spousal contributions of $2,250 per year would produce total values and gains 12.5 percent higher than in the table, and contributions of $2,000 each by working couples would double those numbers.

HOW BIG AN IRA CAN YOU BUILD?

An IRA's capital-building potential is greatest for young people. If they can start now, they can easily build six-figure and, in some cases, seven-figure IRAs. But even people in their middle years can build substantial IRAs to help assure a financially secure retirement—or for any other purpose.

Table 2–5 projects an IRA's growth at an annual 10 percent return for contributors at various ages today, assuming a $2,000 contribution made at the start of each year. (You can make

TABLE 2–4 ■ Tax-Sheltered IRA Gains at Various Rates of Return *(Assumes $2,000 Invested at Start of Each Year)*

8 percent

Plan Years Completed	Total Investment	IRA Value at Year-End	Tax-Sheltered Gain
1	$ 2,000	$ 2,160	$ 160
5	10,000	12,670	2,670
10	20,000	31,290	11,290
15	30,000	58,648	28,648
20	40,000	98,844	58,844
25	50,000	157,908	107,908
30	60,000	244,690	184,690
35	70,000	372,204	302,204
40	80,000	559,560	479,560

10 percent

Plan Years Completed	Total Investment	IRA Value at Year-End	Tax-Sheltered Gain
1	$ 2,000	$ 2,220	$ 200
5	10,000	13,430	3,430
10	20,000	35,062	15,062
15	30,000	69,898	39,898
20	40,000	126,004	86,004
25	50,000	216,362	166,362
30	60,000	361,886	301,886
35	70,000	596,252	526,252
40	80,000	973,702	893,702

12 percent

Plan Years Completed	Total Investment	IRA Value at Year-End	Tax-Sheltered Gain
1	$ 2,000	$ 2,240	$ 240
5	10,000	14,230	4,230
10	20,000	39,308	19,308
15	30,000	83,506	53,506
20	40,000	161,396	121,396
25	50,000	298,666	248,666
30	60,000	540,584	480,584
35	70,000	966,926	896,926
40	80,000	1,718,284	1,638,284

TABLE 2–4 ■ *(concluded)*

Plan Years Completed	Total Investment	IRA Value at Year-End	Tax-Sheltered Gain
		14 percent	
1	$ 2,000	$ 2,280	$ 280
5	10,000	15,070	5,070
10	20,000	44,088	24,088
15	30,000	99,960	69,960
20	40,000	207,536	167,536
25	50,000	414,664	364,664
30	60,000	813,474	753,474
35	70,000	1,581,344	1,511,344
40	80,000	3,059,816	2,979,816

TABLE 2–5 ■ Projected IRA Growth at Annual 10 Percent Return for Contributors at Various Ages Today *(Assumes $2,000 Invested at Start of Each Year)*

Your Age Now	IRA at Age 59½	IRA at Age 65	IRA at Age 70½
25	$569,151	$973,702	$1,662,770
30	345,437	596,252	1,024,490
35	206,529	361,886	628,166
40	120,277	216,362	382,081
45	66,722	126,004	229,282
50	33,469	69,898	134,405
55	12,821	35,062	75,494
60	—	13,430	8,915

these projections for your own age—and for a variety of rates of return—by using the IRA growth tables in Appendix A.)

Even if you're 55 years old today, a 10 percent IRA with $2,000 invested each year would grow to $12,821 by the time you reached age 59½, when you could begin withdrawing money—without paying a tax penalty—if you wish. When you reached age 65, the "traditional" retirement age, the IRA would be worth $35,062. If you continued working and contributing, it would grow to $75,494 by age 70½, when you would be required to stop contributing. Withdrawals would have to begin by the following April 1.

If you're 45 today, at a 10 percent return a $2,000 investment each year would grow to $66,722 by age 59½, $126,005 by age 65, and $229,282 by age 70½.

A 25-year-old worker contributing $2,000 at the start of each year could build an IRA worth $569,151 by age 59½, when penalty-free distributions from the IRA could begin. If contributions continue the IRA would grow to $973,703 at age 65 and $1,662,770 at age 70½.

HOW MUCH INCOME COULD YOUR IRA BUY?

Even after you are required to start withdrawing from your IRA, the money that remains in it continues to grow in a tax-sheltered mode. If it is a large IRA—perhaps opened with a lump-sum distribution from an employer retirement plan—the annual earnings may exceed the amount withdrawn for many years.

If you have so much other retirement income that you don't need your IRA for living expenses when you retire, after you are required to begin making withdrawals you can reinvest the money you take out. This may enable you to take advantage of opportunities in your retirement years that you couldn't have afforded otherwise.

However, most people will probably view IRAs as an additional source of retirement income. How much income an IRA will buy during your retirement (or before, if you wish to use an IRA this way) will depend on how big it is, the rate of return, and how long the IRA is to last.

The minimum amount you must withdraw from an IRA each year after the required distributions following age 70½ have begun is established by the IRS in tables based on your life expectancy or on the combined life expectancies of you and a designated beneficiary. (As an alternative, you can buy an insurance company annuity.) The payout procedure has been greatly liberalized by allowing you to recalculate your life expectancy (and that of your spouse, if your spouse is your designated beneficiary) as often as annually. As a result, most people can structure the payout schedule so they never outlive their IRA. This is discussed in Chapter 11.

Table 2–6 estimates how much retirement income various-sized IRAs could buy at various rates of return if you are willing to exhaust the principal. (Before you establish any payout schedule, however, check with your tax adviser and IRA sponsor to be sure you are meeting the minimum withdrawal requirements as explained in Chapter 11.)

Even a modest $25,000 IRA can be a valuable retirement income supplement. If invested at a 10 percent return over a 15-year payout period, it would provide additional annual income of $3,287 or $269 a month. Paid out over 20 years, it would pay $2,936 a year or $241 a month; and over 25 years, $2,754 a year or $227 a month. (When multiplied by 12, monthly payments are less than annual estimated payments because when money is withdrawn throughout the year rather than at the end of the year, less interest will be earned.)

A $100,000 IRA paid out over 20 years while earning at a 10 percent rate would pay $11,746 a year or $965 a month. A $250,000 IRA invested at that rate for 20 years would pay

TABLE 2–6   ■ $25,000 IRA Annual Payout Estimate

Years to Exhaust IRA	Annual Rate of Return				
	6 percent	8 percent	10 percent	12 percent	14 percent
5	$5,935	$6,261	$6,595	$6,935	$7,282
10	3,397	3,726	4,069	4,425	4,793
15	2,574	2,921	3,287	3,671	4,070
20	2,180	2,546	2,936	3,347	3,775
25	1,956	2,342	2,754	3,188	3,637
30	1,816	2,221	2,652	3,104	3,570
	Monthly Payout Estimate				
5	$483	$507	$531	$556	$582
10	278	303	330	359	388
15	211	239	269	300	333
20	179	209	241	275	311
25	161	193	227	263	301
30	150	183	219	257	296

$29,365 a year or $2,413 a month; and a $500,000 IRA, $58,730 a year or $4,825 a month.

You can easily estimate how much retirement income an IRA of any size would buy at various rates by making adjustments in the following tables. To see what a $300,000 IRA would pay, for instance, just triple the numbers in Table 2–8.

PAYOUT YEARS PROVIDE THE CAPITAL– BUILDING "KICKER"

An IRA's capital-building potential is maximized when its tax-sheltered leverage continues to work as you gradually pay the IRA out to yourself. Table 2–11 illustrates the capital-building kicker that the payout years can provide. Once more, we'll assume a constant 10 percent return.

In this table, $2,000 is contributed to an IRA each year until the IRA's owner is age 65. Then contributions stop, and the IRA is paid out in equal installments over a 25-year period. (The example assumes that the IRA's owner and a designated beneficiary have a combined life expectancy that would permit a 25-year payout under the IRS payout rules.)

TABLE 2–7 ■ $50,000 IRA Annual Payout Estimate

Years to Exhaust IRA	Annual Rate of Return				
	6 percent	8 percent	10 percent	12 percent	14 percent
5	$11,870	$12,523	$13,190	$13,870	$14,564
10	6,793	7,451	8,137	8,849	9,586
15	5,148	5,841	6,574	7,341	8,140
20	4,359	5,093	5,873	6,694	7,549
25	3,911	4,684	5,508	6,375	7,275
30	3,632	4,441	5,304	6,207	7,140
	Monthly Payout Estimate				
5	$967	$1,014	$1,062	$1,112	$1,163
10	555	607	661	717	776
15	422	478	537	600	666
20	358	418	483	551	622
25	322	386	454	527	602
30	300	367	439	514	592

TABLE 2–8 ■ $100,000 IRA Annual Payout Estimate

Years to Exhaust IRA	Annual Rate of Return				
	6 percent	8 percent	10 percent	12 percent	14 percent
5	$23,740	$25,046	$26,380	$27,741	$29,128
10	13,587	14,903	16,275	17,698	19,171
15	10,296	11,683	13,147	14,682	16,281
20	8,718	10,185	11,746	13,388	15,099
25	7,823	9,368	11,017	12,750	14,550
30	7,265	8,883	10,608	12,414	14,280
	Monthly Payout Estimate				
5	$1,933	$2,028	$2,125	$2,224	$2,327
10	1,110	1,213	1,322	1,435	1,553
15	844	956	1,075	1,200	1,332
20	716	836	965	1,101	1,244
25	644	772	909	1,053	1,204
30	600	734	878	1,029	1,185

TABLE 2–9 ■ $250,000 IRA Annual Payout Estimate

Years to Exhaust IRA	Annual Rate of Return				
	6 percent	8 percent	10 percent	12 percent	14 percent
5	$59,349	$62,614	$65,949	$69,352	$72,821
10	33,967	37,257	40,686	44,246	47,928
15	25,741	29,207	32,868	36,706	40,702
20	21,796	25,463	29,365	33,470	37,747
25	19,557	23,420	27,542	31,875	36,375
30	18,162	22,207	26,520	31,036	35,701
	Monthly Payout Estimate				
5	$4,833	$5,069	$5,312	$5,561	$5,817
10	2,776	3,033	3,304	3,587	3,882
15	2,110	2,389	2,687	3,000	3,329
20	1,791	2,091	2,413	2,753	3,109
25	1,611	1,930	2,272	2,633	3,009
30	1,499	1,834	2,194	2,572	2,962

TABLE 2–10 ■ $500,000 IRA Annual Payout Estimate

Years to Exhaust IRA	Annual Rate of Return				
	6 percent	8 percent	10 percent	12 percent	14 percent
5	$118,698	$125,228	$131,899	$138,705	$145,642
10	67,934	74,515	81,373	88,492	95,857
15	51,481	58,415	65,737	73,412	81,404
20	43,592	50,926	58,730	66,939	75,493
25	39,113	46,839	55,084	63,750	72,749
30	36,324	44,414	53,040	62,072	71,401
	Monthly Payout Estimate				
5	$9,667	$10,138	$10,624	$11,122	$11,634
10	5,551	6,066	6,608	7,174	7,763
15	4,219	4,778	5,373	6,001	6,659
20	3,582	4,182	4,825	5,505	6,218
25	3,222	3,859	4,544	5,266	6,019
30	2,998	3,669	4,388	5,143	5,924

With this scenario, even if a couple starts an IRA at a relatively advanced age, they'd reap substantial gains. And if they start at a relatively young age, gains would be remarkable. For instance:

1. Age 55 now—in 10 years a $20,000 investment earning a 10 percent return would have grown to $35,062. For the next 25 years, the IRA would pay an annual income of $3,863—or $319 a month—for a total payout of $92,075 or $4.60 for each dollar contributed.

If both spouses began making maximum IRA contributions at age 55, those numbers would double. Their $40,000 investment would provide an annual income of $7,366 or $638 a month, for a total payout of $184,150.

2. Age 45—a $40,000 investment would build an IRA worth $126,005 by age 65. For the next 25 years, the IRA would pay $13,882 a year or $1,145 a month. The total payout would be $347,050 or $8.68 for each dollar contributed.

3. Age 35—a $60,000 investment over the next 30 years would build an IRA worth $361,887. Over the following 25 years, this would pay an annual income of $39,868 a year or

TABLE 2-11 ■ Total Return from IRA Investments of $2,000 per Year with Fixed 25-Year Payout Plan and Constant 10 Percent Return *(Contributions Stop at Age 65; Entire IRA Pays Out in 25 Years)*

Age Now	Total Invested	Value at Age 65	25-Year Payout after age 65 Annual Income	Monthly Income	Total* Paid out	Dollars Paid* out for Each Dollar Paid in
55	$20,000	$ 35,062	$ 3,683	$ 319	$ 92,075	$ 4.60
50	30,000	69,899	7,701	635	192,525	6.42
45	40,000	126,005	13,882	1,145	347,050	8.68
40	50,000	216,364	23,836	1,966	596,650	11.93
35	60,000	361,887	39,868	3,288	996,700	16.61
30	70,000	596,253	65,688	5,418	1,642,200	23.46
25	80,000	973,703	107,271	8,848	2,681,775	33.52

*Based on annual withdrawals (assumes IRA owner and designated beneficiary have permissible life expectancy multiples).

$3,288 a month. The total payout would be $996,700—or $16.61 for each dollar contributed. The payout if both spouses worked and contributed the limit would be $1,993,400.

4. Age 25—an $80,000 investment over 40 years would build an IRA worth $973,703. For the next 25 years, it would pay $107,271 a year—$8,848 if paid on a monthly basis—for a total payout of $2,681,775 or $33.52 for each dollar contributed.

You could do even better if you were fortunate enough not to have to start withdrawing until after you were age 70½— and you did not require a fixed income and could strictly follow the IRS rules for minimum withdrawals after age 70½. A discussion of this is in Chapter 11.

WILL INFLATION DESTROY YOUR IRA'S VALUE?

Some critics have belittled the IRA program on grounds that over time, inflation will be so virulent that when you get around to taking money out, it will be virtually valueless.

Anything can happen—and in view of the rates of inflation we've already seen, that possibility can't be ruled out. But while this argument will appeal to people seeking an excuse not to save money anyhow, there are powerful arguments on the other side. One is that right at the start, these critics ignore the effect of your tax savings from each year's contributions. These give you that much more immediate purchasing power over the years than would be the case if you gave this money to the government instead. Beyond this, if you can invest your IRA money at an average rate of return that matches or exceeds the inflation rate, which in this country is measured by the consumer price index, you won't lose purchasing power over the years— and, in fact, may gain it.

As discussed in the section on the CPI in Chapter 4, even small investors now have opportunities to better the inflation rate that did not exist before. And, in fact, in the mid-1980s, IRA investors were increasing the buying power of their IRAs because they were substantially bettering the inflation rate.

Finally, it appears that Congress is really serious about making the IRA program a meaningful one that will take some pressure off the social security system. That being so, if inflation was indeed so virulent that 20 or 25 years from now all your $2,000 IRA contribution would buy is a newspaper or a local telephone call, Congress would have increased the IRA contribution limits.

Although it's always possible that inflation could destroy the value of your IRAs, the odds seem to favor taking the risk of a long-term IRA investment program.

3

Tailoring
IRAs to Your Needs

One of the great strengths of the IRA program is that it can be adapted to the needs of people in many different circumstances. This begins with your choice of IRA investments. Along with the financial deregulation movement, the growing popularity of the IRA program itself since 1982 when it was opened to everyone who works has stimulated the development of new investment options.

Over the years, this flexibility also makes it possible to adapt your IRA program to changes in your own circumstances. And as you near retirement and your IRAs grow, you can incorporate them in your overall estate planning.

WHICH IRA INVESTMENTS WILL YOU CHOOSE?

In fashioning an IRA program, you have great flexibility in selecting IRA investments. These range from the safest and simplest to the riskiest and most complex, and include the following.

Certificates of Deposit at Banks and Savings Institutions

These offer safety and—if you select a fixed-rate CD—a predictable return. The fixed-rate CD also offers protection against declining interest rates but would "lock you in" at a lower rate if rates rise sharply. But if you think interest rates will rise, you can buy a variable-rate CD.

Because of financial deregulation, savings interest rates are no longer controlled. These institutions can now offer many more kinds of IRA investments than they could before. In fact, if you know the date on which you plan to retire (or want to withdraw money for any other purpose) and that date is not too many years in the future, you can probably find a bank or savings institution that would sell you CDs maturing on that date.

Bank and savings institution CDs are "liquid" in that you can get your money out when you wish. However, these institutions must charge penalties if you withdraw from a CD before it matures when you are under age 59½, and may charge them if they wish if you are over 59½. (And some charge more than the minimum required by law.) In some cases, the early withdrawal penalty could cut into your principal.

While most banks and savings institutions do not charge fees to open and maintain IRAs, there is a trend toward establishing fees.

Money Market Accounts

Some (not all) banks and savings institutions also offer these as IRAs. They can pay whatever rate they wish but, because the money is available on demand, rates are lower than for CDs. There are no withdrawal penalties. This makes these accounts useful as a "parking place" for IRA contributions you're not sure what to do with, as well as for lump-sum rollovers from company plans.

Money Market Mutual Funds

These are "cash-equivalent" investments that pay returns based directly on the fund's return on its investments in short-term money market instruments, such as U.S. Treasury bills, commercial paper, and jumbo certificates of deposit issued by large banks and some large savings institutions. Money market funds don't have federal deposit insurance, but there are no penalties for taking money out at any time. Often their use as an IRA is as a member of a "family" of mutual funds, but they can also be used as a "parking place" for IRA money until you have decided on longer-term investments.

Stock Mutual Funds

These invest in the stock market and offer the promise of capital appreciation, particularly over the long haul. They also carry the risk of loss if the values of the stocks in the fund fall. Some funds charge a commission ("load"), but others don't.

Mutual Fund "Families"

Built around at least one stock fund, a money market mutual fund, and a bond fund, these give you the versatility of being able to switch from one kind of investment to another when markets—or your circumstances—change. Many mutual fund families also include bond funds for income and "mixed" funds (part stock, part bonds) for moderate growth with income.

Special-Purpose Mutual Funds

If you wish to concentrate in a particular type of investment, you may be able to find a mutual fund that specializes in that field. Some invest only in U.S. Treasury securities, others, in such specialized areas as precious metals, energy, and technology.

Self-Directed Accounts at Brokerage Houses

With these, you buy and sell stocks or make other investments of your own choice. The potential for gain is higher than with most other kinds of IRAs—and so is the risk of loss. You also pay commissions each time you buy or sell.

If you are already a successful stock trader or investor, this may be the ideal type of IRA for you. If you have done little or no successful stock trading or investing in the past, an IRA would be a questionable place for you to begin.

Zero-Coupon Bonds

Very popular with some IRA investors, these can "lock in" today's interest rates for many years into the future, assuring you of an automatically compounded, predictable return. The main risk is that if interest rates rise sharply before the bonds mature, you'd have to sell at a loss if you didn't wait for them to mature—and experience to date suggests that price swings for "zeros" are more volatile than for regular interest-paying bonds. In some cases, commissions may reduce your return to less than that for interest-paying bonds.

Limited Partnerships, Usually in Real Estate or Oil and Gas

A potentially high return is possible but often at high risk. Also, these investments are usually not very liquid. Some may be difficult or impossible to sell if you decide you want out.

Insurance Company IRAs

With some of these, the companies themselves establish the rates they will pay during the buildup years; with others, the rate is based on results of a mutual fund managed by the company. Often there are fees or penalties for withdrawing from these IRAs in the early years, and you may also have to pay commissions. (For more on specific IRA investments, see the last section of this book.)

TAKE A "PORTFOLIO" APPROACH IF YOU WISH

Because there is no limit to the number of IRAs you are allowed to own, when you have accumulated enough money you can diversify into two or more different types of IRAs. And if you roll a large employer plan distribution into an IRA and don't plan to ever roll it back into another employer plan, you could begin a diversification program right at the start.

This makes it possible to take a "portfolio" approach with your IRA investments. You can establish positions in different kinds of investments and keep revising your program to adapt to changing markets or changes in your own circumstances.

Even if you stay with the same general kind of investment, you could diversify with different varieties of that investment and/or different IRA sponsors.

On the other hand, simply because you can make different kinds of investments if you wish, don't get carried away and feel obliged to try them all. Stick to what you know and understand. The tax-sheltered compounding power of IRAs is such that you are assured of doing well with even the safest investments that don't carry the risk of capital loss.

IRAs ARE NOT FOR EVERYONE

Although IRAs can be a useful money management tool for many people in many circumstances, they're not for everyone. You should not contribute to an IRA if:

- Making the contribution would be a financial hardship for you or your family. Don't even consider contributing to an IRA if it would require cutting down on such essentials as food, housing, clothing, or medical care for you, your family, or others who depend on your support.
- You have a more pressing immediate use for the money, such as accumulating the down payment for a home.
- You have better (or more essential) investment options. Through family, personal, or business contacts, some people have investment opportunities that may appear more promising than those available to the general public through IRAs. Other people may be obliged to invest every spare dollar they can find in a personal or family business.
- You have so much money that the advantages of opening an IRA would be virtually meaningless to you. The time involved in opening and contributing to an IRA may not be worth your while for the money you would gain. Or, if you have concentrated your capital in other tax-sheltered investments, you

may not have enough taxable income to make an
IRA worthwhile.

WHO ESPECIALLY SHOULD HAVE AN IRA

For some people an investment program involving IRAs is
especially appropriate. These include the following.

**People who don't have pension or retirement plans
at work.** Typically, these people work for small companies
or businesses. The IRA program was created for these people
in the first place. Many failed to take advantage of the program in the beginning because they didn't know about it. Now
that everyone who works can have an IRA, the word is getting
out. Unless you are already independently wealthy, if you
work where there's no pension or retirement plan and can
afford the contributions, you should have an IRA program to
supplement your social security benefits.

People who move or change jobs often. You may move
because you like moving around, or it may be necessary for
you to move. You may be the spouse of someone with a mobile
occupation—someone on active service in the military, for instance. An IRA could be the only way you'll ever be able to
take advantage of a tax shelter to build a fund for retirement.
Or you may change jobs often simply because you don't like
(or can't keep) the same job for long. If you're this kind of
person, you may never stay at one job long enough to earn
substantial retirement benefits. With an IRA, at least you'll
have something put aside.

Anyone between ages 59½ and 70½. These are the
"golden years" for people in the IRA program. During this
period you can take as much or as little out of your IRA as
you wish without paying the 10 percent tax penalty. If you
can afford the contributions, you have nothing to lose. All you
have to watch out for is tying up your money in investments
for which the sponsor can exact a penalty if you withdraw
before the investments mature. (And in the case of depository

institutions, sponsors are allowed to waive that penalty for depositors aged 59½ or older if they wish.)

AGE IS OFTEN THE KEY FACTOR

In fashioning your IRA program, your age may be the key factor. All research to date suggests that people who save money generally are the biggest users of IRAs. Most commonly, these are people in higher age and income brackets.

As is well known to financial services marketers, as people reach their 40s and 50s they become the prime customers for savings accounts and other investments. At this stage in life, people are usually at the peak of their earning power. Also, their children are becoming financially independent, and the expenses of rearing and educating them are easing off. Typically, the years from 50 or so until retirement are the years of greatest capital accumulation—and, for many people, the first opportunity for it.

When you reach age 59½ and the "golden years" of the IRA program, you can do much more with an IRA than other people can, including using one as an income-leveling device if need be. (For a discussion of this, see Chapter 11, which covers payouts from IRAs.) If you are fortunate enough to have a substantial IRA by the time you reach your 50s, you can be much more independent in thinking about your future, particularly if you also have an employer pension plan. You'll be much less vulnerable if you unexpectedly lose your job. And although you'd have to pay income tax on money withdrawn from your IRAs, you could also tap your IRA to partially or totally fund a part-time or full-time business.

As you near retirement, you'll probably want to emphasize safety in your IRA investment program because you no longer have time to correct mistakes.

The period between your mid-30s and your 50s is when you're most likely to begin serious savings and investment programs, including the IRA program. You still have big living expenses to meet, but typically your income is now increasing to where you have more discretionary income from which to save.

If you start an IRA program in these middle years, you won't be able to build as big an IRA as younger people can, but you can still do pretty well. If you started an IRA program when you were young, at this stage in life you may also be able to use IRAs to help meet such expenses as support for aged parents or college educations for your children.

When you're young, you can afford to take the most chances with IRA investments. On the other hand, when you're young, you're least experienced and more likely to make investment mistakes. And you have more assurance of building a very large IRA with a minimum of risk by sticking to safe, fixed-income investments. That's because the younger you are, the more the financial leverage of compounding is working for you.

Unfortunately, when you're young, you're usually least in a position to make contributions to an IRA even if you wanted to. Yet if you could make them, because of the magic of tax-sheltered compounding you might virtually assure a financially secure retirement in a very short time. Assuming that the contributions for each year are the same amount and you are earning a fixed return, the IRA contributions you make when you are in your 20s may be worth more than all the contributions you could make for the rest of your life.

Example. Because of the power of tax-sheltered compounding, at a constant 10 percent return if you can contribute $2,000 to an IRA at the start of each year between ages 22 and 29—a total of $16,000—when you reach age 65 that $16,000 will have grown to substantially more than an IRA opened at age 30 to which you contributed $2,000 each year between ages 30 and 65.

When you reach age 65 the IRA to which you contributed $2,000 each year between ages 22 and 29 and then stopped contributing would be worth $777,684; the IRA to which you contributed $2,000 each year between ages 30 and 65, a total of $70,000, would be worth only $596,252. (At age 70½, when you would be required to stop contributing, the IRA to which you had made no more contributions since age 29 would be worth more than $1.25 million; the IRA to which you had contributed $2,000 each year beginning at age 30 would be worth a little less than $1 million.)

With that kind of leverage working for you with fixed-rate investments that carry little or no market risk, you should be reasonably sure the odds favor a substantially better return before you make riskier investments.

OTHER THINGS TO CONSIDER

In addition to age, other factors to consider in fashioning an IRA program to your own circumstances include these.

Any family wealth to be inherited. If you anticipate a fairly substantial inheritance, you can afford to take more risks with your IRAs.

Your future financial needs. This includes both your consumption "needs" and your financial obligations. The greater your needs, the more conservative the investment approach you may wish to take.

Your potential earning capacity based on your career choice and personal limitations. Try to make an honest assessment of your future income potential. If you have good reason to believe you are on a career track that will bring you a relatively high income, you can afford more risks.

Your choice of lifestyle. You may decide you'd rather spend your money on things you want to use now than tie up money you probably wouldn't use until you're 60 or 70 years old. If you're fortunate enough to be earning good money at an early age, you may reason that there's plenty of time to save later—and that you'll use most of the money you're earning now to indulge and enjoy yourself. If so, if you open an IRA you won't want to contribute the maximum allowed. Your motive may be simply to establish and have an IRA in place for more serious investing later.

Your personality and self-confidence level. If you're essentially a conservative person, you'll probably feel most comfortable with conservative IRA investments. If you enjoy taking risks, you'll probably seek more venturesome IRA investments, too. You may need a lot of self-confidence to persist in a risky investment program in the face of the losses that may occur. But achieving the superior results hoped for in investments of this type often requires sustaining losses for many months (and sometimes years) before the investments pay off.

Your current and future tax brackets. The higher your tax bracket, the more advantageous an IRA can be for you in terms of sheltering current income from taxation. But if you have a large IRA and are in a high bracket, you should continually reassess your IRAs in light of your estate and the consequences of leaving a large IRA to your beneficiaries. These factors are very complex and for most people will require professional assistance.

Your vulnerability to recession and/or inflation. Some people are more vulnerable to economic and interest rate cycles than others. If your job is subject to economic cycles that could leave you periodically unemployed or, at the very least, having to get by with a lower income, you should avoid illiquid IRAs, or IRAs that could result in your taking a market loss or a substantial sponsor penalty for cashing them in before they mature. These include such investments as very long-term CDs, particularly if they carry early withdrawal penalties higher than the statutory minimum; insurance company IRAs with substantial penalties for withdrawing early; long-term zero-coupon bonds, which you may have to sell at a loss if interest rates have gone up since you bought them; any other "interest rate" investment, including all bonds and bond funds; and any investment in the stock market, including mutual funds and the purchase of stocks in a self-directed IRA.

As a general rule, stocks should never be purchased if you may need the money for living expenses. The risk is that when you need the money, the market (or the price of your stock) may be down. And if your income is reduced or cut off because of a general economic downturn, chances are that the downturn has knocked the stock market down too.

Your opportunities (or the necessity) for investing outside of an IRA. What are your other investment options—or the other investments you must make for one reason or another, such as financing a family business? If you have limited financial resources, you may have to curtail or suspend your IRA program at times and possibly even begin withdrawing from your IRA.

Your personal risk tolerance levels. Can you sleep at night if the value of your investment has been going down? If not, concentrate your IRAs in safe investments with no risk of losing principal.

Your level of financial sophistication. Successful diversification comes with growth and knowledge, and for most people that requires time.

SETTING IRA GOALS

You may do a better job of tailoring an IRA investment program to your needs if you can make realistic estimates of how much your IRA or IRAs might be worth at any given time in the future. If you thought you could assure a financially comfortable retirement with IRAs worth approximately $150,000, for instance, if you contributed $2,000 each year how long would it take you to build that big an IRA at an 8 percent constant return? (Twenty-five years.) If you rolled $134,500 into an IRA from an employer plan, at a constant 10 percent return, what would it be worth with no further additions in five years? ($216,545). Ten years? ($348,759). Fifteen years? ($561,807).

You can make these and many other estimates involving IRA growth at various rates of return with the growth tables in Appendix A of this book. With them, you can project an IRA's growth whether you're making regular additional contributions or not. You can also use the tables to see what your IRA would grow to if you changed the amount you contributed each year, or if the rate of return changed.

As time goes on, be prepared to change your IRA growth estimates as the general levels of interest rates change—particularly if the return on your IRA investments is determined by interest rates. Returns commonplace with reasonable safety on IRAs (and other investments) today are not likely to remain the same for long. Investment returns change constantly, sometimes substantially.

Table 3–1 is a short table that, along with the growth tables in Appendix A, may help you plan your IRA investments. It shows how long it would take to build an IRA worth $25,000, $50,000, $100,000, or $200,000 at various rates of return if you contributed $2,000 at the start of each year.

If you thought you'd need a $50,000 IRA to assure a secure retirement, it shows that at a 10 percent return, you could reach your goal in the 13th year; but if you needed $100,000, it would take until the 18th year.

RELATE YOUR IRAs TO OTHER RETIREMENT INCOME

To the extent possible, relate your IRA investments to your other anticipated retirement income. This includes social security, any other pension benefits, and income from personal savings and investments.

Obviously, if you are still many years from retirement this will not be possible. But the closer you come to retirement, the more accurately you'll be able to make these projections.

Don't forget to allow for inflation. The purchasing power of any fixed-income payments you expect to receive after you

TABLE 3–1 ■ Setting IRA Goals—Regular Deposits
(Assumes $2,000 Invested at Start of Each Year)

Rate of Return (Percent)	Years Needed to Build an IRA Worth			
	$25,000	$50,000	$100,000	$250,000
5%	10	17	25	40
6	10	16	24	36
7	9	15	22	33
8	9	14	21	31
9	8	13	19	29
10	8	13	18	27
11	8	12	18	25
12	8	12	17	24
13	8	12	16	23
14	8	11	16	22
15	7	11	15	21
16	7	11	14	20

retire will be progressively eroded accordingly. As we saw in Chapter 2, even at a "low" 4 percent inflation rate, buying power is reduced by one third in just 10 years.

On the other hand, in estimating your future income from investments, it would be prudent to be conservative. In the early 1980s, double-digit yields on even the safest investments—U.S. Treasury bills—were commonplace. In that kind of an inflationary financial environment, it's easy to lose perspective. Don't forget that during the 1970s, three-month Treasury bill rates averaged 6.32 percent, and rates on three-year U.S. Treasury notes averaged 7.24 percent. In the 1960s, these securities averaged 4.00 and 4.59 percent, respectively.

While financial deregulation has increased the upward bias of all interest rates, it would be dangerous to assume that rates could never, under any circumstances, fall back down to those levels again.

Periodically, the Social Security Administration updates tables showing what your retirement income will be for your age and income. These tables are available at your local social security office.

IRAs AND ESTATE PLANNING

As your IRAs increase in size—or if you roll a substantial sum into an IRA from an employer pension plan—you may wish to assess your IRA program in terms of planning for your entire estate.

Estate planning can be very complex. The larger the estate, the more essential it becomes to obtain professional guidance and periodically review your affairs in light of changes in tax laws and your own situation.

In estate planning, the basic thing to understand about IRAs is that for the purpose of calculating the federal estate tax they will be included in the assets of your estate. This includes IRAs rolled over from employer plans or Keogh plans as well as IRAs you have built from scratch.

Under current law, your estate will have to pay federal estate tax if its net assets (the gross assets less allowable deductions) exceed $400,000 if death occurs in 1985; $500,000 if it occurs in 1986; and $600,000 if it occurs in 1987 or later.

(Note: You may also be subject to a state inheritance tax, for which requirements differ from state to state.)

The federal tax is levied on the *excess* amounts. In 1987 and later, for instance, it would be levied on amounts over $600,000; the first $600,000 would be tax free. Rates in 1987 start at 18 percent for the first $10,000 and go up to 55 percent for amounts that exceed $3 million.

With a $600,000 starting point, most people will not have a taxable estate. However, before you conclude that you won't, work out the numbers for your own situation. With real estate, insurance benefits, your interests in employer pension plans, and jointly held property, antiques, personal property, works of art, and your other assets included, you may find that your estate is larger than you think—or that, given even a moderate rate of growth, it would reach $600,000 sooner than you first believed.

In addition, of course, your heirs or beneficiaries are subject to income tax on money they withdraw from the IRA or IRAs they inherit. As discussed in Chapters 5 and 11, there are several distribution options—and if your spouse is your designated beneficiary, the beginning of distributions can be delayed until the year in which you would have reached age 70½.

If you are married, a key aspect of estate planning is that all assets left to a spouse will escape estate tax until the surviving spouse dies. At that time they become taxable as part of the estate of the spouse. This is the "marital exclusion rule." The rule also applies to an IRA or any part of one left to a living spouse, either as a direct beneficiary in the IRA or under terms of a will. If the surviving spouse marries again, the marital exclusion rule can be applied again. There are no limits to the number of times it can be applied.

When the surviving spouse withdraws money from the IRA for any reason, it is subject to tax as ordinary income. But no matter who inherits an IRA, all money in it will continue to earn tax-sheltered income until withdrawn.

Because all IRA distributions are taxed as ordinary income, if the IRA is also taxed as part of the estate there is actually a substantial double tax on the inherited amount. Prolonging the distributions from the estate allows time to recover some of the estate taxes through the tax-free accumulation of earnings.

If you have a large IRA or IRAs, consider naming more than one beneficiary, including trusts. In some cases this may lower the total income tax that may have to be paid.

In planning your estate, remember that the favorable 10-year forward averaging tax computation is not available to inheritors of IRAs. If the money involved is significant, you may wish to consider your beneficiary's probable tax bracket when selecting the payment method to apply.

Don't forget to review your beneficiaries periodically. Circumstances change. For many reasons, the beneficiaries you named when you opened your IRA may no longer be the people you would prefer leaving your IRA to now.

4

Making the Most of Your IRAs

Congress has given you an unprecedented opportunity to build a tax-sheltered pool of savings with an IRA, but it's up to you to take advantage of that opportunity. Unlike social security, for which contributions are mandatory, the benefits you receive from your IRA will depend on how much money you contribute voluntarily—and how wisely you invest it.

Since the program was opened in 1982 to everyone who works, millions of words have been written about the different *kinds* of IRA investments. In looking for fresh material, money management periodicals and writers are constantly seeking out new (or at least not widely known) IRA investment vehicles—or interviewing experts about the kinds of IRAs *they* have.

Yet, simply following a few commonsense principles in handling any IRA could have a greater impact on how large it grows than the kind of investment it is. No matter what kind of investments they are, here are some simple but effective ways to make the most of your IRAs.

START SOON AND INVEST REGULARLY

You've heard this many times before, but it's worth saying again. Whatever your age or income, to make the most of your

IRA (or any other investment program), start it right away and keep at it.

Not everyone is fortunate enough to be able to put money aside until age 59½ or later—although there could be circumstances where you'd come out ahead paying the tax penalties for taking the money out earlier anyhow. But if you can manage to spend a little less now and put more money into an IRA, that money can multiply many times over.

Investing now gets compound interest working for you right away. Investing regularly makes the growth of your IRA like that of a snowball rolling downhill. It isn't big at the start— but by the time it nears the bottom of the hill, it is many times its original size.

To see how the magic of compounded growth works on a year-in, year-out basis, look at Table 4–1. It shows an IRA's annual growth for 40 years if invested at a constant 10 percent return.

In the first year, your IRA would earn only $200. By the end of the eighth year, it would have earned $2,287, or $287 more than your annual contribution. After 12 years it would earn $4,277, or more than double your annual contribution. The IRA's earnings would triple the size of your contribution in the 15th year, quadruple it in the 17th year, and quintuple it in the 19th year.

After 25 years, your IRA would earn more than nearly 10 times your $2,000 contribution; after 30 years, it would earn more than 16 times your contribution; and after 40 years, it would earn $88,518, or more than 44 times your contribution.

INVEST AS EARLY IN THE YEAR AS YOU CAN

You may have noticed that until now, all tables in this book that estimate an IRA's growth have assumed that investments are made at the start of each year. That's because the sooner you invest in your IRA each year, the faster it will grow. Of all the simple, commonsense techniques for increasing the return on any type of IRA, this is probably the most important. Over the years, following it can put you many thousands of dollars ahead.

Obviously, it's not always possible to make your entire IRA investment each January. At that time, most people are more

TABLE 4–1   ■   IRA Growth at Constant 10 Percent Return
(Assumes $2,000 Invested at Start of Each Year)

Years	Total Investment	IRA Value at Year-End	IRA Earnings during Year
1	$ 2,000	$ 2,200	$ 200
2	4,000	4,620	420
3	6,000	7,282	662
4	8,000	10,210	928
5	10,000	13,431	1,221
6	12,000	16,974	1,543
7	14,000	20,872	1,897
8	16,000	25,159	2,287
9	18,000	29,875	2,716
10	20,000	35,062	3,187
11	22,000	40,769	3,706
12	24,000	47,045	4,277
13	26,000	53,950	4,905
14	28,000	61,545	5,595
15	30,000	69,899	6,354
16	32,000	79,089	7,190
17	34,000	89,198	8,109
18	36,000	100,318	9,120
19	38,000	112,550	10,232
20	40,000	126,005	11,455
21	42,000	140,805	12,801
22	44,000	157,086	14,281
23	46,000	174,995	15,909
24	48,000	194,694	17,699
25	50,000	216,364	19,669
26	52,000	240,200	21,836
27	54,000	266,420	24,220
28	56,000	295,262	26,842
29	58,000	326,988	29,726
30	60,000	361,887	32,899
31	62,000	400,275	36,389
32	64,000	442,503	40,228
33	66,000	488,953	44,450
34	68,000	540,049	49,095
35	70,000	596,253	54,205
36	72,000	658,079	59,825
37	74,000	726,087	66,008
38	76,000	800,895	72,809
39	78,000	883,185	80,290
40	80,000	973,703	88,518

concerned with paying Christmas bills than with putting money where it shouldn't be touched until they are age 59½ —assuming they have any cash on hand at all.

And, in fact, IRA growth tables in this book (and in promotional materials prepared by IRA sponsors) are unattainable because they are idealized examples. Usually you can't even open or contribute to an IRA on the first day of the year because it's a holiday. And for most investments it's not likely you'd earn the same constant rate of return over a long period of time.

Nevertheless, to make the most of your IRA, try as much as possible to bunch your investments close to the start of each year rather than waiting until later in the year—or until just before the tax return deadline in April in the following year, as so many people do. That way, your contributions will be compounding tax sheltered for an extra 15½ months.

And you gain an added modest benefit if you make part or all of your contribution with funds transferred from a taxable investment or savings account, reducing your tax obligation accordingly. If you're in a 33 percent bracket, transferring $2,000 from a taxable savings account paying 10 percent into an IRA will reduce your tax bill by 33 percent of $200, or about $67. If you know you're going to save $2,000 during the year anyhow, why not transfer $2,000 from savings into an IRA at the very beginning of the year, and then replace it from your income during the year?

Concentrating investments at the start of each year won't make much difference in the size of your IRA in the beginning. But the bigger your IRA becomes, the bigger the difference it will make.

Look at what would happen if you contribute $2,000 at the start of each year to an IRA earning 10 percent and someone else contributes $2,000 to an IRA earning the same rate on the April 15 tax deadline the following year (see Table 4–2). After the first year, your IRA will have earned $200 and will be worth $2,200, while the other IRA hasn't even been opened. Thereafter, at the end of each year your IRA's value will always exceed that of the other IRA by the compounded effect of the extra 15½ months' earnings for each year's contribution.

After five years, the start-of-the-year IRA will have earned $1,492 more than the tax-deadline IRA; after 10 years, $3,979

TABLE 4–2 ■ **How Money Grows Faster When Invested at the Start of the Year than on April 15 Tax Deadline the Following Year** *($2,000 Invested Each Year, 10 Percent Annual Return)*

Years Completed	IRA Value If Invested at Start of Year	Total Earnings	IRA Value If Invested at Tax Deadline	Total Earnings	Earnings Difference
1	$ 2,200	$ 200	$ 0	$ 0	$ 200
2	4,620	620	2,142	142	478
3	7,282	1,282	4,497	497	785
4	10,210	2,210	7,089	1,089	1,121
5	13,431	3,431	9,939	1,939	1,492
6	16,974	4,974	13,075	3,075	1,899
7	20,872	6,872	16,524	4,524	2,348
8	25,159	9,159	20,318	6,318	2,841
9	29,875	11,875	24,492	8,492	3,383
10	35,062	15,062	29,083	11,083	3,979
11	40,769	18,769	34,133	14,133	4,636
12	47,045	23,045	39,687	17,687	5,358
13	53,950	27,950	45,798	21,798	6,152
14	61,545	33,545	52,519	26,519	7,026
15	69,899	39,899	59,913	31,913	7,986
16	79,089	47,089	68,046	38,046	9,043
17	89,198	55,198	76,992	44,992	10,206
18	100,318	64,318	86,833	52,833	11,485
19	112,550	74,550	97,658	61,658	12,892
20	126,005	86,005	109,565	71,565	14,440
21	140,805	98,805	122,664	82,664	16,141
22	157,086	113,086	137,072	95,072	18,014
23	174,995	128,995	152,920	108,920	20,075
24	194,694	146,694	170,354	124,354	22,340
25	216,363	166,363	189,531	141,531	24,832
26	240,200	188,200	210,626	160,626	27,574
27	266,420	212,420	233,830	181,830	30,590
28	295,262	239,262	259,355	205,355	33,907
29	326,988	268,988	287,432	231,432	37,556
30	361,887	301,887	318,317	260,317	41,570
31	400,275	338,275	352,290	292,290	45,985
32	442,503	378,503	389,661	327,661	50,842
33	488,953	422,953	430,769	366,769	56,184
34	540,049	472,049	475,987	409,987	62,062
35	596,253	526,253	525,727	457,727	68,526

more; after 20 years, $14,440 more; and after 30 years, $41,570 more. At that time the start-of-the-year IRA, in which you have invested $60,000, will be worth $361,887; the tax-deadline IRA, with $58,000 invested to date, will be worth $318,317.

DON'T SETTLE FOR LESS THAN A MARKET RETURN

Early in the 1980s, when interest rates were very high, some people were buying IRA savings certificates that paid a mere 8 percent return—and tying up their money for periods of four to six years to get it. Yet, other banks and savings institutions were paying IRA buyers 12 percent on 2½-year certificates. Some institutions were marketing six-month money market certificates, which paid as much as 15 percent, as IRAs. (For those, at that time you had to deposit at least $10,000.)

The longer the period involved, the more substantial the effect of a big difference in the rate of return. A 12 percent IRA would more than double the size of an 8 percent IRA in 27 years—$379,396 versus $188,676, if $2,000 contributions are made at the start of each year. In 40 years it would be more than triple an 8 percent IRA's size—$1,718,284 versus $559,560.

Don't allow even a few years to go by with an IRA earning a below-market rate. Remember these numbers if you're tempted to accept a below-market return as a favor to a friend, relative, or business associate with an interest in selling you the IRA—or you're reluctant to take the time to carry or mail an IRA contribution to another sponsor if the IRA pays far below market.

Table 4–3 illustrates the impact of substantial differences of return on an IRA. If you plan to use the IRA for retirement, this impact would be magnified by the lower retirement income your IRA would buy.

UNDERSTAND HOW "LITTLE" DIFFERENCES AFFECT TOTAL RETURN

Even very small differences in the rate of return on your IRA can make a surprisingly big difference in total return over a long period. This applies both to the rate of return itself and, if it is a deposit at a financial institution, to how your money

TABLE 4–3 ■ What a Difference a Rate Makes

Rate of Return Percent	After 10 Years	After 20 Years	After 30 Years	After 40 Years
5%	$26,412	$ 69,438	$ 139,520	$ 253,678
6	27,942	77,984	167,602	328,094
7	29,566	87,730	202,144	427,218
8	31,290	98,844	244,690	559,560
9	33,120	111,528	297,150	736,582
10	35,052	126,004	361,886	973,702
11	37,122	142,530	441,826	1,291,652
12	39,308	161,396	540,584	1,718,284
13	41,628	182,938	662,630	2,290,970
14	44,088	207,536	813,474	3,059,816
15	46,698	235,620	999,912	4,091,906
16	49,464	267,680	1,230,322	5,276,956
17	52,398	304,276	1,515,006	7,334,780
18	55,510	346,042	1,866,636	9,827,182
19	58,806	393,604	2,300,774	13,160,992
20	62,300	448,050	2,836,514	17,625,258

is compounded. All things being equal, if you can get even a small fraction of a percent higher in one investment as compared with another, take it—particularly if it's likely the money will remain in that IRA for a long time.

The qualification is that all things be equal. It wouldn't make sense to make a much riskier investment for a slightly higher rate, or to select one that greatly inconveniences you for one reason or another. But if all conditions are reasonably the same, select the investment that pays the most.

Consider three fixed-rate IRAs identical in all particulars except the annual rate of return. One IRA pays 10 percent, the next 10¼ percent, and the third 10½ percent (see Table 4–4).

Investing $2,000 at the start of each year at those constant rates of return, after five years you'd be ahead of the 10 percent IRA only $98 in the 10¼ percent IRA and $196 in the 10½ percent IRA. After 10 years, the difference would be $504 in the 10¼ percent IRA and $1,015 at 10½ percent.

Table 4–7 shows the effect of commissions on a lump-sum You'd be $3,928 ahead in the 10¼ percent IRA and $7,989

TABLE 4–4 ■ **Over a Long Period, Even a Little Change in the Rate of Return Can Make a Big Difference** *(Assumes $2,000 Invested at the Start of Each Year)*

Plan Years	10 Percent	10.25 Percent	Difference	10.5 Percent	Difference
1	$ 2,200	$ 2,205	$ 5	$ 2,210	$ 10
2	4,620	4,636	16	4,652	32
3	7,282	7,316	34	7,351	69
4	10,210	10,271	61	10,332	122
5	13,431	13,529	98	13,627	196
6	16,974	17,121	146	17,268	294
7	20,872	21,080	209	21,291	419
8	25,159	25,446	287	25,737	578
9	29,875	30,259	385	30,649	774
10	35,062	35,566	504	36,077	1,015
11	40,769	41,417	648	42,075	1,307
12	47,045	47,867	821	48,703	1,658
13	53,950	54,978	1,028	56,027	2,077
14	61,545	62,818	1,273	64,120	2,575
15	69,899	71,462	1,563	73,063	3,163
16	79,089	80,992	1,903	82,944	3,855
17	89,198	91,499	2,300	93,863	4,665
18	100,318	103,082	2,764	105,929	5,611
19	112,550	115,853	3,303	119,261	6,711
20	126,005	129,933	3,928	133,994	7,989
21	140,805	145,456	4,651	150,273	9,468
22	157,086	162,571	5,485	168,262	11,176
23	174,995	181,439	6,444	188,139	13,145
24	194,694	202,241	7,547	210,104	15,410
25	216,363	225,176	8,813	234,375	18,011
26	240,200	250,462	10,262	261,194	20,994
27	266,420	278,339	11,919	290,829	24,410
28	295,262	309,074	13,812	323,577	28,315
29	326,988	342,959	15,971	359,762	32,774
30	361,887	380,317	18,431	399,747	37,860
31	400,275	421,505	21,229	443,931	43,655
32	442,503	466,914	24,411	492,753	50,250
33	488,953	516,977	28,024	546,702	57,749
34	540,049	572,172	32,124	606,316	66,267
35	596,253	633,025	36,772	672,189	75,936
36	658,079	700,115	42,037	744,979	86,900
37	726,087	774,082	47,995	825,412	99,325
38	800,895	855,630	54,735	914,289	113,394
39	883,185	945,537	62,353	1,012,500	129,315
40	973,703	1,044,660	70,957	1,121,020	147,319

ahead in the 10½ percent IRA. In 30 years, you'd be $18,431 ahead at 10¼ percent and $37,860 ahead at 10½ percent. After 40 years, your 10¼ percent IRA would be worth $70,957 more and the 10½ percent IRA, $147,319 more.

COMPOUNDING MAKES A DIFFERENCE, TOO

If the IRA is a deposit in a financial institution, the frequency at which the money is compounded can also make a big difference, especially for a large sum kept on deposit for many years.

The deregulation of savings accounts has resulted in a greater variance in the compounding methods used by banks and savings institutions. How yields on these investments can be compared is discussed in Chapter 15.

But for an at-a-glance understanding of how important compounding differences can be over the years, look at Table 4–5. It shows how an IRA earning a nominal 10 percent interest rate would grow with various compounding methods if you contribute $2,000 at the start of each year.

The IRA compounded daily will be worth $261 more than the annually compounded IRA after five years; $1,356 more after 10 years; $10,743 more after 20 years; $51,254 more after 30 years; and over $200,000 more after 40 years.

TABLE 4–5 ■ Compounding Makes a Difference, Too *(10 Percent Interest—Assumes $2,000 Invested at Start of Each Year)*

Years	Annual	Semiannual	Quarterly	Monthly	Daily	Advantage Daily over Annual
5	$ 13,431	$ 13,529	$ 13,580	$ 13,616	$ 13,692	$ 261
10	35,062	35,566	35,833	36,018	36,419	1,356
15	69,899	71,462	72,298	72,877	74,140	4,240
20	126,005	129,933	132,048	133,522	136,748	10,743
25	216,364	225,175	229,956	233,300	240,663	24,300
30	361,887	380,315	390,390	397,468	413,141	51,254
35	596,254	633,021	653,278	667,574	699,415	103,161
40	973,704	1,044,651	1,084,049	1,111,982	1,174,566	200,862

With many IRAs, including variable-rate savings certificates, you don't know the future rate of return. You must base
your estimate on past performance and future projections. Even
under those circumstances, if it appears that one IRA investment has been consistently doing a little better than another
with the same characteristics, weigh the odds in your favor
by selecting the one that has been doing best.

UNDERSTAND HOW COMMISSIONS AFFECT INVESTMENT RETURNS

Paying a fee or commission to make an IRA investment is
often worth it. If you can afford and understand the risk in a
self-directed IRA in which you buy and sell stocks, you must
pay brokerage commissions for each purchase or sale. But if
you know what you're doing and make good investments, you
may outpace more conservative investments. Or your research
may lead you to a "load" mutual fund that provides above-
average returns even after deducting the front-end sales
charge, often 8½ percent.

On the whole, though, most people who lack the financial
sophistication and resources needed for self-directed plans and
other more esoteric IRAs may be better off investing 100 percent of their money rather than having the tax-sheltered power
of their IRA contributions reduced by fees or commissions.
Money you pay in commissions can't work for you.

This is especially true if you're not going to contribute to
your IRA for very long. The shorter the time you expect to
keep your IRA, the higher the rate of return you must earn
just to match the return without a fee or commission. On the
other hand, the longer you continue contributing to the IRA
with a fixed fee or commission, the smaller the gap between
the rate you must earn on the IRA with the commission to
match the return of the IRA with no commission.

Table 4–6 shows this relationship. If you pay an 8½ percent commission when you contribute $2,000 to an IRA instead
of investing $2,000 in the first year, you are investing only
$1,830, or $170 less. If both IRAs increase 10 percent in value
during the first year, the $2,000 IRA would be worth $2,200
at year-end, but the $1,830 IRA would be worth only $2,013.

TABLE 4–6 ■ IRA with Commission versus IRA with No Commission *(Assumes $2,000 Invested at Start of Each Year, 8.5 Percent Commission, and Constant 10 Percent Rate of Return)*

Plan Years Completed	IRA with 8.5 Percent Commission	IRA with No Commission	Difference	Return with Commission Needed to Match IRA with No Commission (Percent)
1	$ 2,013	$ 2,200	$ 187	20.22%
2	4,227	4,620	393	16.57
3	6,663	7,282	619	14.81
4	9,342	10,210	868	13.76
5	12,290	13,431	1,141	13.08
6	15,532	16,974	1,442	12.59
7	19,098	20,872	1,774	12.23
8	23,020	25,159	2,139	11.95
9	27,335	29,875	2,540	11.73
10	32,082	35,062	2,980	11.55
15	63,958	69,899	5,941	11.00
20	115,295	126,005	10,710	10.72
25	197,973	216,364	18,391	10.56
30	331,126	361,887	30,761	10.45
35	545,572	596,253	50,681	10.37
40	890,938	973,703	82,765	10.31

For the $1,830 IRA to be worth as much as the $2,000 IRA by the end of the year, the $1,830 IRA would have to increase in value by a hefty 20.22 percent—a little more than double the rate of return on the IRA without commissions.

In time, this gap would narrow. Assuming the same level of annual contributions, after five years the IRA with the 8.5 percent commission deducted each year would have to increase in value at a 13.08 percent rate to be as valuable as the non-commission IRA earning 10 percent, still a significant difference. After 10 years this would drop to 11.55 percent, after 15 years, to 11.0 percent, and after 20 years, to 10.72 percent. Nevertheless, the *dollar* difference would still be substantial and would continue to increase each year. This means that if you're thinking of contributing to an IRA that charges a fixed commission—a load mutual fund, for instance—you should plan on remaining in the program for many years to offset the impact of commissions on your return.

You should also have good reason to anticipate a higher return on the IRA with the commission than on the noncommission IRA. Otherwise there would be no point selecting an IRA that charged a commission. If both gain 10 percent in value annually and contributions of $2,000 are made to both every year, the IRA requiring the 8.5 percent commission would be worth $2,980 less than the no-fee IRA in 10 years, $10,710 less in 20 years, $30,761 in 30 years, and $82,765 less in 40 years.

Table 4–7 shows the effect of commissions on a lump-sum IRA, typically a sum rolled over into an IRA from an employer pension plan. Growing at a constant 10 percent rate and with no additions, a $100,000 lump sum with no commission would be worth $13,689 more in five years than one that required

TABLE 4–7 ■ Effect of Commission on Growth of Lump-Sum IRA *(Assumes $100,000 Lump-Sum Investment, 8.5 Percent Commission, and Constant 10 Percent Rate of Return)*

Plan Years Completed	IRA with 8.5 Percent Commission	IRA with No Commission	Difference	Return with Commission Needed to Match IRA with No Commission (Percent)
1	$100,650	$ 110,000	$ 9,350	20.22%
2	110,715	121,000	10,285	15.00
3	121,787	133,100	11,313	13.31
4	133,965	146,410	12,445	12.47
5	147,362	161,051	13,689	11.97
6	162,098	177,156	15,058	11.64
7	178,308	194,872	16,564	11.40
8	196,138	214,359	18,221	11.23
9	215,752	235,795	20,043	11.09
10	237,327	259,374	22,047	10.98
15	382,218	417,725	35,507	10.61
20	615,566	672,750	57,184	10.49
25	991,375	1,083,470	92,095	10.39

an 8½ percent commission; $22,047 more in 10 years; and $57,184 more in 20 years.

To match a 10 percent return with no commission over a five-year period, the with-commission IRA would have to earn at a rate of 11.97 percent. This would fall to 10.98 percent for 10 years and 10.49 percent for 20 years.

DIVERSIFY YOUR IRA INVESTMENTS—FOR TWO GOOD REASONS

Diversification is a basic rule of investment. The traditional reason for diversifying is to be sure you don't have all of your IRA eggs in one basket. If the bottom falls out of that basket, you'll suffer a major financial setback.

There's no need to diversify with your IRA investments right away, although that might be a good habit to get into. But when your IRA begins to grow, consider alternative investments. You could either roll over or transfer assets into the new IRA or IRAs, or stop making contributions to the old IRA and begin contributing to the new IRA or IRAs.

In addition to the traditional reason, there's another good reason for diversifying IRA investments. It's that unlike most investments, IRAs are subject to IRS rules and regulations. Some penalties for breaking the rules, intentionally or unintentionally, are annoying but mild. But others could disqualify the entire IRA. This would throw all the money in it into your ordinary income for that year and subject you to additional tax penalties besides.

To protect yourself if you have a substantial amount of IRA money—either through investments you have built up over the years or because you rolled a large sum into an IRA from an employer pension plan—split it into two or more IRAs. That way, if a serious technical error is made in handling or moving one IRA, the others would not be affected.

DON'T HESITATE TO MOVE IRAs AROUND

As noted, one of an IRA's great advantages as a personal finance tool is its flexibility. You're not locked into it forever. If you're not satisfied with its performance (or for any other reason), you may move your money out of that IRA and into another one. You can revise your strategy quickly to adapt to changes in financial markets—or in your own circumstances.

Take care to follow IRS rules when moving money from one IRA to another. Those rules are discussed in Chapter 9, which you should read before proceeding with any IRA move. But within those rules you have a great deal of flexibility.

It's possible to overreact to market fluctuations by moving money around too often. A mutual fund's performance may vary considerably from quarter to quarter or even year to year, for instance. But if you're investing for the long term and the fund is long-term oriented and has a good overall record, this should not overly concern you.

There's also a risk of falling into the habit of switching IRA money into each new hot investment or investment fad that comes along. Many of these new investments may have unproven track records—or may cause your IRA to be eroded by fees and commissions even though the new investments do no better than the ones you abandoned.

When it comes to your IRA, don't be in a hurry to be "first on the block" with a new kind of investment. Let someone else go first—and learn if the new investment has flaws or risks that were not immediately apparent.

Make every IRA investment with the hope that it is for the long term and will work out well. But when an investment clearly begins to demonstrate that it is not living up to the promise that you thought it had—or if after a thorough analysis you conclude you could do much better with some other investment—don't hesitate to switch, perhaps seeking professional advice if the sum involved is large.

Under some circumstances, it pays to take a sponsor penalty for pulling out of an IRA investment. IRA savings certificates at banks and savings institutions usually require a penalty if money is withdrawn before maturity. However, if the return you can get by switching to a different certificate or investment is high enough, you'd come out ahead.

Making this calculation involves determining what the original investment would be worth if you held it to maturity. Then subtract the penalty to determine how much you'd have left for the new investment if you switch, and estimate what the new investment would be worth on the old investment's maturity date. If the new investment will be worth much more, the switch would be worth the effort.

Moving your IRA or IRAs could also be part of an overall investment strategy. It hardly pays to open a self-directed IRA that invests in stocks unless you have a fairly large sum. Otherwise your IRA would be eaten up by commissions and odd-lot differentials for buying small amounts of stock. But you may decide to first build an IRA worth $10,000 or $20,000 in bank or savings institution certificates or a money market mutual fund—and then switch to a self-directed plan in which you buy stocks when the sum is big enough to make it worthwhile.

For a while, only people who had rolled money into IRAs from employer plans had IRAs big enough for meaningful stock market investments. But now that the IRA has been universal since 1982, many people who have been committing $2,000 to their IRAs each year have IRAs big enough to make a switch to a self-directed IRA that purchases stock if they wish.

Changes in your own circumstances could also dictate moving IRAs around. If you came into a windfall inheritance that assured a comfortable retirement, you may decide you can afford to take more chances with your IRAs. But if you lose other assets and your IRAs become a substantial part of your holdings, you may wish to begin making more conservative IRA investments. And on the whole, the closer you are to retirement, the more careful you may want to be with IRA funds.

By all means take advantage of opportunities to move IRA moneys that do not require a rollover or transfer from one sponsor to another. If you have an IRA with a family of mutual funds, you can switch assets from one fund to another at a minimal expense without worrying about breaking IRS rollover and transfer rules.

DON'T PUT IRA MONEY AWAY AND FORGET IT

As time goes on, keep an eye on alternative IRA investments. Back in the 1970s, stock market gurus were talking about "one-decision stocks." Supposedly these stocks were such good investments that you could buy them, put them away, and forget them. People who bought those stocks got burned. Investment fashions changed—and many "one-decision" stocks became financial disasters for people who believed the gurus and held on to them.

The point is—*never* put IRA money away and forget it. Monitor your IRAs constantly. Are they doing as well as other IRA investments? If not, why not? And are other investment vehicles now better suited to your circumstances?

The universal IRA has stimulated a lot of creative thinking on the part of IRA sponsors. To bring investments within reach of people with only $2,000 maximum to commit at one time, many new investment approaches were brought to the marketplace when IRAs became universal—and there will be more innovations in the future.

Also, the deregulation of savings rates at banks, savings institutions, and credit unions has resulted in new types of savings vehicles, some of which may also be better suited for you than the IRA investments you have now. To make the most of your IRAs, keep abreast of the changes occurring in financial markets and adjust your IRA investments accordingly.

USE YOUR IRA AS LONG AS YOU CAN

Even though you may have opened an IRA to help finance your retirement, you probably have other sources of retirement income, including social security, interest and dividends from other savings and investments, and perhaps an employer pension plan.

You'll usually come out ahead maintaining your IRAs— and their tax-sheltered earning power—as long as you can. If you must supplement your retirement income from these other sources, consider drawing down funds that produce taxable income first.

As long as you are paying income tax, all things being equal, the tax-sheltered IRA should earn a better return than you could enjoy on other investments after you pay taxes or on most tax-exempt investments. Consider liquidating those investments first, allowing the IRA to continue earning (and perhaps growing) at the tax-sheltered rate. But don't forget to factor in any impact of a higher income on the portion of your social security payments that may be subject to income tax.

By April 1 of the year after you reach age 70½ you *must* begin withdrawing from your IRA according to life expectancy tables prepared by the IRS (or through insurance annuities based on the insurance company's own mortality tables).

If you can afford to get by with as little money from the IRA as possible, your strategy at this point should be to reverse the procedure used during the IRA's buildup years. Just as you tried to bunch contributions at the start of each year during the buildup period, now try to bunch withdrawals at the end of the year. At its extreme, this would mean not making *any* withdrawals until the last day of the year. An explanation of the IRS withdrawal rules and how to stretch out withdrawals if you wish is in Chapter 11.

KEEP YOUR EYE ON THE CPI

In building your IRA, keep trying to earn a return that betters the rate at which prices in general are rising—which is to say, the inflation rate. If you can consistently do that, you'll always be ahead of inflation because you have a powerful investment kicker—the fact that your IRA's earnings are compounding tax sheltered. The larger your IRA becomes, the more effective this kicker can be.

For many years, it was difficult for most people to better the inflation rate with their savings because of ceilings on the interest paid at banks and thrift institutions. But now there are no rate ceilings on savings instruments at these institutions, and they can pay savers whatever they please.

There are also new savings and investment options in the marketplace. These include money market mutual funds, which grew rapidly because they could pay small investors the money market rates formerly available to big investors, as well as "zero-coupon" securities that can provide fixed rates of return for many years out, in effect compounding your earnings automatically.

Consequently, there are now opportunities for beating the inflation rate that did not exist before—opportunities that include federally insured savings instruments that do not hold the risk of capital loss found in the stock and bond markets.

In the United States, the rate at which prices of goods and services rise or fall is measured by the consumer price index (see Table 4–8). The Bureau of Labor Statistics issues these reports every month. If you're not already doing so, start looking for these reports, which are widely carried in newspapers and on radio and television newscasts.

The CPI is not a perfect measure of inflation, but at the moment it is the best inflation measure we have. There can be big swings in the monthly CPI rate for one reason or another. If the CPI rate is higher than the rate your IRAs are

TABLE 4–8 ■ Consumer Price Index, 1960–1984
(Based on Annual Average)

Year	Index	Percent Change
1960	88.7	
1961	89.6	1.0
1962	90.6	1.1
1963	91.7	1.2
1964	92.9	1.3
1965	94.5	1.7
1966	97.2	2.9
1967	100.0	2.9
1968	104.2	4.2
1969	109.4	5.4
1970	116.3	5.9
1971	121.3	4.3
1972	125.3	3.3
1973	133.1	6.2
1974	147.7	11.0
1975	161.2	9.1
1976	170.5	5.8
1977	181.5	6.5
1978	195.4	7.8
1979	217.4	11.3
1980	246.8	13.5
1981	272.4	10.4
1982	289.1	6.1
1983	298.4	3.2
1984	311.1	43

earning now and then, it's nothing to worry about. And there may be periods—hopefully, not many—when inflation is rising at such a rapid rate that it is outpacing all IRA investments comparable with yours month after month. But if the CPI rate is consistently higher than the return on your IRAs—and higher-yielding IRA investments with equivalent safety and convenience are available—then switch your retirement money into those investments.

For a historical perspective, Table 4–8 indicates what the CPI has been doing since 1960. As you can see, it began rising in the late 1960s and reached new and dangerous heights as the 1970s drew to a close. It would have been difficult for most people to beat the inflation rate in many of those years.

But the inflation rate then dropped and averaged only about 4 percent between 1982 and 1984, a period during which it would have been easy to better the inflation rate even with taxable investments—and during which you could easily have more than doubled the inflation rate with an IRA. If you made your first IRA investment when the IRA was made universal in 1982 and continued to contribute every year since, your IRAs should have grown much faster than the inflation rate.

And if the inflation rate turns up again, the new IRA investment options open to savers and investors may make it easier to continue beating inflation in the future.

Part Two

HOW
IRAs
WORK

5

IRA
ABCs

Some general rules apply to individual retirement arrangements no matter how or where they are set up. This chapter provides a broad overview of how IRAs work and refers you to more detailed discussions of key points later in the book. Even if you're not concerned with the finer points of IRA law at the moment, read this chapter so you understand the fundamentals.

It also tells what you must do—and don't have to do—when you file your tax return. And it touches on some more obscure points of IRA law that could become very important if they apply to you.

HOW IRAs MUST BE SET UP

All IRAs must be set up in the United States. However, you may make contributions to the offices of qualified IRA sponsors even if those offices are located outside the United States.

If you work outside the United States during part or all of the year, you may contribute to an IRA only for that portion of your compensation on which you pay U.S. income tax. This effectively excludes many people who work abroad for private companies as well as for other governments, as opposed to members of the armed forces, the diplomatic corps, and other U.S. government employees.

Employees of private companies or other governments may exclude up to $80,000 of overseas pay from U.S. taxable income, but none of this can go into an IRA. If you could put it into an IRA, you'd be deducting it from your income for a second time.

However, you could still open or contribute to an IRA if you make more than $80,000 of overseas pay and it is subject to U.S. taxation, as well as on the basis of any supplemental qualifying taxable income earned in the United States.

An IRA must be set up for your exclusive benefit or for the benefit of your beneficiaries. Unless it is an individual retirement annuity or an endowment contract issued by an insurance company, it must have a trustee or custodian. The trustee or custodian must be a bank, federally insured credit union, savings and loan association, person, or other entity found eligible to act as a trustee or custodian by the IRS. In practice, this will be taken care of automatically by the IRA sponsor. You are not allowed to be your own trustee or custodian.

Except in cases of rollovers, all contributions must be made in cash (which can include checks, money orders, money market fund withdrawal orders, etc.) Rollover contributions can be made in property other than cash, but *only* if this is exactly the property rolled over. Typically, it is stock in the company sponsoring the plan.

The money or other assets in your IRA must be fully vested at all times. This means if it is in a plan where you work, you must have the right to take all of it with you if you leave that job.

No part of your IRA can be used to buy a life insurance policy, and the assets in your IRA cannot be combined with other property except in a common trust or investment fund.

If you have income that qualifies, you can start or contribute to an IRA for any year up to (but not including) the year in which you reach age 70½, even though you may also be receiving retirement income from social security or some other pension plan or IRA. Your IRAs do not affect your social security benefits or any other pension benefits to which you are entitled. IRAs are intended to supplement all other pension benefits and cannot result in your losing any other retirement income. However, under some circumstances they could increase your retirement income to the point where a portion of your social security benefits would become taxable.

Within the limits set by law, the IRS doesn't care how often you contribute or how large or small your contributions are. However, individual IRA sponsors may set their own minimum contribution requirements.

DEADLINES FOR OPENING AND CONTRIBUTING TO IRAs

You can set up or contribute to an IRA at any time between the beginning of one tax year and the due date for filing your federal income tax for that year, *not* including extensions. Most people are on a calendar tax year. Their filing deadline is April 15 (or April 16 or 17 if April 15 is a Saturday or Sunday) of the year following the tax year.

If you file your return before the deadline, you *are* allowed to deduct the contribution on your return before you actually make it. You could file your return in January, for instance, and delay opening an IRA or making the final contribution until as late as April 15. If you are entitled to a tax refund and receive it before April 15, you could then use the refund to make part or all of your IRA contribution for that year.

Until the 1984 tax year, many people were stretching the period in which they could do this by applying for extensions of their tax filing date, typically to August 15. However, the IRS has stopped this practice by requiring that irrespective of whether you receive a filing date extension, contributions for the previous tax year must be made by the statutory deadline, which for all taxpayers on a calendar year is April 15. Unless you are on a different tax year, all contributions made between April 16 through the end of the year will apply only for the year in which made.

Consequently, you normally have a 15½-month period in which to set up and contribute to an IRA for any given tax year. But if you make any contributions between January 1 and April 15, be sure you clearly instruct the sponsor as to the years for which your contributions are to apply. This is an area in which the IRS has tightened the reporting requirements for IRA sponsors. If you make your final 1986 contribution in April 1987, for instance, be sure the sponsor credits the contribution to 1986, not 1987.

If you wish, you can also set up an IRA with a sponsor before making any contributions. This might make sense if it involved a payroll or other regular deduction plan—automatic withdrawals from your checking or savings account, for instance—that would take effect soon after you authorized it.

WHAT INCOME QUALIFIES?

Any money you're paid for doing something is "compensation" and qualifies as income for the purpose of setting up an IRA. This includes all wages, salaries, tips, professional fees, bonuses, and commissions as well as royalties for books, songs, and inventions and any other payments for your personal services. Beginning with the 1985 tax year, it includes taxable alimony and separate maintenance payments. Prior to 1985, to include alimony as compensation you had to meet a number of special conditions, which effectively excluded most people receiving alimony.

Compensation also includes your *net* income from self-employment, whether as a self-employed professional or as an owner and sole proprietor operating your own business. Net income is your *gross* income from self-employment less any expenses related to your self-employment or own business income. These expenses would be deducted on your tax return and must be subtracted from your self-employment gross income to arrive at your net income from that source for that year. (This must be further reduced by contributions to Keogh plans or SEP IRAs.)

People who work full time will easily earn more than $2,000, the minimum net income required to make the maximum $2,000 IRA contribution. Whether you can afford a $2,000 contribution is something else again.

Many people who earn less than $2,000 of qualifying income during the year may wish to contribute 100 percent of that amount. They include people who are supported by a spouse or have nonqualifying sources of income, such as interest, dividends, and rents, and also have a small qualifying income. This could be from part-time work, self-employment, or a side business.

You *are* allowed to combine incomes from different sources to reach the total amount of qualifying income. If you had net income of $500 from free-lance writing or a side business and $1,600 from a part-time job, your total income for purposes of establishing an IRA would be $2,100, or $100 more than the $2,000 needed to contribute the maximum. And if one or more part-time businesses shows a loss for the year, you are *not* required to deduct those losses from any income from salary or wages. In other words, side income always adds to qualifying income and can never reduce it.

If you are an active partner in a partnership and provide services to the partnership, your income from the partnership also qualifies as income for setting up an IRA. The key word is *active*. If you are an inactive partner who simply invests in the business and doesn't provide services, your share of the partnership income does not qualify. Also, income received as a shareholder in a Subchapter S corporation does not qualify.

By the same token, earnings and profits from other investments for which you do no more than put up money do not qualify. This includes interest, dividends, rents, and short- and long-term capital gains. All amounts that you exclude from your taxable income, such as certain amounts earned by U.S. citizens working abroad, don't qualify either. And you are not allowed to use unemployment benefits or pension income as the basis for an IRA.

If your income is entirely from investments, interest, and dividends, you may be tempted to set up a corporation or otherwise structure your investments to pay yourself a fee or salary for managing them and then establish an IRA on the basis of the fee or salary. Be forewarned that the IRS has thought of that. It classifies paying yourself "unreasonable compensation" for managing your own investments as a "prohibited transaction." If it concludes that your fee or salary for managing your own investments is "unreasonable," it will disqualify that IRA. All the money in it will be thrown into your income for that year, and you may be subject to additional tax penalties.

Also, any such corporation may be deemed a "personal holding company." This introduces another series of tax problems. Never take such a step without competent professional advice.

CAN YOU BORROW TO BUY AN IRA?

In a word, yes.

There is some confusion on this point. While you may borrow money to buy tax-exempt investments—municipal bonds, for instance—the IRS will not allow you to deduct the interest on those loans. The reason is that if you're not going to be taxed on the income from the investment, it isn't fair for you to deduct the cost of borrowing money to make the investment.

IRAs, however, are not tax exempt. Sooner or later, all the money in an IRA becomes subject to taxation. And so if you borrow money and use it to contribute to an IRA, you *can* deduct the interest under current IRS regulations.

In fact, borrowing to open or contribute to an IRA will make good economic sense for many people, especially if you plan to keep the money in the IRA for a relatively long period of time. The loan should be paid off in a few years or less. Meanwhile, you gain the IRA's double economic advantages. It reduces your tax for the year in which the contribution is made, and over the years the earnings or gains compound while tax sheltered.

The loan's actual cost is reduced by whatever you save in taxes by deducting the interest if you itemize deductions on your return. If you're in a 25 percent bracket, in effect the government will pay one dollar of every four of the interest. If you're in a 50 percent bracket, your actual cost will be half the stated cost.

As the economics of this kind of borrowing become better understood, it's likely more people will fund part or all of their IRA contributions this way. Some financial institutions now seek to make loans of this type. It wouldn't pay to borrow to open an IRA if you couldn't afford to repay the loan—or if repaying it would work an economic hardship on you or your family. But if an IRA contribution deadline nears and you don't have the cash available, consider looking into the economics of making the contribution with a loan.

WHAT ARE YOUR INVESTMENT OPTIONS?

There are three kinds of individual retirement arrangements—individual retirement accounts, individual retirement annuities, and individual retirement bonds.

If you have a pension, retirement, or profit-sharing plan at work that provides for it, you can also contribute up to $2,000 to that plan and deduct your contribution on your tax return rather than opening an IRA or IRAs of your own. The pros and cons of doing so are discussed in Chapter 8.

Individual retirement bonds were issued by the U.S. government, but they are no longer being sold. As discussed in the last section of this book, even if you are under age 59½ you may now cash in any you own and roll the proceeds over into some other type of IRA if you wish.

Individual retirement annuities are issued by life insurance companies. They build in value during the years you make contributions and, if you wish, can be used to provide guaranteed payments to you when you retire, with a number of payment options.

Individual retirement annuities (and endowment contracts) are not allowed to have fixed premiums. (If the premiums were fixed, you would be obligated to make IRA contributions in future years even if you found you couldn't afford them—or, worse still, even if you no longer earned compensation that qualified to support the contributions.) Annual premiums for IRA annuities or endowment contracts are not allowed to exceed $2,000.

While you are not allowed to buy life insurance as an IRA, you may buy it in connection with an IRA if the premiums are paid separately and are not part of your IRA contributions.

Any other individual retirement arrangements you make are called individual retirement accounts. These include savings accounts at banks, savings and loan associations, and credit unions; accounts at mutual funds and families of mutual funds; self-directed plans (meaning you make the investment decisions and can buy stocks, bonds, or anything else that attracts IRA sponsors); as well as a wide range of other qualifying investments including zero-coupon bonds, real estate and oil and gas partnerships, securities of the Government National Mortgage Corporation, and deeds of trust.

One thing you can no longer do (at this writing, anyhow) is set up a self-directed IRA to invest in "hard" assets—such things as coins, stamps, antiques, gold or silver bullion, gemstones, works of art, and collectibles. The 1981 Tax Act in effect outlaws any "hard-asset" IRA established after December 31, 1981.

Your investment options don't stop with one IRA, however. You may have as many IRAs as you wish, provided you don't contribute more than the law allows each year. You could open a savings account for $2,000 this year, a mutual fund IRA next year, and an individual retirement annuity in the following year—or spread your maximum allowable contributions among two or more different IRAs during the same year.

After you start, you're not required by the IRS to make additions to your IRA every year. If you need money for something else or your income falls, you can contribute less than the maximum—or even skip contributions. However, you are *not* allowed to carry forward unused contributions into following years.

If you decide to change IRAs, the IRS allows you to move the assets into another IRA or IRAs. However, some IRA sponsors penalize you for withdrawing before your investment matures or for not holding it for a specified period of time. Penalties of this type may be required by federal regulations for premature withdrawals from deposits in banks and savings institutions. And IRS rules must be followed in making the move. If the move isn't handled properly, the entire IRA could be thrown into your income for that year—and you may have to pay a 10 percent penalty besides.

Generally speaking, you can switch assets from one IRA to another as often as you wish, *provided* it is a transfer made directly from one trustee or custodian to another, and the assets are never under your control.

For each IRA, you are also allowed one rollover per year in which you may handle the assets directly yourself. You have up to 60 days in which to complete the rollover of these assets, giving you in effect an interest-free loan for that period. But these rollovers must be at least 12 months apart per IRA.

Of great importance to people with retirement plans at work, if you are given a lump-sum distribution from your employer's pension, retirement, or profit-sharing plan when you quit your job, are fired, or retire—or if your employer terminates the plan—any part or all of this money can also be rolled into an IRA within 60 days and sheltered from taxation. If you don't mix these assets with other IRAs, you may later roll them back into another employer's plan if the new employer will allow it. The decision whether to roll the assets from your employer plan into an IRA could be one of the most important you'll ever make.

HOW LONG CAN YOU CONTRIBUTE—AND WHEN CAN YOU TAKE MONEY OUT?

Rules covering withdrawals from IRAs and how long you may continue contributing to them are generally the same for all IRAs except individual retirement bonds, which stop paying interest when you reach age 70½ whether you cash them in or not. These rules are:

1. You cannot take money out of an IRA before age 59½ without paying substantial tax penalties unless you are disabled. Chapter 6 discusses these penalties and other potential problems with the IRS.

2. Between ages 59½ and 70½, you may withdraw as much or as little as you wish each year. At the same time, if you wish you may continue contributing to your IRA to the limit allowed (assuming you are earning compensation that qualifies). Even if you are no longer working, some compensation that qualifies includes royalties, commissions, fees, or other payments earned currently for work you did in the past.

3. After the beginning of the tax year in which you reach age 70½, you are no longer allowed to contribute to an IRA except if for the previous year. However, if you are one of the relatively few people in what is called a Simplified Employee Pension (SEP), your employer may continue contributing to your IRA after you reach age 70½ even if you are no longer allowed to do so.

4. During the year in which you reach age 70½, you must decide whether to cash in your IRA and pay taxes on it, buy an annuity, establish a payout plan based on your life expectancy or that of you and your beneficiary, or begin a payout schedule that will pay the IRA out during your lifetime or the combined lives of you and your beneficiary or over a shorter period.

Under greatly liberalized payout rules, beginning in 1985 your life expectancy (and that of your spouse, if your spouse is your beneficiary) can be recalculated as frequently as annually as you grow older. Consequently, in most cases it is now possible to ensure that, if you wish, you will never outlive your IRA or IRAs.

5. If you have more than one IRA, you are *not* required to establish the same withdrawal procedures for all of them. You could fully withdraw from as many as you wished at age 59½ without triggering any tax penalties, withdraw all or part of others as you pleased up to age 70½, and then fully withdraw from as many as you wished under permissible payout programs for the remainder. The required payout programs, which must begin by April 1 after the year in which you reach age 70½, need not be identical. However, the minimum amount that must be withdrawn to avoid a serious tax penalty each year must be calculated for each IRA.

While these are IRS rules, some IRA sponsors may have more restrictive rules or penalties for withdrawing from specific investments.

Current government rules covering IRA plans at insured banks, savings and loan associations, and credit unions say that these institutions *may* waive premature withdrawal penalties for fixed-term savings instruments for people aged 59½ and older. However, they are not required to do so— and many don't.

If they wish, these institutions also have the right to refuse to allow any withdrawal from fixed-term savings instruments until these instruments mature. In practice, hardly any institutions would do this, but they could if they wished. You may also have to pay substantial penalties or fees for pulling out of other IRA investments, especially some insurance company annuity plans, in the early years.

PAYING TAX ON YOUR IRA

Federal income tax on money contributed to your IRA over the years and on your IRA's earnings or gains is not eliminated; it is merely deferred.

Contrary to what some overenthusiastic IRA marketers may suggest, an investment in an IRA is not "tax free." In the end, there is no free lunch. Sooner or later, the money accumulating in your IRA or IRAs must become subject to income tax, whether paid by you, by your heirs, or by your estate.

Your moment of truth with the IRS arrives when you (or your heirs or estate) start withdrawing money from your IRA. The withdrawals (technically called distributions) are subject to taxation as ordinary income for the years in which made, and the new four-year income-averaging computation can be used if it is to your advantage.

In promotional materials, IRA sponsors often state that taxes should be lower when you retire and begin withdrawing "because you will probably be in a lower tax bracket." However, this isn't necessarily so—although that should be no reason for concern. It's quite possible that if you open your IRA early enough and contribute regularly over the years, you would build such a large IRA that when you retire you would not be in a lower bracket. If your IRA is big enough, your retirement income might even put you in a higher bracket.

Astoundingly, IRAs (and Keogh plans) have been criticized for this. But what's wrong with having so much retirement income that you don't fall into a lower tax bracket when you stop working? And possibly having more income in retirement than you enjoyed during your working years? If IRAs can do this for you, how much more fortunate you are than people who find their incomes drastically reduced when they must stop working.

One of the great things about an IRA is how it uses a tax-sheltered mode to build a much larger sum, whether for retirement or any other purpose, than most people could build with taxable investments. You're much better off building a substantial fund with an IRA during your working years and then paying taxes on it as you withdraw money than you'd be paying little or no tax because you have little or no income.

Your goal isn't to be in a lower tax bracket; it is to be more financially secure. Paying taxes on the income from an IRA is a small price to pay for the security it can buy.

WHAT YOU MUST DO AT TAX TIME

When IRAs were first authorized, *all* taxpayers with IRAs were required to file a separate IRA reporting form along with their regular tax return. If you didn't file this form, you were subject to penalties. This caused a lot of confusion and got the the IRA program off to a questionable start.

But the IRS has simplified the rules. You are no longer required to file a separate IRA reporting form with your tax return unless you owe penalty taxes for that year.

If you have one or more IRAs but didn't contribute to any during the year and are not subject to penalties, you don't have to do anything about your IRAs at tax time. It's not even necessary to note anywhere on your return that you have an IRA or IRAs.

If you have contributed to an IRA for that tax year, you should deduct it on either the Form 1040 or the Form 1040A, the "short" form. However, you cannot use the Form 1040EZ.

If all you've done during the tax year is contribute an allowable amount to an IRA or IRAs, your main obligation when you file your federal tax return is to enter the amount contributed—and then subtract it from your gross income, reducing your taxable income accordingly. It is not necessary to break this amount down into parts if you contributed to more than one IRA. But you must also indicate if any part of your contribution was made during the three and a half months between the end of the tax year and the tax filing deadline, usually April 15.

If you have withdrawn any money from an IRA or IRAs during the year, this amount must be listed on Form 1040. This includes any taxable premature distributions from your IRAs as well as allowable distributions if you are age 59½ or older or are disabled.

If you receive a lump-sum distribution from a qualified employer plan and roll it into an IRA during the year, it must be reported according to instructions for filling out that year's Form 1040. These often change from year to year.

A separate IRS form must be filled out and attached to your Form 1040 if you owe *penalty taxes* for that year. This is Form 5329, "Return for Individual Retirement Arrangement Taxes." These include taxes for excess contributions, premature distributions, prohibited transactions, or excess accumulations.

If you owe penalty taxes but are not required to file a Form 1040 for that year, file the completed Form 5329 with the IRS at the time and place you would have originally filed your tax return. Include a check or money order payable to the IRS for the tax you owe.

Interest earned on IRA assets while they are in your possession between rollovers is taxable as ordinary income during the year in which earned.

WHICH IRA EXPENSES CAN YOU DEDUCT?

If you itemize your deductions, the cost of professional advice about your IRAs is deductible. Lawyers frequently divide their bills into deductible and nondeductible items.

The IRS says in its *Publication 590* that administration fees charged by some IRA sponsors "which are billed separately" are deductible "to the extent that they are ordinary and necessary." If your IRA's trustee does not bill you separately for these fees, it would be advisable to pay them with a separate check. Clearly mark the check as being for these fees.

Generally, you cannot deduct ordinary transaction costs, such as the commission on the purchase or sale of stocks. (Note: You cannot deduct those for non-IRA investments either. The difference between the purchase and sale prices *after* commissions and fees are deducted is your net capital gain or loss.)

SUPPORTING TAX DOCUMENTS

All IRA sponsors are required to send you a full account of your IRA by June 30 following the end of your tax year. (It's not possible for them to provide this information much sooner because so many people wait until April to make their final contributions.) It's up to you to keep track of your contributions and to report the total for that year on your return. These reports from IRA sponsors are for your information only and should not be forwarded to the IRS. However, keep them in your files in case your return is audited.

If you receive a *total distribution* from any IRA during the year, the sponsor must send you a Form 1099R, "Statement for Recipients of Total Distributions from Profit Sharing, Retirement Plans, and Individual Retirement Accounts." This form contains the amount distributed and indicates the type of distribution. These are a premature distribution, rollover, disability, death, prohibited transaction, normal distribution, excess contribution refunded (including earnings), transfer to an IRA for a spouse because of divorce, or "other." The Form 1099R is for your information only and need not be attached to your tax return.

If you receive periodic payments from your IRA, the sponsor must send you a Form W2P, "Statement for Recipients of Periodic Annuities, Pensions, Retirement Pay, or IRA Payments." These include regular payments to people who have become disabled as well as people aged 59½ or older who have started withdrawing from their IRA. A copy of this form should be attached to your return. (Note: Generally, a "periodic" payment from an IRA is a regular payment specified in a written agreement.)

IRAs SET UP BY EMPLOYERS AND LABOR UNIONS

An employer trust account can be set up for you by your employer, union, or employee association. Typically, employers that do this are small firms that do not want to be burdened with the red tape and other requirements of a regular employer pension or retirement plan.

With this kind of IRA, the employer, union, or employee association makes all the arrangements. It decides where to invest the money and makes contributions to the IRA trustee on your behalf. You are allowed to deduct the contributions on your tax return, and your records are maintained separately from those of other participants in the plan. When you leave the company or union, you take this IRA with you as your own and may then do with it as you wish.

If you have this kind of IRA, your maximum contributions to it by your employer and any by you to IRAs you set up on your own is $2,000 (or $2,250 in the case of spousal IRAs). If your employer contributes the full $2,000, you may not contribute to any IRAs of your own. If the employer contributes less than $2,000, you may contribute the difference either to your own IRA or to the one set up for you by your employer, assuming your employer allows it. Usually it would be advisable to contribute the difference to an IRA of your own so it will be under your control.

(Note: This is not the same as a SEP IRA, discussed in Chapter 12, which has higher contribution limits and different rules.)

CAN YOU GIVE AWAY OR TRANSFER AN IRA?

Technically, you can give away an IRA at any time. However, the entire gift would be included in your taxable income for that year. Consequently, this move should be avoided. If the gift was made before you reach age 59½, you'd also have to pay the 10 percent early distribution penalty.

A transfer of interest in your IRA or any part of it—to satisfy a creditor, for instance—would have the same consequence as a gift.

Don't even consider giving an IRA away or transferring any part of one to someone else without getting professional advice. Even then, do so only if confronted with very unusual financial problems.

WHAT HAPPENS TO YOUR IRA IF YOU DIE?

When you set up an IRA, you are asked to name a beneficiary or beneficiaries. If you die before you withdraw all of your IRA, the balance will be paid to your beneficiary or beneficiaries. Up to this point, that sounds simple. However, there are several beneficiary options, and professional advice may be called for here.

When your IRA reaches a substantial size, you may want advice in deciding whether to specify how your death benefits should be distributed—and if the answer is affirmative, what to specify. And if your beneficiaries have options to exercise and don't fully understand the implications of those options, certainly they should seek advice before doing anything—particularly if the IRA is substantial.

There have been several recent changes in the law covering what IRA beneficiaries may or may not do. If the required distributions that start after you have reached age 70½ have already begun when you die, the remaining assets in your IRA must be distributed to your beneficiaries at least as rapidly as the method being used on the date of your death. But if you die before these required distributions have begun, the beneficiaries have several options. These are discussed in more detail in Chapter 11, but will be summarized briefly here.

Until 1984 one option open to all beneficiaries was to treat the IRA (or their portion of one) as their own—but now only a spouse is allowed to do that. Under current law, if a spouse so desires, the spouse may in effect be placed in the "shoes" of the deceased. This would be a great advantage if the spouse has other means of support and wants the money in the IRA to continue growing in a tax-sheltered mode for as long as possible.

If your spouse elects to treat the IRA inherited from you as his or her own, distributions can be delayed until the date on which you would have reached age 70½. The distributions would be covered by the regular IRA payout rules.

Of course, if the spouse needs or wants the money immediately, he or she can take all or part of it in a lump sum and pay taxes on it.

For beneficiaries other than your spouse, under current law if the required distributions that must be made after you have reached age 70½ have not begun, in general death benefits must be distributed to your beneficiaries within five years of your death. However, if the distributions are started no later than one year after your death, the money can be distributed over a period not to exceed the beneficiary's life or life expectancy.

In the past, you could leave up to $100,000 from an IRA to anyone without incurring estate taxes. However, this exclusion was repealed effective for estates of decedents dying after December 31, 1984.

CAN YOU CONTRIBUTE TO AN IRA AFTER YOU DIE?

The question is more than academic. Under some circumstances it could involve thousands of dollars for the executor of an estate or the IRA's beneficiaries.

In a discussion of this question in *Savings Institutions* magazine, a tax deferral specialist for the U.S. League of Savings Institutions said that while it is likely that the IRS would challenge a posthumous IRA contribution, there are good arguments for allowing it. She observes that nothing in the IRS Code or regulations specifically prohibits or permits a posthumous contribution.

The IRS argues that to be a valid IRA trust, the trust must be established "for the exclusive benefit of an individual." It concludes that an individual who is deceased will not benefit in any way from an IRA contribution.

But one court case involving an IRA rollover found otherwise. An estate tried to roll over a lump-sum distribution received by an employee who died prior to rolling it over; the rollover was completed within the 60-day period allowed for rollovers. The IRS refused to recognize the rollover on grounds that only the employee had the right to make it. But the court decided that the power of an executor to act in the same manner as the decedent included the power to make a rollover into an IRA. From this, it could also be argued that the same logic could be extended to the executor making a posthumous IRA contribution.

Obviously, this is an area where you should consult with a tax counsel before taking any action.

IRAs NOT SAFE FROM CREDIT CLAIMS

Are assets in IRAs protected from creditors? Apparently not, according to a 1984 court case in the state of New York. A state supreme court judge rejected a claim that only spouses, former spouses, or children of an account holder can get access to an account holder's IRA, and then only in cases of negligence in making alimony or child support payments.

The account holder was trying to keep a creditor from claiming an $8,000 IRA in a savings bank as part of a $277,500 judgment for fraudulently obtaining money from the creditor. The account holder argued that he would suffer bank penalties, lost interest, and tax penalties if his IRA was awarded to the creditor.

But the judge found that the federal legislation creating IRAs provides only protection from current income taxes for the holder of an IRA and not protection from creditors. He ruled that an IRA is a "self-settled trust," or funds voluntarily paid over by a depositor for his own ultimate benefit, revocable at will. As such, the judge said that if the self-settled trust is subject to the settler's control and can be abrogated when the settler wishes, it is subject to attack by creditors.

6

Pitfalls
and Penalties:
Avoiding Problems
with the IRS

Although IRAs offer great investment opportunities, they are also creatures of the IRS—and if you break IRS rules regarding IRAs it usually triggers tax penalties.

Some of these penalties are more vexing than damaging, but others may have serious financial consequences. In some cases your IRA will be disqualified no matter how large it has become, throwing all of the assets into your ordinary income for that year. If this puts you in the 50 percent tax bracket, you'll have to give half of your IRA to the government—and you may have to pay a 10 percent penalty besides, leaving you with only 40 percent of your IRA to reinvest for taxable returns.

But for any IRS rule violation, the penalty applies only to that IRA. Any other IRAs you may have are not affected, another good reason for diversifying your IRA assets—especially if they are so large that they represent a substantial part of your net worth.

Usually, people who get into trouble with the IRS do so because they don't understand an IRA's limitations. When you open an IRA you may be thinking more of projections of its future growth than of the fine print that spells out those limitations and your own obligations. Understandably, the sponsor is more concerned with emphasizing an IRA's benefits than with dwelling on pitfalls that may lie ahead. And some people selling IRAs are themselves uninformed or misinformed about the rules and the trouble you can get into by breaking them, so understanding these rules is your responsibility.

Many rules that got people into trouble with the IRS in the early years of the IRA program were eliminated when Congress expanded it in 1982 to everyone who works. You no longer need worry about whether you are an "active participant" in another pension or retirement plan at any time during the year, a provision that until 1982 disqualified large numbers of IRAs.

But other danger areas remain. Especially try to avoid getting involved in what the IRS calls a *prohibited transaction,* which can trigger the most severe penalties. You also risk penalties that could be very costly when you engage in IRA rollovers and transfers.

While it's easier to avoid now, there are still circumstances that could find you making an *excess contribution,* which in some IRS literature is called an *excess payment.* You may be able to correct the excess by withdrawing it, and the consequences for making one are usually less severe than for other rules violations. But the rules themselves are complicated.

The other side of that coin comes after you are age 70½ and must begin a regular withdrawal program from your IRA. If you don't withdraw enough money each year the IRS can penalize you for what it calls an *excess accumulation.* (See Chapter 11 for an explanation of these rules.)

A penalty box in Table 6–1 (see pp. 108–9) summarizes the major IRS rule violations regarding IRAs and the penalties that may be assessed.

Finally, along with those from all other pension and retirement plans, distributions from IRAs are now subject to backup income tax withholding rules. It's easy to avoid withholding by electing not to have tax withheld—but the election won't be valid unless you've complied with the information-reporting requirements of this law.

PREMATURE DISTRIBUTIONS

One very common violation of IRS rules occurs when people find they need some or all of the money in the IRA before they reach age 59½—and then proceed to withdraw it. Often this happens because they get carried away by the idea of opening an IRA. They fail to look realistically at their own financial resources and their ability to do without the money until they are near retirement.

Sometimes people simply don't trouble to read and understand the rules even though they are clearly and prominently explained in the sponsor's literature. But despite the most realistic assessments and the best of intentions, people may find that they need money for an emergency.

Nobody likes to pay a tax penalty to the IRS. But under some circumstances, the penalty for a premature distribution may not be all that serious. When you make a premature distribution, the amount must be included in your gross income for the year in which it was withdrawn. Unless you're permanently disabled, you'll also have to pay a 10 percent tax penalty on the premature distribution.

Example. You've been building an IRA for many years and find you need $10,000 for a medical emergency. When you withdraw the $10,000, it's added to your gross income for that year. Unless you have lost at least $10,000 of ordinary income from some other source, this will probably push you into a higher tax bracket for the added amount of income. If you're not permanently disabled you'll also have to pay the 10 percent penalty, which is $1,000.

The money that remains in your IRA, however, is not affected. This is an important point. All the premature withdrawal penalty affects is the amount withdrawn.

These are IRS penalties only. Depending on the kind of IRA, the IRA sponsor may charge a penalty or withdrawal fee for withdrawing money before the end of an agreed-upon period.

You are not allowed to "make up" the premature distribution by putting money back into your IRA or IRAs in future years. Consequently, another (and often little-appreciated) aspect of this penalty is the "hidden" loss of the tax-sheltered compounding power represented by the sum withdrawn.

THE "HIDDEN LOSS" CAN BE SUBSTANTIAL

The longer you would have allowed the money to remain in your IRA, the greater this hidden loss. Instead of having the full amount earning for you at a tax-sheltered rate in the future, all you'll have remaining will be what's left after the penalty is assessed and taxes are paid—and the earnings on what's left will be taxable.

For instance, each $1,000 earning a constant 10 percent return would grow to $2,593 in 10 years, $6,727 in 20 years, and $17,449 in 30 years. If you withdrew $10,000 that could have earned at this rate when you are at age 49½, you will have reduced the amount that would have been available penalty free had you waited until age 59½ by nearly $26,000. If you withdrew it at age 39½, you will have reduced it by more than $67,000; and if you withdrew it at age 29½, you will have reduced it by about $175,000.

If you didn't spend all the money, your "hidden loss" would be reduced by the earnings on what remains of the money after it is distributed to you. This would be what's left after you pay tax on the distribution as ordinary income and pay the 10 percent tax penalty as well.

Let's assume you're in a 33 percent tax bracket, for 1985 filed a joint return, and had an aftertax income of between $36,630 and $47,670. For each $1,000 prematurely distributed, you'd have to give the government $333 for income tax. You'd also have to pay a $100 tax penalty, for a total of $433. This would leave you with only $567 remaining per $1,000 to begin with.

■ **"Hidden Loss" of IRA Compounding Power Due to Premature Distribution** *(Assumes Constant 10 Percent Annual Return)*

Amount Prematurely Withdrawn	What Tax-Sheltered Sum Would Have Grown To		
	10 Years	20 Years	30 Years
$ 1,000	$ 2,593	$ 6,727	$ 17,449
5,000	12,965	33,635	87,245
10,000	25,930	67,270	174,490

Even if you invested all of this in a taxable mode, in a short time you'd be many thousands of dollars behind. After 10 years, for each $567 invested at a constant (but taxable) 10 percent return, after paying 33 percent to the government each year you'd have $1,084, or $1,509 less than the $2,593 for each $1,000 earning at a tax-sheltered rate in the IRA.

After 20 years, for each $567 invested you'd have $2,074, or $4,653 less than the $6,727 for each $1,000 in the IRA; and after 30 years, you'd have $3,967, or $13,482 less than the $17,449 for each $1,000 in the IRA.

Before deciding to take a premature distribution from an IRA, sit down with paper, pencil, calculator, or computer and try to estimate how much "hidden loss" you'd suffer in addition to the obvious penalties—taking the money as ordinary income and paying the 10 percent penalty. Include this estimate with the other factors you must weigh in deciding whether to take the premature distribution.

Note also that this "hidden loss" is also part of the penalty you must pay if you must take an involuntary distribution of a large sum from an IRA. This could happen if you make a technical error in moving money or other assets from one IRA to another or from a company plan to an IRA—or because the IRS disqualifies your entire IRA because of certain serious rule violations discussed later in this chapter.

WHAT THE IRS MEANS BY "DISABLED"

Unfortunately, the only way to avoid paying penalties for taking money out of an IRA before age 59½ is to be classified as "disabled." Obviously, there can be honest disagreements about exactly what "disabled" means. This is bound to start some people who suddenly need their IRA money thinking about becoming "disabled" just enough to meet the letter of the law—and to do so with "disabilities" that may be more imaginary than real.

However, the IRS has fairly precise guidelines as to what "disabled" means. Unless you measure up to them, you'd better be prepared to pay the penalty if you take money out of an IRA before you reach age 59½.

According to the IRS, you are "disabled" only if you are "unable to engage in any substantial gainful activity." The disabling condition, which could be physical or mental, must have lasted or be expected to last for a long period or must be expected "to lead to death."

The IRS adds that a condition that can be corrected is *not* a disability. You will not be considered disabled if, "with reasonable comfort and safety, the condition can be lessened so that the person can engage in substantial gainful activity."

To be certified as "disabled," you must attach appropriate medical statements to your tax return. For the first year, this means a doctor's statement about the disability. You must also attach a statement explaining the effect of the mental or physical condition, why you're not able to engage in "substantial gainful activity," and the date the condition began.

From then on, each year's tax return must have an attached statement saying the condition has not lessened substantially and that it still affects "engaging in any substantial gainful activity."

CAN A SPONSOR REFUSE TO PAY YOU?

Most literature prepared by IRA sponsors does not stress the point, but if you insist on withdrawing money from your IRA before age 59½, in virtually all cases you can get it.

The exceptions would be if the sponsor's right to refuse was expressly stated in your agreement with the sponsor, as is the case with some depository institutions, and the sponsor actually exercised that right. To avoid public relations problems, most of those sponsors would allow you to take the money anyhow.

SPONSORS MUST REPORT ALL DISTRIBUTIONS

Sponsors are required to report all distributions from an IRA to the IRS, just as they report your interest and dividends. Consequently, one way of triggering an IRS audit would be to fail to report the premature distribution on your own tax return. The IRS computer capability for matching sponsor reports with individual returns has been greatly expanded and can be expected to continue to improve. Now that IRAs can be opened by everyone who works, it can be expected that the IRS will watch this area of possible abuse closely.

In addition, you must pay an automatic penalty of 5 percent of the total unreported income on distributions.

DOES IT EVER PAY TO TAKE A
PREMATURE DISTRIBUTION?

While we strongly advise against breaking IRS rules, the fact is that *as the rules are now written* there are circumstances where it could pay you to withdraw money from an IRA before age 59½.

Probably this step should not be undertaken without consulting an attorney, accountant, or tax adviser—especially if it involves a substantial sum or there is a large sum in your IRA. The closer you get to age 59½, the more cautious you should be about jeopardizing the entire IRA by making a technical misstep or being unaware of a change in IRS rules and regulations or in the tax law itself.

Circumstances could arise, however—the loss of a job or other relied-upon income, catastrophic medical bills, or a need for more cash to keep your business from going bankrupt— that would make the need for immediate cash more important than the penalties for withdrawing the money. Under those circumstances, the longer you've maintained your IRA and the more it has grown, the more likely that after paying the penalty you'd come out ahead.

For instance, a $2,000 investment each year for 20 years at a 10 percent return would build an IRA worth about $126,000, toward which you had invested only $40,000. If your income was entirely cut off because you lost your job, you could make gradual withdrawals from the IRA to cover your living expenses until you found another job. These withdrawals could be at the same rate at which you were earning income or less, so you wouldn't be thrown into a higher tax bracket.

If it took you a whole year to find another job and your living expenses and other financial obligations required withdrawing $40,000 from the IRA, your total tax penalty would be the 10 percent premature distribution tax, or $4,000. Meanwhile, your IRA would continue earning at the tax-sheltered 10 percent rate and would be worth about $100,000 at the end of that year.

You'd have suffered a setback in your IRA program. But the penalty you paid for meeting all living expenses and other financial obligations for you and your family during that year would make it a bargain. In fact, even if the money withdrawn did push you into a higher tax bracket, in time your IRA would grow to where you could take the withdrawal into your income and come out ahead of investments with comparable safety on which you had to pay taxes all along.

SHOULD YOU BUILD LONG–TERM STRATEGIES AROUND TODAY'S PENALTIES?

Inevitably, some people are devising long-term strategies around the fact that under many circumstances the 10 percent penalty isn't all that serious. Some tax advisers, financial institutions, and money management writers and publications have suggested using IRAs to meet savings goals even if it involves withdrawing money before you reach age 59½.

One financial institution suggested in its advertisements that sometimes an IRA "can be a shortcut to saving for a house or a car." A major accounting firm has advised financial institutions to develop schedules showing investment accumulations for IRAs with and without penalties. The schedules were to include "crossover points" showing where you'd come out ahead even though you withdrew money before age 59½. For instance, for people in a 30 percent bracket the crossover point would be reached after 11 years with an 8 percent return, and after 7 years with a 12 percent return.

Certainly the 10 percent premature distribution penalty shouldn't deter anyone from opening an IRA. And people who build investment strategies around deliberately violating the intent of the law by taking money out of an IRA before they reach age 59½ may very well profit greatly. However, it's also possible that this strategy could backfire. As we have emphasized elsewhere, the IRA program is in a constant process of change. No IRA rules or regulations are written in stone. Congress will keep changing the law, and the IRS continually revises its rules and regulations.

If growing numbers of taxpayers begin deliberately violating the spirit of the law by basing investment strategies on taking money out of IRAs before they reach age 59½, Congress may at least consider increasing the premature distribution penalty. If some future Congress raises the penalty to 15 or 20 percent or more, all of the "crossover points" based on the current 10 percent penalty would be meaningless.

For the record, it should also be noted that the securities industry is trying to persuade Congress to drop the premature distribution penalty entirely. But anyone thinking of building a long-term investment strategy around the current 10 percent penalty should be aware of the risk that when they want to start taking money out, the penalty could be higher than it is now.

SOME PROHIBITED TRANSACTIONS DISQUALIFY YOUR ENTIRE IRA

The penalty for engaging in what the IRS calls a *prohibited transaction* can be more serious than for taking a premature distribution. For some prohibited transactions, the entire IRA will be disqualified.

A prohibited transaction is defined as "any improper use" of your IRA account or annuity. Three specific transactions that can trigger the disqualification of your entire IRA are:

- Borrowing money from it.
- Selling property to it.
- Receiving "unreasonable compensation" for managing it.

Having your entire IRA disqualified for one of these prohibited transactions would be serious enough at any time. But if it happened after you had built an IRA for many years to six-figure size or larger, or had rolled over a large sum from an employer pension plan, the consequences could be financially disastrous.

If you had a $300,000 IRA and engaged in one of these transactions, however small, you'd have to take the entire $300,000 into your income for that year, knocking you into the highest tax bracket. If that was the 50 percent bracket, it would cost you $150,000—half the value of the entire IRA—right off the top. If you were under age 59½ and were not disabled, you'd also have to pay the 10 percent premature distribution penalty, adding another $30,000 to your tax bill. When it was all over, instead of a $300,000 IRA, you'd have only $120,000 to invest at taxable rates of return.

Actually these three prohibited transactions are simple and reasonable restrictions aimed at preventing self-dealing. If you're strapped for cash, you'd be better advised simply to take a premature distribution from an IRA for what you need, especially if you don't need much, rather than trying to borrow from your IRA. Borrowing from almost any other source would be a better alternative. (Note: Actually borrowing *from* your IRA is not the same as pledging part or all of your IRA as security for a loan, for which the penalty is less severe, as discussed later.)

Selling property to your own IRA would also put you in an obvious self-dealing situation, as would paying yourself unreasonable compensation for managing it.

If you engage in any of these prohibited transactions, your IRA will stop being tax sheltered as of the first day of the year in which the transaction occurs, and the fair market value of all assets in the IRA must be included in that year's gross income. "Fair market value," according to the IRS, means "the price at which the IRA could change hands between a willing buyer and a willing seller when neither has any need to buy or sell, and both have reasonable knowledge of the relevant facts."

PROHIBITED TRANSACTIONS BY AN EMPLOYER

If you're in an IRA set up by your employer, labor union, or employee association and the prohibited transaction is engaged in by the employer, union, or employee association, you do *not* have to pay any penalties. Your account will not lose its IRA status, and you won't be subject to the premature distribution tax.

But if you participate in the prohibited transaction with your employer, union, or employee association, you will have to suffer the consequences. Your account or annuity will no longer be treated as an IRA, and if you are under age 59½ and not disabled, you'll have to pay the 10 percent premature distribution penalty.

OTHER PROHIBITED TRANSACTIONS

There are two other prohibited transactions for which the penalties are not as severe. These are (1) using your IRA as security for a loan and (2) investing in collectibles (after 1981).

If you use any part of your IRA to secure a loan, that part is treated as a distribution. You must include it in your gross income for that year. If you're under age 59½ and are not disabled, you'll also have to pay the 10 percent tax on premature distributions.

Pledging part of your IRA for a loan, however, does *not* disqualify the entire IRA. The part not pledged to secure the loan retains its IRA status. However, if you have an IRA annuity contract and borrow against it, you must include the entire contract's fair market value as of the first day of the tax year in your gross income. If you are under age 59½ and are not disabled, you'll also have to pay the 10 percent premature distribution tax.

The ban on IRA investments in collectibles took effect in 1982. Collectible IRA investments made before that year may be retained and need not be liquidated.

The IRS defines collectibles as including "art work, rugs, antiques, metals, gems, stamps, coins, alcoholic beverages, and certain other tangible property." After 1981, any new IRA investment in collectibles will be considered distributed to you and included in your income for the year in which you made the investment. If you're under age 59½ and are not disabled, you'll also have to pay the 10 percent premature distribution tax.

Collectibles dealers are trying to persuade Congress to make collectibles permissible as IRA investments again but so far haven't made much progress.

EXCESS CONTRIBUTIONS

The danger of making an excess contribution was reduced substantially when Congress opened the IRA program to everyone who works.

Before 1982, your IRA contribution was limited to $1,500 or 15 percent of qualifying income, whichever was less. You had to make this calculation in addition to determining what your income for purposes of contributing to an IRA would be. These requirements led to many complications. Sometimes they resulted in people making excess contributions even though they did all they could to follow the letter of the law.

To make an excess contribution based on your annual income now, you'd have to contribute more than 100 percent of your income that qualifies for purposes of an IRA. Your income would have to be less than $2,000 if it's your IRA alone or no more than $2,250 if a spousal IRA is involved. Most people can easily see if they are violating those rules.

Nevertheless, there are still many ways to make an excess contribution. Often the penalties for doing so aren't serious—but under some circumstances they can be very serious and costly. In any event, the complicated rules covering excess contributions illustrate why there's nothing "simple" about IRA tax laws.

The most serious tax consequences for making an excess contribution stem from rollovers and transfers involving large sums. If a technical error is made in these moves, part or all of the assets being moved may not qualify as tax free and could become excess contributions, costing you thousands of dollars.

The tax consequences for simply contributing more to your IRA than you thought you were allowed to contribute are less serious but are annoying and involve you in additional red tape at tax time.

One problem arises if you plan to contribute the limit but aren't sure what your limit is. You may have financial support or income from other sources, with additional part-time qualifying IRA income from part-time work, self-employment, or a part-time business.

Only *net* income counts toward an IRA. Related business expenses that you deduct on your tax return must be subtracted first. Misunderstandings or errors in making these calculations could result in an excess contribution.

You could also make an excess contribution if you misunderstood the rules about "compensation" and included income from investments or other nonqualifying sources, such as a business in which you are not an active investor or partner.

You'd also wind up making an excess payment if you contribute $2,000 early in January but something happens to cut off your income for the remainder of the year—a serious illness, accident, or loss of a job. It's true that the sooner you make your IRA contributions each year, the faster they'll grow. But it would be prudent not to make a substantial contribution in early January if you're not reasonably sure of earnings sufficient to cover it—in severance pay if you lost your job, if nothing else.

Excess contributions could also result if you're in a plan where the employer makes contributions for you—to a SEP IRA or to an IRA set up by an employer or labor union—and the employer contributes too much. In some cases, even though the employer made the payment, it will be up to you to withdraw the excess contribution.

Finally, you could make an excess contribution simply through carelessness. You might forget that you contributed a few hundred dollars to an IRA back in January, or fail to give proper instructions to an IRA sponsor as to which year in which you wish a payment to apply. This could happen for any contribution made between January 1 and April 15 of any year. Your IRA payments between those dates could apply either to the current year or to the previous one.

It's also possible that, despite your instructions, a sponsor will credit your payment to the wrong year. A letter from the sponsor could clear up the matter—if the sponsor was willing to cooperate and admit the mistake.

PENALTIES AND OPTIONS FOR EXCESS CONTRIBUTIONS

The penalty for an excess contribution is a 6 percent excise tax for each year it remains in your IRA. If you're under age $59\frac{1}{2}$ and not disabled, you'll also be subject to the 10 percent premature distribution tax on the excess contribution's earnings.

More important, if your total contribution for the tax year in which the excess contribution takes place is more than $2,250—apparently indicating a clear intent to contribute more than is allowed—you also risk having the entire excess contribution included in your gross income whether you have deducted it on your tax return or not. This could result in you paying double the tax on the excess.

This picture isn't as grim as it appears at first glance, although it would still be best to avoid making an excess contribution. But if your total contributions come to no more than $2,250, you can avoid most of these penalties by withdrawing the excess payment and its earnings before the date on which your tax return is due. (And, of course, you must *not* deduct the excess payment on your tax return.)

This will excuse you from the 6 percent excise tax and from having the excess contribution included in your gross income. However, if you are under age 59½, you'll have to pay the 10 percent premature distribution tax on the earnings or other income of the excess contribution. The earnings will be included in income for that year.

You also have the option of allowing the excess contribution to remain in your IRA and carrying it over to the following year (or years). To qualify, your total contributions for the tax year (including the excess contributions) must be no more than $2,250. (You are *not* allowed to carry *back* an excess contribution, applying it to an earlier year in which you may have contributed less than allowed.)

If you take the carry-forward option, you'd pay the 6 percent excise tax on the excess contribution for the year in which you made it and carry the excess forward into the following year.

Example. You contributed $2,200 to an IRA for 1985 when you were allowed to contribute only $2,000. You carry the excess $200 forward into 1986 and can contribute only up to $1,800 in that year. For 1985 you would pay an excise tax of $12 ($200 × .06 = 12), plus a 10 percent penalty tax on the earnings of the $200. These earnings would also be taxable.

But, if your total contribution for the tax year including excess contributions is more than $2,250, you are not allowed to carry the excess forward. If the excess is still in your IRA after you file your tax return, you'll have to include it in your gross income even though you didn't originally deduct it.

In effect, this could force you to pay tax on the excess twice. If the excess is $750 and you're in the 30 percent bracket, you must pay an additional tax of $225 ($750 × .3 = 225) even though you didn't deduct the $750 on your return. If you're under age 59½ and are not disabled, you'll also have to pay a 10 percent premature distribution tax of $75, increasing your total tax bill by $300.

Simple? Of course not. IRAs are indeed great investments—but nobody except some IRA sponsors ever said IRAs were simple.

BACKUP INCOME TAX WITHHOLDING

After a bitter fight, in 1983 Congress repealed a law that would have mandated the withholding of income tax from most interest and dividend payments. However, as part of the final compromise on repeal it tightened tax-reporting procedures by passing the Interest and Dividend Tax Compliance Act of 1983, which established a backup withholding system.

Many people are still unaware of the ramifications of this law should they run afoul of it. The key to the IRS reporting system is your taxpayer identification number, which in official literature is often referred to as your TIN. (For individuals, your TIN is your social security number.) If you fail to give the interest or dividend payer your TIN or provide an incorrect TIN, ordinarily the payer is required to withhold a portion of each payment to you at the source for federal income tax. (And, of course, when this money is forwarded to the government you will have been identified to the IRS as someone who, for one reason or another, is not complying with the law.)

Since January 1, 1984, when opening an account at a financial institution, brokerage house, or any other source of taxable interest or dividend income, you must sign a document certifying the correctness of the TIN you are providing. (For accounts opened before that date, institutions are required to ask you for your TIN or to verify that a TIN you have already provided is correct.) To assure "due diligence," the government fines financial institutions and other payers of taxable interest and dividends $50 for each missing or obviously incorrect TIN— as well as for each TIN identified by the IRS as incorrect on the basis of its cross-checking program.

How would an institution know your TIN is "obviously incorrect?" By the number of digits in it. All correct social security numbers have nine digits separated by two dashes, as follows: 000–00–0000. If the TIN on an institution's records is obviously incorrect—even if, it later develops, it's because of a simple mistake made by you, the institution, or the institution's computer—the institution must withhold.

Consequently, whether it involves an IRA or some other account or investment, whenever you receive a communication about withholding from a financial institution or other source of interest or dividend income, take time to read it! It could require action on your part that, if not taken, would result in the withholding of tax on payments to you. Once a payer withholds, it cannot give the money back. You may correct the error or supply a missing TIN, but you'll have to take credit for the amount withheld when you file your tax return.

NO WITHHOLDING ON IRAs—UNTIL YOU TAKE MONEY OUT

Insofar as IRAs are concerned, backup withholding does *not* apply to the interest or dividends earned by your IRA. Even if you fail to provide a TIN, or you provide one that is incorrect, there will be no withholding—at that point. The reason is that because interest or dividends are merely credited to an IRA, they are tax sheltered.

However, the backup withholding program does apply to any distribution from an IRA to you, including regular retirement payments or the distribution of the entire account if you attempt to take it in a lump sum for any purpose, including rollovers.

The backup withholding rules cover payments from all pension and profit-sharing plans and annuities, not just IRAs.

For all of these plans, tax will be withheld from payments to you *unless you elect not to have them withheld.* The paying institution is required to notify you of your right to elect against withholding and to give you an election form to fill out if you wish to exercise this right.

And so for most people receiving payments from an IRA or some other pension or retirement plan, avoiding withholding from these payments will be a simple matter. All you'll have to do is fill out a form, which the interest- or dividend-paying institution is supposed to give you. But for the non-withholding election to be valid, you must have supplied the paying institution or sponsor with your correct TIN. If you haven't supplied a TIN or the TIN you have supplied has been found to be incorrect, the payer will be required to withhold even if you have elected not to have tax withheld—and for some types of payments, it will be at a higher-than-usual rate.

For a discussion of how backup withholding applies to different types of distributions from IRAs and the rates at which income tax is withheld, see Chapter 11.

HAVE CONTRIBUTIONS CREDITED TO THE CORRECT YEAR

Along with the backup withholding system, the government is tightening all of its income tax reporting procedures. When you open or contribute to an IRA, try to be sure that the sponsor credits your contribution to the correct tax year.

The period during which mistakes are most likely to be made is between January 1 and April 15 of every year. During this period your contributions could apply either to the past tax year or to the current one.

In the past, although sponsors were required to report IRA contributions, many were not required to report the year to which they were to apply. But now they must report the year to which your contributions apply, too. Sponsors that fail to do so can be fined $50 for each failure.

Finally, when you make an IRA contribution, be sure *you* know the year to which it is to apply. If you have several IRAs, or make a number of small contributions for each tax year instead of a single large one, it's easier than you think to make an excess contribution because you've overlooked a contribution made earlier.

PREMIUMS FOR IRA DEPOSITS A "GRAY AREA"

People who have received premiums or "gifts" from financial institutions for opening or adding to IRAs may be surprised to learn that the IRS has raised questions about this practice. The IRS reasons that because you receive the premium now, it could be viewed as a distribution from your IRA.

In fact, regulations have been proposed that would classify receiving some premiums as a prohibited transaction, causing the loss of the deduction and the tax deferral for the deposit. If these regulations become final as proposed, they would be retroactive. This would create tax problems for people who received these premiums and who probably aren't even aware that the practice has been questioned.

What *seems* likely is that premiums falling inside the limits established to determine whether they are to be considered "interest" paid to depositors would be exempt from the prohibited transaction rules. According to those limits, if the deposit is $5,000 or less, the premium must cost the institution no more than $10. If it costs more than $10, it is considered part of the interest paid and the institution must report it as such to the government. For deposits of more than $5,000, the maximum premium cost to the institution before it must be treated as interest is $20.

What this means to you is:

- In general, be cautious of *all* offers of premiums or "gifts" for opening or adding to IRAs. Particularly if a substantial sum is involved—as with a rollover from a company plan or from another IRA—check with a professional tax adviser first. It isn't worth putting your whole IRA under a cloud just to get a premium for making a deposit. The IRA program is generous enough on its own merits.
- Especially, *do not* accept premiums that cost the institution more than $10 if your IRA deposit is $5,000 or less, or more than $20 if your deposit is more than $5,000. It is already established that those premiums will be reported as payment of interest to you.

The only way to learn a premium's cost to a financial institution is to ask. Because institutions buy in large volume, their costs for some premiums may be much less than you think. But if people at the institution are unable to tell you the cost, don't make the IRA deposit—or, if you make it, don't accept the premium until you're sure it won't create problems with the IRS.

TABLE 6–1 ■ Penalty Box

Taking money out before age 59½ (if you are not disabled)	Premature distribution	Take amount of distribution into income for that year. Pay 10 percent penalty for that amount.
Contributing more than the limit	Excess payment or excess contribution	If total contributed is $2,250 or less, pay 6 percent excise tax each year on excess amounts remaining in your IRA. If excess is withdrawn before due date of tax return and no deduction taken, no excise tax due. However, if under age 59½ and not disabled, pay 10 percent premature distribution tax on earnings of the excess contribution. If total contributed is more than $2,250, include excess withdrawn in gross income even if it was never deducted.
Borrowing money from your IRA	Prohibited transaction	Account no longer treated as IRA as of first of the year. All assets considered distributed and included in your income for that year. If under age 59½ and not disabled, also pay 10 percent premature distribution tax.
Selling property to your IRA	Prohibited transaction	Same as above.
Receiving "excess compensation" for managing your IRA	Prohibited transaction	Same as above.
Using IRA as security for a loan	Prohibited transaction	Part used as security considered distributed and included in your income for that year. If under age 59½ and not disabled, also pay 10 percent premature distribution tax.
Borrowing on IRA annuity contract	Prohibited transaction	Value of entire annuity considered distributed and included in income for that year. If under age 59½ and not disabled, also pay 10 percent premature distribution tax.

TABLE 6–1 ■ (concluded)

Investing in collectibles after 1981	Prohibited transaction	Amount invested considered distributed and included in your income for that year. If under age 59½ and not disabled, also pay 10 percent premature distribution tax.
Beginning April 1 after year in which you reach age 70½, fail to withdraw minimum amount	Excess accumulation	Pay 50 percent excise tax on the excess accumulation. (Can be excused if you demonstrate "good reason" for not withdrawing enough.)

BE WARY OF UNUSUAL INVESTMENT ARRANGEMENTS

The old saying that if something looks too good to be true, it probably is, also applies to some IRAs. Any time an IRA sponsor promises to pay you substantially more than comparable IRAs are paying but requires that you enter into some out-of-the-ordinary arrangement to earn the higher return, be careful. Check it out with a tax adviser and/or the IRS, particularly if a large sum would be involved.

Actually, avoiding problems of this type is simply a matter of exercising common sense. For instance, some financial institutions have offered "dual-rate" IRA plans. These paid unusually high interest rates for IRA deposits—but required that you put an equal amount in another account that paid little or no interest.

The IRS took a dim view of these arrangements and warned that "serious tax consequences" could be faced by people who invest in them. It reasoned that because the high-interest IRAs required a second account to qualify, the interest in excess of the institutions' regular IRA rate should be considered interest earned on the accompanying account, not the IRA.

The institutions offering these plans believed they were acting within the law. But anyone looking at the unusual terms of these arrangements, coupled with the substantially higher-than-usual returns they offered, should have been fore-warned that the deal required closer scrutiny.

HOW LONG SHOULD YOU KEEP IRA RECORDS?

It would be prudent to keep all records concerning your IRAs for at least as long as you maintain your IRAs. You'll need those records in case of an IRS examination or audit. But while it's not likely the IRS will examine your return after three years have passed from the date of filing, there are many other situations where these records might be useful—or even essential.

They may be needed to establish your rights to the assets in the IRA. They may also be needed by your heirs or estate to establish their rights to the assets if you die—or by whoever handles your affairs if you become permanently disabled in such a way that you are unable to handle your affairs yourself.

They may become essential if an IRA sponsor becomes insolvent or if the sponsor's records are lost or destroyed. Records could conceivably be lost in a fire, earthquake, or other disaster. Questions about your IRA could also arise if records are lost or misplaced in a takeover of one financial institution by another.

The larger your IRA and the more it represents in terms of your total financial assets, the more important keeping all these records in a safe place becomes. It would be a good idea to put them in a safe deposit box and/or make copies of them to be held by others, such as your attorney or your beneficiaries.

7

Women,
Husbands and Wives,
and Widows

The IRA program can be particularly useful to many women, including many who don't work themselves but whose husbands are eligible to have IRAs. All women who work can do everything with an IRA that a man can. They may also use IRAs to help compensate to some extent for the loss of retirement benefits if they stop working to rear children or for any other reason.

And IRAs are especially useful for married couples. If both spouses work and can afford the contributions, it can double the amount that can be sheltered and built in an IRA.

Even if only one spouse works, the added benefits can be substantial. In that case, the law allows what's called a "spousal" IRA to be created for the nonworking spouse. Although the total contribution limit for this couple is only $250 more than for a single IRA, over time the fund that can be built for retirement or any other purposes can be substantially higher.

Periodically, proposals have been made in Congress to increase the spousal contribution. Sooner or later, it is likely that Congress will pass this kind of legislation.

More important, the spousal IRA offers an opportunity—perhaps the only one many nonworking spouses, usually wives, will ever enjoy—to have an independent retirement fund under their control. And because up to $2,000 of the total $2,250 limit can be contributed each year into the IRA of the nonworking spouse if desired, for a nonworking spouse the IRA program holds all the capital-building potential of a regular IRA.

As with any IRA, couples should undertake commitments only if they're in a position to afford them. In many marriages, both partners must work because they need the money for living expenses. Little or nothing would be left over for an IRA.

Other couples could afford an IRA only by dipping into savings—assuming they had savings. And if they might need those savings before reaching age 59½, this would not be prudent.

Still other couples could afford an IRA or IRAs—perhaps easily—by cutting expenses here and there. But for one reason or another, they may prefer not doing so. It might require them to give up things they value more than they value an IRA at that point in their lives.

These are personal decisions. What means most to you? A vacation? A new car or wardrobe? Eating out several times a week? Having a child? Financing an older child's education? An investment opportunity? A hobby? A coveted work of art? Starting a business or keeping one going? Supporting an aged parent? Or earmarking more money for an IRA?

Alternative uses for the money you and your spouse could contribute to an IRA are endless and involve all aspects of your lives. As with all important domestic decisions, if a couple disagrees on goals and priorities, it may lead to spirited—and sometimes bitter—arguments. In short, if you're married, IRA decisions could affect both you and your spouse profoundly—and both of you should be involved in making them.

HOW IRAs CAN HELP WIVES—AND WIDOWS

The IRS words its IRA rules and regulations carefully to make it clear that they apply evenly irrespective of the sex of one spouse or another. In reality, the "nonworking spouse" is usually a woman.

Whether a wife works or not, IRAs offer opportunities for capital-building and retirement income that were not available to her before. One day this extra source of retirement income could prove more important than she realizes.

In recent years, the treatment of a nonworking spouse insofar as pension and retirement benefits to the working spouse are concerned has improved. Although companies are not required by law to have pension plans—and many smaller firms don't have them—once a plan is established, the Employee Retirement Security Act of 1974 (ERISA) requires that they provide for annuities to spouses of deceased employees. The surviving spouse must be paid regular income equal to at least half of the pension paid to the retiree.

To do this, however, the plan may reduce the pension paid to the retiree with a reduced annuity called a "joint and survivor" annuity. Until 1985, married workers had the right not to accept the reduced annuity and the payments to the surviving spouse irrespective of the wishes of the spouse to whom the survivor's payments would be made.

This was changed by the Retirement Equity Act of 1984. Effective in 1985, it requires that the employee's spouse give written consent for any election, including a lump-sum distribution, other than a joint and survivor annuity.

The 1984 act included a number of other important provisions affecting women. It reduced the maximum age a retirement plan can require that an employee attain before becoming a plan participant from 25 to 21. Maternity leaves are no longer treated as a break in service, and a worker can leave his or her job for as long as five years (more in some cases) and still receive credit for participation and vesting purposes after the break in service.

The purpose of these changes was to recognize that under previous rules, many women had great difficulty building retirement credits because they had to drop out of the work force during their child-rearing years. But the new law comes too late to help women who had to drop out of the work force to rear children before this law was passed.

They and millions of other women could face serious financial problems as they grow older, particularly if there are no joint savings or other substantial assets. Most women must live their final years alone. Three fifths of all women older than 65 are unmarried, and two thirds of women over 75 are widows. Elderly widows rarely remarry and on the average live 16 years longer than their husbands. With higher divorce rates adding to the number of elderly women living alone, today only two fifths of women older than 65 live with their spouses.

Despite the growth of the private and public employee pension systems, a Social Security Administration study of newly retired people who left the work force in the early 1980s found that monthly pensions were received by only 53 percent of the married men. Only 10 percent of newly retired married women had pension income, with slightly more unmarried women having some.

When a husband who did not have a pension dies, all a widow may have left other than social security is what income she could draw from an IRA. Many women also lose part or all of the husband's pension rights if there is a divorce.

At least to some extent, an IRA can help women offset these potential disasters. Even if the IRA is her husband's, its value is not reduced when a woman's husband dies. One hundred precent of the money is still there. If he has designated her as his beneficiary, she can take all of it within five years, buy an annuity, or, in effect, place herself in her late husband's "shoes" and make the IRA her own.

A spousal IRA can give a nonworking wife the advantage of having a retirement fund in her own name, one she can do with as she pleases just as though it was built with her own earnings. And, in fact, it *can* be built with her own money if the contributions are made from her savings or from interest, dividends, rents, or other investment income she receives, even though this income does not qualify for an IRA based on her own earnings.

If the nonworking wife later goes to work, she can change the spousal IRA into a regular IRA by simply taking her contributions as deductions on her tax return or on a joint return filed with her husband.

IRAs are also particularly advantageous for working wives. In many cases, wives must follow work patterns during their lifetimes that make it difficult to establish retirement income of their own in any other way. Although the Retirement Equity Act of 1984 will help to some extent, interrupted work patterns will still make it difficult for many women to build substantial retirement credits at work. With an IRA, however, working wives can begin building a retirement fund of their own.

Even a wife who works full time throughout her marriage can benefit from an IRA by building her own independent source of retirement income. It will help protect her against the loss of retirement income if her husband should die or there is a divorce. If her IRA is large enough, it could assure her financial independence in old age after her husband's death. It could also help offset the inequity that finds a working wife's contributions unrecognized in calculating social security benefits if her husband's earnings have been higher.

IRAs AND SINGLE WOMEN

An IRA program is also especially appropriate for many single women. If you never marry, an IRA gives you the same opportunity all other workers have of sheltering some income from taxation each year and using the money to build your own source of retirement income. The earlier in your working life you can start contributing to an IRA, the more substantial the capital pool you can build.

If you marry and quit your job, at least you'll have one source of retirement income (or capital pool you can use for any other purpose) of your own, rather than having to depend for retirement finances on decisions your husband-to-be might make or on other forces beyond your control.

Even if you never return to the work force to make more contributions after you're married, the tax-sheltered earnings alone will increase the IRA's value substantially over the years.

This is particularly true if you have been able to put some money in an IRA while you are still very young and can harness an IRA's tax-sheltered compounding power over a long period. If you drop out of the work force at age 25 and make no more contributions to it, at a constant 10 percent return each $1,000 in your IRA would be worth more than $45,000 when you reach age 65. A $2,500 IRA at age 25 would be worth $113,000, and a $5,000 IRA would be worth $226,000, and so on. If you had been able to contribute $2,000 for each year between ages 22 and 25, a total of $8,000, and then stopped making contributions, that IRA would grow to about $462,000.

IRA RULES FOR WORKING COUPLES

If both spouses work, each can have his or her own IRA or IRAs—and the rules governing IRAs in general apply to each. Their maximum combined total contribution is $2,000 each, or $4,000.

A working couple's IRAs must be established and maintained separately. Funds cannot be commingled in a jointly owned IRA. Because they are separate, these IRAs need not be with the same IRA sponsors or the same type of investment. One spouse may have IRA contributions deducted from paychecks by an employer, while the other splits them among savings accounts, mutual funds, and insurance annuities.

Each spouse has control over what is done with his or her IRA. This includes naming beneficiaries and transferring or rolling over the IRA from one investment to another.

In practice, most couples will consult with one another before making investment and other decisions involving their IRA or IRAs—but they don't have to. Of course, they *are* required by the IRS to report contributions, withdrawals, and any violations of IRS rules and regulations and penalties due on their tax return.

However, it's not necessary for working couples with their own IRAs to file a joint return, as they'd have to do with a spousal IRA. If both spouses work, if they wish they may file separate returns—although, in most cases the joint return would be more advantageous.

If the working couple can afford to contribute the maximum to their IRAs, their capital-building potential will double. If each contributes $2,000 a year that earns at a constant 10 percent return, after 30 years they'd have IRAs totaling nearly three quarters of a million dollars. After 40 years, their IRAs would be worth nearly $2 million.

As with any other IRAs, contributions need not come directly from wages or other sources that qualify as income for the purpose of having an IRA. You can make your IRA contributions from savings or other nonqualifying sources, including interest, dividends, capital gains, rents, and gifts. To make the maximum $2,000 contribution, all either spouse need do is earn at least $2,000 of compensation that does qualify during that tax year.

But a couple that is unable to contribute the limit and may even have to skip years when there is no money to spare for IRAs can still build a much larger retirement pool than a single worker in similar circumstances. Irrespective of the age of the other spouse, each may continue contributing to the IRA (assuming there is qualifying compensation) until the year in which he or she becomes age 70½, at which time withdrawals must begin by the following April 1.

WHEN ONLY ONE SPOUSE WORKS: THE SPOUSAL IRA

When one spouse works and the other doesn't, the IRS allows them to establish a "spousal" IRA. This involves setting up an IRA for the spouse who does not earn compensation. To qualify for a spousal IRA, the working spouse must have an IRA, too—and the couple must file a joint tax return. The maximum total annual contribution to both IRAs is $2,250 or 100 percent of income, whichever is less.

The spousal IRA gives couples with a nonworking spouse the opportunity to contribute $250 a year more toward an IRA than a single person with a $2,000 limit can contribute. The couple must be married at the end of the tax year and meet all other IRA requirements.

The opportunity to contribute an extra $250 each year won't make a great difference in the beginning, but the dollar difference becomes significant as time goes on.

According to Table 7–1, after contributing $2,250 each year for five years at a constant 10 percent return, the spousal IRA would have a total of $15,109 compared with $13,430 for the maximum single IRA contribution—a difference of $1,679. After 10 years, the spousal IRA total would be $39,445, compared with $35,062 for the single IRA, a $4,383 difference. After 20 years, the spousal total would be $141,755, compared with $126,004 for the single IRA, a $15,751 difference. After 30 years, it would be $407,122, compared with $361,886 for the single IRA, a $45,236 difference.

TABLE 7–1 ■ **Sample Spousal IRA Gains** *(Assumes Constant 10 Percent Return with Investments Made at Start of Each Year)*

Plans Years Completed	(Single IRA Maximum) $2,000	(Spousal IRA Maximum) $2,250	Difference
5	$ 13,430	$ 15,109	$ 1,679
10	35,062	39,445	4,383
15	69,898	78,635	8,737
20	126,004	141,755	15,751
25	216,362	243,407	27,045
30	361,886	407,122	45,236
35	596,252	670,784	74,532
40	973,702	1,095,415	121,713

HOW WILL YOU DIVIDE YOUR SPOUSAL IRA?

The other aspect of a spousal IRA is that it gives the non-working spouse—usually the wife—an opportunity to have an independent tax-sheltered fund for retirement or any other purpose. But how much of each year's contributions should go into the IRA of the nonworking spouse?

Until 1982 the IRS required that contributions to spousal IRAs be divided equally between the two spouses. If one had a $500 contribution during the year, the other had to have a $500 contribution too.

Some people incorrectly believe this is still the case, but the law has been changed. Since 1982, a spousal IRA can be divided in almost any way. The only limitation now is that the higher account may receive no more than $2,000 in one year. In practical terms, this means up to $2,000 can be contributed to the IRA of the nonworking spouse each year, with only $250 for the IRA of the working spouse. But it also means $2,000 can be contributed to the IRA of the working spouse, leaving only $250 to the IRA of the non-working spouse.

This requires couples with a spousal IRA to make what could be a very difficult decision on how to allocate the contributions. Many factors have to be weighed. They include any assured retirement income from other sources, the assets owned jointly or separately by the couple, and the income-producing potential of both spouses. Also, which spouse has the better judgment? Will the offspring make demands on their retirement funds, a not unusual situation today? And if one spouse has a company retirement plan, should not the other get the bulk of the spousal IRA?

If you wish, you can vary the way spousal IRA contributions are divided from year to year to adapt to changing conditions. Up to $2,000 could go into the IRA of the working spouse for tax year 1985, for instance, with only $250 going to the IRA of the nonworking spouse. But for the 1986 tax year, this could be reversed. The IRA of the nonworking spouse could get $2,000, with only $250 going to the IRA of the working spouse.

The change in the tax law did *not* change the status of contributions made in the past. These cannot now be switched from one spouse's IRA to the other's.

There is still some general misunderstanding about who has control over the spousal IRA. Even though contributions are based on compensation earned by the working spouse, the nonworking spouse has complete control over the IRA opened in his or her name. This includes the right to name a beneficiary or beneficiaries and to transfer or roll the IRA over into another investment. The IRA for the nonworking spouse need not be in the same institution or even the same kind of investment as that for the working spouse.

The spousal IRA is set up just as any other IRA. If the working spouse already has an IRA, all that need be done is establish one for the nonworking spouse.

BEWARE THE "SPOUSAL INCOME TRAP"

It's always a good idea to maximize IRA earnings by making contributions early in the year. But don't forget that if you contribute early to a spousal IRA and the spouse then earns some income, however small, later in the year, the situation will have changed—and the spousal contribution will have been invalidated. The consequences will depend on how much was contributed to the IRA of the nonworking spouse, and on how much the formerly nonworking spouse then earned.

If the contribution to the IRA of the nonworking spouse was less than the amount the spouse later earned, there is no problem. On your tax return, simply treat the contribution as one to a regular IRA. If you contributed $1,000 to a spousal IRA and that spouse later earned $1,000 or more, you would simply list the $1,000 on your tax return as a regular IRA contribution for the spouse. But if the spousal contribution is more than the spouse later earned, you'll have to make some adjustments.

Example.   Early in the year, a man contributes $2,000 to his nonworking wife's IRA as a spousal IRA and another $250 to his own, for the $2,250 maximum. But in October, his wife earns $150 working in a local election. They don't realize it at the time—but by earning the $150, the wife has invalidated the $2,000 spousal IRA contribution. All she is now entitled to contribute to her IRA is a maximum of 100 percent of her earnings, or $150. The remaining $1,850 is now an excess contribution, a technical error not called to their attention until they meet with their tax adviser early in the following year.

In this case, the remedy will be to withdraw the $1,850 excess contribution, as well as the earnings on it, before the deadline for filing that year's tax return, usually April 15. There would be no tax on the $1,850 withdrawn but, if the wife is under age 59½, there would be a 10 percent penalty tax on the earnings, which would have to be reported on Form 5329. Meanwhile, the husband could contribute another $1,750 to his IRA before April 15, bringing it up to the $2,000 individual contribution limit.

The moral: If you make a spousal IRA contribution, be alert to adjustments you may have to make if the nonworking spouse later earns some income, however small, during that tax year and invalidates the spousal IRA. The earlier in the year you make the spousal contribution, the easier it is to forget the contribution and fall into the "spousal income trap."

HOW LONG MAY SPOUSAL CONTRIBUTIONS CONTINUE?

If you are the working spouse, when you reach age 70½ you must stop contributing to your own IRA. However, contributions of up to $2,000 to your spouse's IRA (assuming you have the qualifying income) can continue to be made until the year he or she reaches age 70½.

By April 1 of the year following the year in which you reach age 70½, you must begin taking distributions from your own IRA. However, your spouse doesn't have to start receiving distributions until April 1 following the tax year in which he or she reaches age 70½.

If your spouse is older than you, you must stop contributing to your spouse's IRA in the tax year in which he or she reaches age 70½—and your spouse must then begin taking distributions by the following April 1.

You may still continue contributing to your own IRA as long as you have compensation that qualifies. However, starting with the year in which your spouse has reached age 70½, your annual contributions to your own IRA will be limited to the ceiling for an individual—currently $2,000 or 100 percent of your income.

WORKING JUST A LITTLE COULD PAY OFF A LOT

Although a spousal IRA allows an additional $250 to be sheltered from taxation each year, that's a far cry from being able to shelter up to an additional $2,000. A couple whose everyday living expenses are being comfortably met by the working spouse would come out much further ahead if the other spouse worked just enough to make a bigger contribution.

In view of the likelihood that she will outlive her working husband, this would be a prudent step for a nonworking wife to take—assuming she's in good health and has no objection to working. If she worked just long enough each year to earn the $2,000 or so needed to qualify for the maximum contribution, she'd soon have a substantial retirement fund that would be hers no matter what happened to her marriage in the future. It would provide some independence and protection in case her husband died and she was cut off from part or all of his retirement benefits, or they later divorced and she lost all rights to his benefits.

Assume that a couple is age 55 with the husband earning enough to meet all of their needs and the children are grown and gone. If the wife worked just enough to earn $2,000 for each of the next 10 years and contributed the limit to an IRA each year, at a constant 10 percent return she'd have more than $35,000 ($35,062) when her husband retired at age 65— and it would be hers to do with as she pleased.

If she went to work at age 50 and contributed $2,000 for each of the next 15 years, the couple would have an additional $70,000. And if she started at age 45, in 20 years they'd have more than $125,000 in her IRA or IRAs.

This advice may be easier given than followed. Where you live, there may not be many opportunities for finding a source of income paying up to $2,000 or so each year, but possibilities exist. Stores may be happy to hire a responsible adult willing to work part time, especially at busy seasons like Christmas. Many offices would welcome part-time help, too. If you have office skills, you could register with a temporary office help firm and work just enough to earn as much as you please.

Baby-sitting or cottage industry income—from the sale of arts and crafts, for instance—also qualifies. If you earn less than $2,000 after paying expenses, you could contribute and deduct the entire sum. You'd owe no added taxes on those earnings until you begin withdrawing from your IRA or IRAs. (But you would have to pay social security tax.)

SHOULD YOU PUT YOUR SPOUSE TO WORK FOR $2,000?

If you own or control a corporation, are the sole proprietor of a business, or have a business partnership, it may occur to you to put a nonworking spouse to work just long enough to earn the $2,000 maximum IRA contribution—assuming the spouse agrees. This is perfectly legal if:

The spouse actually performs useful duties. If he or she merely shows up at the office and spends the day working crossword puzzles or making social telephone calls, it won't suffice. Work must be performed, and the work must relate to your business.

In the case of a corporation, you withhold social security taxes. You can't have it both ways. If your spouse is going to take a deduction for an IRA, he or she must also pay the taxes other employees pay. However, social security taxes are neither withheld nor paid for wages paid to your spouse if he or she is employed by you in an unincorporated business.

The rate of pay is reasonable for the duties. If your spouse's principal duty is answering the phone and greeting visitors to your office, the IRS will not allow you to compensate him or her at the same rate you compensate attorneys, accountants, or other providers of professional services.

If you are unable to demonstrate actual services performed and it appears that in putting your spouse to "work" you are merely shifting income, the deduction for the spouse will be disqualified and penalties will be assessed. But if service was rendered and the compensation is reasonable, the wages will qualify for an IRA.

IRAs AFFECT THE TWO–EARNER MARRIED COUPLE DEDUCTION

If a couple filing a joint return has an IRA or IRAs, it may affect the two-earner married couple tax deduction—but not to a great extent.

A two-earner married couple filing a joint return is allowed to deduct from gross income up to 10 percent of the first $30,000 of income earned by the lower-earner spouse. But if the lower-earner spouse also has an IRA, the IRA deduction must be taken first. This will reduce that spouse's earned income for purposes of the two-earner deduction.

For instance, if the lower-earning spouse earned $20,000, the deduction without an IRA would be 10 percent of that, or $2,000. But money contributed to an IRA would have to be subtracted from the $20,000 before calculating the penalty deduction.

If the lower-earning spouse had contributed $2,000 to an IRA, this would reduce the sum on which the penalty tax deduction is calculated to $18,000. Ten percent of that would be $1,800, or a $200 smaller deduction than if the lower-earning spouse did not have an IRA.

You'll always come out ahead with the IRA. All you're giving up is 10 percent of your two-earner deduction. In return, you're getting 100 percent of the IRA deduction—and the tax-sheltered money in the IRA may grow manyfold.

WHAT IF THERE'S A DIVORCE?

If there's a divorce, an IRA (or part of an IRA) can be transferred from one spouse to the other by the divorce decree or other written document related to the divorce. This transfer is *not* considered a distribution by the IRS and is taxfree. Beginning on the date of the transfer, the IRA (or partial IRA) is treated as the property of the spouse who receives it.

Since the IRA program was opened to all workers in 1982, it has become increasingly commonplace to include IRAs as part of a domestic relations settlement. But until 1984 the essential legal ingredients were provided by state courts, which had varying success in penetrating qualified employer plan assets and IRA assets of divorcing couples.

The Retirement Equity Act of 1984 was the most significant federal legislation in this area to date. It provides for state courts to issue what are called Qualified Domestic Relations Orders. These are judgments, decrees, or orders of a court that provide for support, alimony, or the payment of property rights to an "alternate payee" without jeopardizing the protective tax features of IRAs and qualified employer pension plans.

Consequently, in any state, a court can now award all or part of one party's IRA to the other party without it being taxed as a distribution to the party who established the IRA. If the IRA was originally set up for the husband, for instance, part or all of it can be transferred to the divorced wife with no adverse tax consequences for the husband even if he is under age 59½.

The wife takes the IRA or partial IRA and from then on treats it as her own. However, it seems clear that if she does not roll the assets over into an IRA immediately, she will be taxed on the amounts received.

Also of great significance if your spouse is covered by an employer pension plan, if you are given a distribution from the plan as part of a domestic relations decree you may roll part or all of it into an IRA. The amount must be received within a single tax year.

After it is placed in an IRA, this money is subject to the usual IRA rules, including the right to roll it over into another IRA. However, the special lump-sum tax benefits ordinarily available to participants in a qualified plan at work are not available to the divorced spouse (or other alternate recipient, such as a child.) And if you roll over only part of the distribution, you must include the part that you keep as income for the year in which you receive it.

These new rules involving divorced or separated persons are complicated. Professional guidance is recommended to assure that your legal and tax rights are preserved.

ALIMONY IS NOW "COMPENSATION"

Starting with the 1985 tax year, all taxable alimony and separate maintenance payments that are ordered by a court can be considered "compensation" for the purpose of contributing to an IRA. This is a major liberalization of the law as it affects a nonworking spouse.

The regular IRA rules apply. The nonworking divorced spouse may contribute up to the lesser of $2,000 or 100 percent of compensation, including taxable alimony, to an IRA.

Although contributions into the IRA of a nonworking divorced or legally separated spouse were allowed before 1985, it was under such strict conditions and limitations that most divorced spouses were unable to take advantage of the rule.

8

IRAs and Your Retirement Plan at Work

If you're not participating in an employer pension, profit-sharing, or thrift plan at work, skip this chapter. But if you are participating in one—or find yourself participating in one in the future—the information in this chapter could be of great importance to you.

If your employer allows it, you can make voluntary contributions to your employer's retirement or pension plan and deduct those contributions instead of (or as well as) contributing to an IRA. In the lexicon of the IRS, these are called qualified voluntary employee contributions (QVECs).

Many employers will not allow you to make these voluntary, tax-deductible contributions to their plans. But if your employer does allow it, you may contribute up to $2,000 to your employer's plan instead of to your own IRA. Or, if you wish, you may split your contributions between your employer plan and one or more IRAs of your own.

If you're in a company plan that allows you to make voluntary deductible contributions, you must decide whether your voluntary contributions will be deductible or nondeductible. If your financial resources are limited, you may also have to decide whether you'll come out ahead by setting up your own IRA or contributing to an employer plan—or by making voluntary nondeductible contributions to a company thrift or savings plan that are matched by contributions from your employer.

WHAT ARE YOUR INVESTMENT OPTIONS?

Before 1982, you were not allowed to deduct voluntary contributions to an employer plan from your income. They had to be made with aftertax dollars. The benefit was that your contribution's earnings would compound tax sheltered in the plan. And if you later took a lump-sum distribution from the plan, you enjoyed very favorable tax treatment.

If your employer plan still allows nondeductible voluntary contributions, you may still continue making them.

You are not allowed to deduct any voluntary contributions to a company thrift or savings plan that are matched by your employer. These do not affect the amount you may contribute to an IRA.

The total of your deductible employer plan contributions and the amount you contribute to your IRA or IRAs can be no more than $2,000 annually, but you may split the $2,000 any way you wish. You could make a $1,200 deductible contribution to your employer's plan and contribute another $800 to an IRA—and make nondeductible contributions to your employer plan, too.

If you participate in more than one employer plan during the year, you may make deductible contributions to all of them and to an IRA or IRAs as well—provided the total deductible contributions is not more than $2,000.

If you deduct your employer plan contribution, the amount you deduct is not subject to withholding by your employer.

CHARACTERISTICS OF EMPLOYER PLANS

A "qualified employer plan" means any IRS-qualified pension, profit-sharing, bonus, or annuity plan for employees. This includes profit-sharing, stock bonus, and bond purchase plans. It also includes government, military, and teacher pension and retirement plans and annuities at all levels of government—federal, state, and local—as well as plans under which tax-exempt educational, political, and other organizations buy annuities for their employees.

One big advantage of an employer plan is that it is built with the employer's money. Contributions are made on your behalf but are not considered part of your income for tax purposes. This money continues to compound earnings that are sheltered from taxation each year.

Another big advantage is that you enjoy favorable tax treatment on distributions when you retire. You can use 10-year averaging for a lump-sum distribution, which reduces the tax bite considerably. You may also enjoy favorable capital gains treatment for unrealized gains on employer stock, and when you die your beneficiary can take advantage of a $5,000 death benefit exclusion from taxable income.

Ten-Year Averaging

Basically, 10-year averaging allows you to pay tax on a lump-sum distribution just as though you had received it in equal amounts over a 10-year period rather than in a single year. Even when the lump sum reaches $100,000, the total tax due is less than the top 20 percent capital gains rate, although it surpasses that for higher sums.

Smaller distributions fare even better because of a minimum distribution allowance. Half of the distribution or $10,000, whichever is less, is not subject to federal taxes. This means that for distributions up to $20,000, you pay tax on only half. This tax computation is independent of your computation on your other income.

Another potential tax advantage of an employer's lump-sum distribution is that employer contributions made before 1974 can be treated as long-term capital gains if you wish, rather than using 10-year averaging for that portion of the distribution. You or your tax adviser would have to figure the tax both ways to see which is best. For examples of 10-year averaging, see Chapter 10.

Employer Plan Pros and Cons

As you can see, an employer retirement plan is great to have if you are an employee. The bulk and sometimes all of the benefits stem from the employer's contributions, but you don't pay tax on those contributions as part of your income. And, just as with an IRA, you don't pay tax on the earnings of those contributions as they continue to compound over the years. You may also enjoy substantial tax advantages for lump-sum distributions when compared with IRAs, which cannot use 10-year averaging.

On the other hand, the employer dictates the plan's terms and makes the investment decisions. You may have to work for the employer for a specified period of time before you're entitled to retirement benefits or have vested rights, which means being able to take your share of the plan with you when you leave the company.

If you're in a profit-sharing plan, you're not assured of any contributions from the company unless the company operates profitably and there are profits to share.

And, you have no control over your contributions to the plan. You have no say as to how your contributions will be invested. If you're dissatisfied with the progress of those investments, you cannot take the money out and invest it somewhere else.

If your employer allows it—and so far the majority of employers do *not* allow it, although there are some major exceptions—should you make a nondeductible contribution to an employer plan? Or, should you make a deductible contribution to your employer's plan or to an IRA or IRAs of your own?

Under some circumstances, the favorable tax treatment you may enjoy upon receiving a lump-sum distribution when you retire may be the determining factor. You would, of course, have to be reasonably sure that you'd be offered a lump-sum distribution. Not all plans offer one.

This is a difficult projection to make. It would also depend on your other financial resources and your life expectancy after taking the lump-sum distribution.

Contributing to your employer's plan is convenient, especially if your contributions will simply be deducted from your paycheck. If you're one of those people who find it difficult to save in any way other than through "forced savings" plans, this may be best for you.

If you want to put $2,000 into your company pension plan (or into an IRA through a company payroll deduction program) for next year, the company could deduct $38.46 from your paycheck every week beginning the first week of January. Of course, this means you won't be able to maximize the tax-sheltered earning power of your contributions by bunching them near the start of the year, but you'll be able to build your IRA relatively painlessly.

Also, weigh the probable return from the employer's plan against what you may be able to receive elsewhere. Some employer plans have done much better than others. If the employer's literature shows that the plan is earning substantially less than what an IRA could earn with reasonable safety, consider setting up your own IRA or IRAs instead.

One of an IRA's major advantages is that it is more flexible than an employer plan. You always own 100 percent of it and can decide what to do with it. If you move to another part of the country, change jobs, or become aware of a better investment opportunity, you can move the IRA accordingly.

But what happens to your voluntary deductible contributions if you change jobs? Can you take them with you? Or, must you leave them with the company plan until you are age 59½? Get the answers to these questions before making your decision.

With your IRA, you're not tied to the fortunes of your employer's plan. As with any other investments, just because your pension plan has done well in the past doesn't mean it will always continue to do well. A change in the management of the plan—or of the company itself—could result in a change in the plan's investment policies.

Also, how well is your company doing? If it's a leader in its field or is clearly holding its own, you should have no hesitation about making voluntary contributions to its pension or retirement plan—assuming the plan's return is reasonably as good as what you could earn on your own.

But, if your company is in trouble, it may be prudent to put your discretionary retirement dollars into an IRA rather than in that company's retirement plan. Certainly, if the company is reporting losses every quarter, must depend on consortiums of bankers to keep afloat financially, and is closing some income-producing properties and selling others just to meet expenses, you'd be well advised to avoid further voluntary contributions.

At this writing, IRA voluntary contributions are not covered by the Pension Benefit Guarantee Corporation, the federal agency that insures the assets of employer pension plans. (However, they would be a preferred claim against the assets of the plan.) In any event, if there is any question about the solvency of your company plan, stop contributing to it and contribute the maximum to an IRA instead.

Another factor is the time you expect to continue working for the company. If you don't plan to remain long enough to earn vested rights in the plan, contributions made by your employer may be forfeited. In this case, you'd also be better off setting up your own IRA. This is especially true if you change jobs often, either because of the nature of your work or because you don't like staying at one place too long.

If you can afford it, one strategy would be to contribute $2,000 to your own IRA each year—and then contribute as much as you can to your employer's plan on a nondeductible basis. This would give you the full $2,000 deduction while earnings on the nondeductible contributions continue to pile up tax sheltered in your employer plan too, with the possibility of substantial tax advantages if you later take a lump-sum distribution.

EMPLOYER THRIFT AND SAVINGS PLANS

Another set of factors comes into play with employer thrift and savings plans to which your employer makes matching contributions.

You are not allowed to deduct any of your own contributions that are matched by your employer. As a rule, these plans allow you to invest from 2 to 6 percent of your pay. The employer then matches some or all of your contributions.

Typically, an employer might match your contribution by 50 percent. If you contributed $2,000 to that plan, the company would contribute another $1,000, giving you an immediate 50 percent return on your investment.

That's a very tough deal to beat. Even though you cannot deduct your contributions, no IRA will give you an immediate return remotely comparable to this. If the plan is earning any kind of reasonable return, your investment results will be much better than those of most IRAs.

If you can't afford to invest in both and must decide between investing in an IRA and making nondeductible contributions to a plan where the employer makes a substantial matching contribution, usually your best bet will be the company thrift plan. Another advantage is that with the company thrift plan, you may be allowed to make withdrawals before you reach age 59½ without penalty.

However, many thrift plans have one big drawback if you don't remain with the company long enough. It's that you must be vested before you can keep the employer's contribution. If you quit or are fired before you are vested, you lose your rights to the employer's contribution.

Also, there's a point at which the matching contributions aren't big enough to overcome the tax advantage of deducting each year's contribution to an IRA. *Money* magazine reports that a study by the employee benefits consulting firm of Towers Perrin Forster & Crosby in New York City showed that for the employee to come out ahead, the employer should match at least 25 percent of your contributions.

SIMILARITIES BETWEEN DEDUCTIBLE EMPLOYER CONTRIBUTIONS AND IRAs

In general, the rules covering deductible employer plan contributions and IRAs are similar. For instance:

- If you receive a distribution of deductible contributions from a qualified employer or government plan, you must pay a 10 percent penalty tax for the tax year in which you receive it if you are under age 59½. However, there is no penalty if you are 59½ or older or in the case of death or permanent disability.
- You are not allowed to make voluntary contributions to the employer plan and deduct them after the year in which you reach age 70½. However, one difference is that, unlike with an IRA, you are *not* required to begin withdrawals from an employer plan at age 70½ if the plan itself does not require it.
- Contributions can be made after the end of the tax year to April 15 of the following year. This gives you

a lot of flexibility in allocating contributions between employer plans and IRAs.

Warning. If you're in an employer plan that allows deductible contributions, it is your responsibility to notify the plan administrator if you intend your contributions to be nondeductible instead. Unless the administrator has designated some other date, this notification must be made by April 15 of the year following the tax year. If you fail to notify the administrator, it will be assumed that your contributions to the plan will be deductible. Whether you want them to or not, they'll count toward your $2,000 IRA contribution limit for that year. If you contribute $2,000 to an IRA and then contribute $500 to an employer plan that allows deductible contributions but fail to tell the administrator that it is to be a nondeductible contribution, you'll have made a $500 excess contribution to your IRA.

DISTRIBUTIONS ARE TAXED JUST AS IRAs ARE TAXED

One thing you do *not* gain by making deductible contributions to an employer's plan rather than to an IRA is the favorable tax treatment on the distribution of the portion of the plan represented by your deductible contributions. The portion of the plan represented by your employer's contributions continues to enjoy it, but the portion resulting from your voluntary contributions is taxed as an IRA distribution would be taxed.

If you're given a lump-sum distribution from an employer plan, the portion represented by your deductible contributions (and their earnings in the plan) must be included in your gross income for that year. Four-year averaging is available, however. You may also defer taxes by rolling this money into an IRA—and later, into another employer plan, assuming the other plan permits holding the distribution as accumulated deductible employee contributions.

If taken in other than a lump sum the distribution of your deductible voluntary contributions and their earnings must be under the annuity rule. This means regular payments must be made over your anticipated life span or the money must be used to buy an insurance annuity.

In that case, the tax treatment of distributions gets tricky. The IRS assumes that your deductible contributions to the plan (and the earnings or gains on them) will be distributed after everything else. The exception would be if the employer's plan states otherwise. In any event, this complicates figuring the tax on the distributions. Once again, you'll probably need professional help.

EMPLOYER PLANS NOW HAVE "AUTOMATIC ANNUITY" PAYOUTS

There's one new and important difference between company plans (and most other retirement plans) and IRAs. It's that if you are married, company plans are now required to provide automatic survivor benefits for your spouse unless you elect otherwise—and your spouse must approve the change.

Under the Retirement Equity Act of 1984, with these plans you are now required to take retirement (or preretirement) benefits in the form of a joint and survivor annuity unless you elect not to. Moreover, if you elect not to take your retirement benefits in this form—if, for instance, you'd prefer taking a lump-sum distribution from your company's plan and rolling part or all of it into an IRA—your spouse must give consent in writing, witnessed by a plan representative or a notary public.

This requirement does *not* apply to IRAs. With an IRA, you can arrange any kind of payout the IRA permits without having to obtain your spouse's consent.

With a company plan, however, the spouse must give consent for any payout other than a joint and survivor annuity, as well as for the preretirement distribution of this money. In effect, this gives every worker's spouse "veto power" over any use of pension benefits other than for a joint and survivor annuity.

A qualified joint and survivor annuity is for the life of the participant, with a survivor annuity for the spouse that is not less than one half or greater than the annuity payable during the joint lives of the participant and spouse. It must be paid to your spouse if you die while still working, and it may not be terminated or reduced because of the spouse's remarriage.

Annuities are usually associated with insurance policies, and often policies are purchased with your account balance in the employer's plan. However, very large plans may fund their own annuities.

There are many complex aspects to this new provision in our pension laws, and it is not within the scope of this book to examine them except as they relate to IRAs. But, if you are married and are covered by an IRS-qualified pension or retirement plan at work, you should be aware that if you wish in the future to roll some or all of the assets of that plan into an IRA, the decision will not be all yours to make.

MANY EMPLOYERS OFFER IRA PAYROLL DEDUCTIONS

For a number of reasons, most employers will not allow you to make voluntary deductible contributions to their retirement or pension plans. To do so they'd have to amend their present plans or get involved in a lot of paperwork and costly changes to set up new programs.

As an alternative, many employers have established payroll deduction programs for investments in regular IRAs. There is great variety in how these programs are organized. Sometimes the employer gives the employees the option of having the money deducted from their paychecks and sent to the IRA of their choice. Other employers offer specific IRA packages. Often these have been set up by investment management firms, insurance companies, mutual funds, or other IRA sponsors. These packages usually give employees a wide choice of investments. (Employers prefer that you have a choice because they don't want to be held responsible if you select an investment that doesn't do well. If they offered just one IRA and you lost money investing in it or even didn't do as well as the average investment, it would create morale and other problems.)

Typically, these packages include several mutual funds—a money market fund and perhaps a stock, bond, or government securities fund. IRA packages are also provided by banks and savings institutions with a variety of insured savings plans. In short, although your contributions are deducted from your paycheck at work, you still face the problem of sifting through all the sponsor literature and deciding which IRA is best for you.

On the other hand, sponsors of these packages often allow investors to participate in investments at lower commissions than would be charged if you made these investments on your own. Usually, you also have the option of switching money from one investment vehicle to another without worrying about breaking IRS rules and triggering a big penalty, which is a major advantage.

Convenience is another advantage in contributing to an IRA through payroll deductions—and the "forced savings" aspect of this approach may be essential for some people.

However, the payroll plan may limit you to IRAs you don't like or that you don't believe are appropriate for your circumstances. You may also wish to set up your IRAs elsewhere if you don't think you'll be with that company for long.

Some employers have decided not to get involved with IRAs at all, except perhaps to distribute some explanatory literature. As an executive of one firm put it to *Business Week*, "There is just so much you can deduct from a person's paycheck."

PAYROLL DEDUCTION PROS AND CONS

A payroll deduction is certainly the easiest way to start an IRA. And this "forced savings" approach will help millions of people build larger IRAs than they could have otherwise.

However, it also has major drawbacks. One is that your choice of investments is limited to those selected by your employer. You must invest either in the employer's own qualified pension or retirement plan and/or in investment options selected by your employer. Before signing up for a payroll deduction plan, compare the track records of those investments with investments you could make elsewhere.

And be sure you understand the nature of these investments. If you don't know what a mutual fund or a money market fund is, don't commit your retirement dollars to them until you do know. Any investment that you understand and feel comfortable with is appropriate for an IRA, but don't sign up for any payroll deduction option unfamiliar to you.

Take your time. Study the choices in your payroll deduction plan. One advantage of these plans is that you can usually move money around in them from one investment to another without worrying about trouble with the IRS.

TECHNICAL PAYROLL PROBLEMS

There are some technical problems involved with any IRA program that depends on a payroll deduction plan. One is that, in many cases, the deduction plan must of necessity be built around the convenience of the payroll computer system, not yours. If it is prohibitively expensive to allow you to bunch contributions early in the year—or to extend them into the following year—the computer program will not accommodate your special circumstances.

Another is that when an employer deducts your IRA contributions from your paycheck, the IRS authorizes adjusting your income tax withholding to reflect the new exemption in your gross income. However, not all companies will do this. If this change is not made, you could wind up overwithholding.

What's more, the government does not pay you any interest during the time it holds your money. Before signing up for a payroll deduction IRA, learn if your employer is going to adjust your withholding accordingly.

The other side of this coin involves what could happen if you start a payroll deduction IRA plan for which your employer adjusts your withholding accordingly, but you later drop out of the plan. If your company's payroll department fails to readjust your withholding schedule, you could wind up owing the government more money than you thought at income tax time.

9

IRA-to-IRA
Rollovers and Transfers

Sales literature prepared by many IRA sponsors gives the impression that once your money is in their IRA it will remain there forever—or at least until you are happily retired and begin making withdrawals.

Actually, you have a lot of flexibility in moving money (and other assets) around from one IRA to another. If you decide you don't like the IRA's performance or believe there are better investment opportunities in other IRAs, you can move funds without paying any tax penalties, provided you follow the IRS rules.

This flexibility is one of the great advantages of an IRA as a money management tool. It allows you to restructure your IRA investments to maximize profits (or cut your losses) by adapting to changing conditions or perceptions.

If you conclude that the stock market will be down for the next few years, you can get out of it. If you think stocks will soar and register gains greater than what savings certificates or money market funds are paying, you can get in it. Or, if you made an investment that isn't doing well, you can dump it.

You may also wish to move IRA funds for personal reasons. If you change jobs, move from one city to another or even from one part of town to another, you may wish to move your IRA to a sponsor with an office more convenient to your new job or home. If you opened an IRA simply because you had a business or personal relationship with that sponsor and that relationship ends, you may want to switch to a sponsor that can deduct contributions for your new employer. Or you may decide to move an IRA simply because people you deal with in a sponsor's office are rude or make mistakes processing your accounts.

Rollovers can also be made into an IRA or IRAs from a qualified employer pension plan under some circumstances— and can be rolled back into another employer plan if the second employer will permit it. Those rollovers, which are covered by special rules, are discussed in the next chapter.

But after those employer plan assets are rolled into an IRA, you can move them from one IRA to another if you wish. So long as they remain in an IRA, they are governed by the same IRA-to-IRA rollover and transfer rules as any other IRA.

TWO WAYS IN WHICH TAX–FREE MOVEMENTS CAN BE MADE

There are two ways in which tax-free movements of assets in and out of IRAs can be made—rollovers and transfers.

Both are allowable contributions, but obviously you cannot deduct them from income on your tax return. Your IRA deductions are limited to your regular contributions, if any, for that tax year.

Rollovers and transfers give you great flexibility in moving assets, but each move must be made with care. Before undertaking a move, be sure you understand the rules covering that particular move—and the penalties for violating those rules, knowingly or unknowingly.

There are no IRS dollar limits on amounts that can be rolled over or transferred. On the one hand, this gives you great flexibility. On the other, it means you could suffer a major financial setback if you make a mistake when rolling over a large sum.

Some people tend to overuse the rollover and transfer devices. Some investments require time and patience to work out. Before making a move, give yourself a cooling-off period to review all aspects of it.

Is the new investment really all that better? Or, are you getting caught up in an investment fad that could fade as fast as it arose? And, up to this point, what has been your track record in moving other IRAs? Have the new investments usually worked out better than the old ones? Or, would you have been better off sticking with the old ones?

PENALTIES APPLY ONLY TO THAT IRA

If a mistake *is* made in rolling over or transferring an IRA, any IRS penalties apply only to that IRA and do not affect any other IRAs you own.

This is another good argument for not putting all of your IRA dollars in the same investment basket once your IRA begins to reach what to you is a substantial size. Even if you wish to concentrate on one type of IRA investment, split your contributions among several sponsors. That way, if you make a technical error in a rollover or transfer, your entire IRA portfolio won't be penalized.

IRA–TO–IRA ROLLOVERS—THE ONE–YEAR RULE

A *rollover* is a tax-free movement of part or all of the cash or other assets from one retirement program to another. Either the actual physical transfer is made by you, or at some time in the process the assets are under your direct control.

Most commonly, rollovers involve people moving money between IRAs—receiving a check from one IRA sponsor, for instance, and then using it to set up an IRA with another sponsor.

IRA-to-IRA rollovers must be at least one full year apart to qualify as tax free. It isn't enough to have one rollover at some time in 1986 and another at some time in 1987. At least one full year must elapse before that IRA may be rolled over again. If you make an IRA-to-IRA rollover on October 1, 1986, that IRA wouldn't qualify for another rollover until October 1, 1987.

If you made a rollover before the full year elapsed, it would be considered an excess contribution. If you withdrew the money before the date on which you filed your tax return, you'd have to take it into your ordinary income for that year. If you are not disabled and are under age 59½, you'd also have to pay the 10 percent premature distribution tax.

If you didn't withdraw the money before filing your tax return and the attempted rollover was for more than $2,250, you'd still be required to withdraw the entire sum, take it into ordinary income, and pay the 10 percent penalty, if applicable. But if it was for less than $2,250, you could keep it in the IRA and the penalty would be a 6 percent excise tax for that year. You'd also have to reduce your IRA maximum payment for the following year accordingly.

Example. In examining your return, the IRS finds that you made a $12,000 IRA-to-IRA rollover that didn't meet the once-a-year requirement. Because the rollover was for more than $2,250, you'd have to take the $12,000 out of the IRA and into your income as a premature distribution and pay tax on it. If you're in a 40 percent bracket, your tax bite for the disallowed rollover would be $4,800. In addition, if you are under age 59½ and are not disabled, you'd have to pay the 10 percent penalty, in this case $1,200, for a total of $6,000 in penalties and income taxes.

And, of course, from then on instead of $12,000 earning at a tax-sheltered rate, all you'd have would be $6,000 earning at a taxable rate.

Example. You make a $1,500 IRA-to-IRA rollover that doesn't meet the once-a-year rule. Because the rollover is for less than $2,250, instead of withdrawing it and paying tax on it as ordinary income (and paying the 10 percent penalty if you are under age 59½ and not disabled), you may pay the 6 percent excise tax on the rollover as an excess contribution for that year, which is $90 ($1,500 × .06 = $90). The $1,500 then becomes a deductible IRA contribution for the following year, and you could contribute up to another $500 to a regular IRA or $750 to a spousal IRA.

THE SAME PROPERTY MUST BE ROLLED OVER

In IRA-to-IRA rollovers, you must roll over to the new IRA exactly the same amount or property you received from the old IRA. If you receive stock from the first IRA, you must contribute the same stock to the second IRA. You cannot sell the stock and roll over the proceeds or sell it, buy back an equivalent amount of stock, and roll the new stock over.

If you receive money in a rollover and the money earns interest or dividends between the time you take it from the first IRA and roll it over into the second one, the interest or other earnings cannot be included in the rollover. You must keep it and report it as ordinary income for that year. Similarly, interest and dividends paid to you during this period on stocks or bonds being rolled over must be taken into your ordinary income. However, you do *not* have to take into your income *accrued* interest that may accumulate during this period but is not paid until after the rollover is completed.

In considering an IRA-to-IRA rollover, don't forget to weigh penalties or fees that could be levied by IRA sponsors. These include early withdrawal penalties at banks, savings institutions, and credit unions that under some circumstances could cut into your principal. They may also include substantial "back load" fees charged by many insurance companies for leaving their plans before a specified period. Self-directed IRAs and mutual funds may also have withdrawal fees.

Factor these other fees or penalties into your decision to be sure the rollover you're contemplating is really all that good a move. You may find that by delaying your rollover a few weeks or months and waiting for an investment to mature, you could avoid an expensive sponsor penalty.

YOU HAVE 60 DAYS TO COMPLETE IRA–TO–IRA ROLLOVERS

You have 60 days in which to complete rollovers from one IRA to another. This creates an interesting situation. As we've seen, in a rollover you may take physical control of the money or other assets. When the first sponsor gives you a check for funds to be rolled over, you needn't take it directly to the second sponsor. You could put it in your own checking or savings account or do virtually anything else you please with it for the next 60 days. For all practical purposes you could give yourself an interest-free loan to meet a big college tuition bill for one of your children, buy a car, make a down payment on a house, pay off a gambling debt, take a world tour, or whatever, provided you rolled over a like sum into the second IRA within 60 days.

Some tax advisers won't even tell their clients about this 60-day option unless asked. They know that people who start playing these games with IRA money are running great risks, particularly if the rollover involves a large sum. If you are making a six-figure rollover, the consequences of not completing it within the 60-day period could be a financial disaster.

If the rollover is not completed within 60 days, the IRS will require that you include the entire amount withdrawn from the first IRA as income for that year and pay tax on it. If the attempted rollover was for $200,000 and you are in the 50 percent tax bracket, you'd have to give the government $100,000 for failing to complete the rollover on time. If you are below age 59½ and not disabled, you'd owe another $20,000 as the 10 percent premature distribution penalty.

If any payment is made to the second IRA, it is viewed by the IRS as a regular payment. You may deduct only the portion that qualifies for an IRA. If you had made no other IRA contributions that year, the maximum would be $2,000. But if you had attempted to roll over $200,000 as in the previous example, you would have to withdraw all of it before you file your tax return because the excess is above the $2,250 limit.

In short, if something goes wrong with a rollover involving big money during this 60-day period, you could find yourself in big trouble.

LET SOMEONE KNOW WHAT YOU'RE DOING

The longer you hold IRA assets during the 60-day rollover period, the greater the chance something could go wrong. For one reason or another—illness, an incapacitating accident, simple forgetfulness, or death—the assets received from the first IRA may never get to the second one within 60 days. If this happens the person who is penalized—or that person's beneficiaries, if the person dies and the beneficiaries are unaware that the rollover was in progress—would blame the tax adviser for providing information on the procedure.

Nevertheless, the option is there and, under some circumstances, is useful. Ordinarily, if you know what you're going to do with money or other assets received in a rollover, it would be best to complete the rollover as soon as possible.

But this option does give you the ability to pull money out of an IRA quickly if you see you've made a serious investment error, have concerns about the sponsor's financial condition, or want to get out of that investment for any other reason. It could also be useful if you're moving from one part of the country to another and want time to investigate IRA sponsors where your new home will be located. Finally, it would be a convenience if you knew you'd have no trouble finding money to complete the rollover and wanted to take advantage of an immediate investment opportunity or great bargain by giving yourself a temporary loan.

If you decide to make a rollover of a large sum for any reason, let someone close to you or someone who handles your financial affairs know about it. This could be your spouse, a family member, business associate, attorney, or financial adviser. If you are in the process of rolling over a large sum and suddenly are unable to communicate with anyone because of an accident, stroke, or other incapacitating illness, this person may be able to arrange to complete the rollover in time for it to remain tax free. Doing so may require that someone have your power of attorney, which should be arranged in advance of the rollover.

TRANSFERS FROM ONE IRA TO ANOTHER

While IRA-to-IRA rollovers must be made at least one year apart, transfers from one IRA to another can be made at any time.

The difference between a rollover and a transfer is that with a transfer, the assets are never under your direct control. Rather than moving assets from one IRA to another yourself, the transfer is made directly between the IRA trustees, custodians, or contract issuers.

To make a transfer you instruct the trustee, custodian, or contract issuer of the first IRA to transfer the funds or other assets to the trustee, custodian, or contract issuer of the second IRA. This must be done in writing.

The trustee or custodian of the second IRA should be informed that the transfer is to take place. And, in fact, often the sponsor of the second IRA will help prepare the paperwork and arrange the transfer for you. This transfer can also be handled by tax advisers, insurance brokers, and financial planners.

However, it is best to do the actual signing of these documents yourself and be directly involved in the process until you receive confirmation that the transfer has been completed from both sides of the transfer. Keep track of the transfer— and if the paying trustee or custodian is slow to act, nudge them a little.

When a transfer is made, at no time must assets be in your possession even if just long enough for you to carry a check across the street from one office to another—or even down the hall. If this happens, the transfer becomes an ordinary IRA-to-IRA rollover and is governed by those rules.

If you haven't made a rollover of that IRA in more than a year, all you've lost is the chance to make another tax-free rollover for a year. But if you've broken the once-a-year rollover rule, the entire sum is now an excess contribution and could trigger all the IRS penalities. It could result in the entire amount becoming taxable income for that year and subject you to the 10 percent premature distribution penalty besides.

TRANSFERS ARE USUALLY PREFERABLE TO ROLLOVERS

The main drawback to a transfer is that it usually takes more time to arrange. It may take up to a several weeks (or more) to complete a transfer, while under some circumstances you could complete a rollover in a single day.

In making transfers, some IRA sponsors may be in no hurry to transfer your money or other assets to their competitors—or they may simply have inefficient office procedures for handling a transfer. For obvious reasons, they may be more interested in concentrating on procedures for getting IRA money into their financial institutions than in getting it out.

Transfers out of self-directed brokerage firm accounts take the longest time. That's because to make the move, the securities in the account must be registered in the name of the new account. For this reason, transferring mutual fund shares out of a brokerage account may also be time consuming.

If a sponsor doesn't complete your transfer within a reasonable time—other than where the ownership of securities must be transferred, two weeks would seem more than ample time under most circumstances—start phoning and writing the first sponsor to demand that the transfer be carried out. If this doesn't produce results, take your case to whatever government agency or agencies regulate that sponsor (assuming the sponsor is under government regulation.)

All things being equal, if there's no need for speed you'll be better off arranging a transfer than making a rollover. There's no limit to the number of transfers you can make. Making a transfer would preserve the right to move that IRA again in less than a year with a rollover if you believed it had to be moved very quickly—if you saw the investment turning sour, for instance. With a rollover you could cut your losses by getting your money out in one day, rather than seeing them deepen as you waited for the trustees or custodians to complete transfer arrangements.

With a transfer you also avoid the risk of something happening to prevent the rollover from being completed within 60 days after you take possession of the assets.

10

Rollovers into IRAs from Other Pension Plans

From the beginning of the IRA program, people have used IRAs as a tax shelter for lump-sum distributions from employer pension and retirement plans. Now that more people are beginning to understand IRAs, this use is increasing.

You may not have any other pension or retirement plan now—or you may believe you'll remain covered by your company plan until you retire, at which time you expect to take monthly benefit checks rather than a lump-sum distribution.

But, during your working lifetime, circumstances could change greatly. Some of the most important financial decisions you will ever make during your lifetime may involve rolling assets from other pension plans into an IRA—and later, possibly rolling them back into another employer plan.

Some differences between IRAs and qualified employer plans—which include government and teacher plans as well as those offered by private employers—are discussed in Chapter 8. Insofar as they relate to potential rollovers of lump-sum employer plan distributions in and out of IRAs, the major difference is that in general the tax treatment of a lump-sum distribution from an employer plan is more favorable than for an IRA. A portion may be taxable as long-term capital gains, and some or all of it may be subject to a favorable 10-year averaging rule. (You'll find a table with examples of how 10-year averaging works later in this chapter.)

On the other hand, money rolled into an IRA from an employer plan will continue to pile up tax-sheltered earnings. In time this could more than offset the less favorable tax treatment given IRA distributions when you begin withdrawing money.

Complicating your choices if you are given a lump-sum distribution that you could roll over into an IRA during your working years is the fact that you may wish to use the IRA as a "conduit" and roll it back to a new employer plan at some later date—if the new employer will allow it.

Consequently, when you are given a lump-sum distribution from a qualified pension, profit-sharing, or stock bonus plan, there are many important implications. You may have only 60 days in which to make decisions that could profoundly affect your financial situation for many years.

The rules covering employer plan rollovers are also among the most complex related to IRAs. Again, this is a situation where professional advice may be needed.

WHEN CAN EMPLOYER ROLLOVERS BE MADE?

Circumstances under which the IRS will allow a tax-free lump-sum rollover from an employer pension, profit-sharing, or stock bonus plan into an IRA include these:

- If you leave your job for any reason, whether voluntarily or because your services have been terminated.
- If your employer ends a pension plan or permanently stops making payments to a profit-sharing or stock bonus plan and gives you your complete share.
- If you are age 59½ or older.
- If you die, and your spouse is your beneficiary. In that event, your spouse may roll your death benefits from the plan into an IRA.
- If the rollover is made under a domestic relations order—that is, if it is part of a divorce or separation settlement.

Although your complete share in the employer plan need not be paid to you in a single installment, to qualify as a tax-free rollover into an IRA it must be received within a single tax year. If you were paid part of the distribution in 1985 and part in 1986, you could not roll over either portion because this would not meet the one-year test. (This assumes that, along with the vast majority of taxpayers, you are on a calendar year.)

Ordinarily, rollovers into IRAs from employer plans involve total distributions from the plan. But, under some circumstances, you are now allowed to take a partial distribution from your employer plan and roll it into an IRA. However, as will be seen, for some people there would be disadvantages to doing so.

As discussed in Chapter 8 and at the end of this chapter, if you are married you must now have the written consent of your spouse to do anything with your employer plan benefits other than accept a joint and survivor annuity. This includes taking a lump-sum distribution from an employer plan for any purpose, including a rollover into an IRA.

YOU CANNOT "QUIT" SELF-EMPLOYMENT

One exception to the rules covering distributions from retirement plans involves the self-employed. The IRS will not allow you to "quit" self-employment and give yourself a lump-sum distribution from a Keogh plan (or your IRA) before you are age 59½. Obviously, if you were allowed to do this you could obtain the use of the money while avoiding the 10 percent premature distribution tax.

If you stop being self-employed, you must still keep the money in a Keogh plan (or IRA) until age 59½—or pay the tax penalty if you take it out before then.

However, if you are self-employed and become permanently disabled, even if under age 59½, you *are* allowed to take a lump-sum distribution of everything in your Keogh plan or IRA without a tax penalty. Of course, you would have to report the distribution as income and pay tax on it.

EMPLOYER PLAN ROLLOVERS MUST ALSO BE MADE WITHIN 60 DAYS

As with IRA-to-IRA rollovers, rollovers from an employer plan must be completed within 60 days of the date the assets are distributed to you.

Particularly if you did not expect to receive the distribution— if, for instance, you were given the distribution because you were unexpectedly terminated from your job—this gives you very little time to make what could well be the most important financial decision in your life. The sum in an employer plan distribution could be the largest you will ever handle. Its disposition could have a great effect on your financial security—and that of your beneficiaries.

During the time the assets are under your control after the distribution, you must take any money earned by those assets into your income for that year. If you deposited a $100,000 employer plan distribution in a money market savings account, the earnings from the $100,000 should not be rolled into an IRA later. You should contribute no more than $100,000 to the IRA if you decide to complete the rollover.

If the assets are distributed to you in more than one payment, it appears that the 60-day period starts from the date of the last payment. As noted earlier, however, all of the payments must be received within a single taxable year.

THESE ROLLOVERS CAN BE MADE AT ANY TIME

One important difference between employer plan rollovers and IRA-to-IRA rollovers is that rollovers out of or into employer plans are not subject to the once-a-year rule. They can be made at any time.

If you lose your job and roll an employer plan distribution into an IRA, you could roll that money right back into another employer plan if you got a new job and the employer allowed the rollover.

However, when the assets are in your IRA, movements to any other IRA would be covered by the IRA-to-IRA rules. If you moved them to another IRA with a rollover, the move would be covered by the once-a-year rule. But, if you had them transferred directly from one IRA trustee or custodian to another, you could move them as often as you wish.

TO KEEP THE "ROLL BACK" OPTION, DON'T MIX ASSETS

After you roll assets from an employer plan into an IRA, unless you have taken only a partial distribution from the plan, the law allows you to roll them back (along with any tax-sheltered earnings while they were in the IRA) to another employer plan at a later date.

For most people, retaining this option would be a good idea. Even if you now have no intention of ever rolling these assets back to an employer plan, you might change your mind later.

But, if you wish to roll these assets and their IRA earnings back into another employer plan at any time in the future, you must never mix these assets with any other IRA assets.

Do not roll money or any other assets from an employer plan into any other IRA if you wish to retain this option. Even if the IRA you roll the assets into has only a few dollars in it, you'd lose the right to make a tax-free rollback later.

Instead, set up a separate IRA for the assets being rolled over from the qualified plan. As long as you wish to retain this option, don't make any more contributions to this IRA. If these assets are mixed with those of any other IRA, you will not be allowed to roll them into another employer plan.

If you attempt to roll this IRA into another employer plan, the entire amount will be considered distributed to you and taxable for that year. If you are under age 59½ and are not disabled, you'll also have to pay the 10 percent premature distribution penalty. If you made this technical mistake while handling a six-figure IRA, it could be a financial disaster.

YOU NEEDN'T ROLL ALL THE ASSETS OVER

When you receive a distribution from a qualified employer plan under conditions that permit rolling it into an IRA, you are *not* required to roll *all* of it over. If you wish, you may roll over part of the assets tax free and keep the remainder.

However, there is an important trade-off if you split the distribution. It is that you will *not* be allowed to use the favorable 10-year averaging treatment for the amount you keep. You will be eligible for the regular 4-year averaging treatment if you qualify, but the special 10-year tax treatment for qualified employer plan distributions cannot be used.

You may also split the rollover by rolling assets into more than one IRA. The same rules about later rolling those assets back into another employer plan apply. To retain the option, these IRA assets must never be mingled with other assets. However, if you commingle the assets of one of these IRAs with those from some other source, only that commingled IRA is disqualified from rolling back into an employer plan tax free.

These rules give you a lot of flexibility, particularly with a large employer plan distribution. If you receive a $100,000 distribution from an employer plan, you could keep $20,000 as part of your ordinary income for that year and split the remainder by setting up eight separate IRAs for $10,000 each—or as many IRAs as you wish, for that matter—in a wide variety of investments. If you were willing to give up the option to roll this money back into another employer plan later, you could also roll these assets into one or more existing IRAs.

NONDEDUCTIBLE VOLUNTARY CONTRIBUTIONS CANNOT BE ROLLED OVER

For years, some employer plans allowed employees to make voluntary contributions that you were not allowed to deduct from your income. Although the employer's plan sheltered the earnings of those contributions from taxation, the contributions were made with aftertax dollars. Before 1982, all voluntary employer plan contributions were of this type.

If you roll your share of an employer plan into an IRA, you are not allowed to roll over the portion that consists of those voluntary, nondeductible contributions. Before completing the rollover, take those contributions out and keep the money. Your employer should give you a statement totaling your voluntary contributions.

That money doesn't have to be added to your income, however. It has already been taxed—or will be included by the employer in your current year's earnings statement, if the contributions were made in the current year.

Example. You're given a $100,000 lump-sum distribution from an employer plan, but $5,000 of that represents your own nondeductible contributions. You subtract the $5,000 and may roll over up to the remaining $95,000 into an IRA tax free. If you roll over any portion of your nondeductible contributions, that portion will be viewed as an excess contribution even though you have already paid tax on this money.

DEDUCTIBLE VOLUNTARY CONTRIBUTIONS CAN BE ROLLED OVER

As we saw in Chapter 8, if an employer allows it, you are now permitted to make voluntary contributions to your employer's plan and deduct them instead of making contributions to an IRA.

If the employer later gives you a lump-sum distribution, these voluntary deductible contributions *can* be rolled over into an IRA or another qualified plan. Your employer should give you a statement telling you what they are.

If you decide to keep these voluntary deductible contributions rather than rolling them over into an IRA, they will be considered distributions from the plan. You'll have to take them into income for that year and pay tax on them. If you are under age 59½ and are not disabled, you'll also have to pay the 10 percent premature distribution penalty.

The rollover rules covering voluntary deductible contributions are complicated, to say the least. It shouldn't be surprising if some IRA sponsors don't fully understand them. And so, if you can show that your rollover resulted in an excess payment because the sponsor gave you incorrect information, the IRS has said it will allow you to withdraw the excess without having to include it in your gross income.

ROLLOVERS OF SOME PARTIAL DISTRIBUTIONS NOW ALLOWED

Under some circumstances, you do not have to receive a distribution of all of your assets from an employer plan in order to make a rollover into an IRA. Rollovers of certain partial distributions are permitted by the Tax Reform Act of 1984. Formerly, there had to be a distribution of all of your assets in the plan if you wished to roll all or any part of them into an IRA.

To roll a partial distribution into an IRA, the distribution must be equal to at least 50 percent of "the balance to your credit" under the plan or a tax-sheltered annuity. In addition, it must not be one of a series of periodic payments.

For partial rollover purposes, the "balance to your credit" in the plan does not include any of your deductible (voluntary) contributions and the earnings on them. Also, only the taxable portion of the partial distribution may be rolled over into the IRA. You are not allowed to roll over your voluntary nondeductible contributions.

A partial distribution from an employer plan cannot be rolled into another qualified employer plan, as can be done with a full distribution. To make a tax-free rollover, the partial distribution must be rolled into an IRA—and no portion can later be rolled back into another qualified plan. However, if both plans permit it, you could move a partial distribution from one employer to another by *direct transfer* instead of a rollover.

There are several potential disadvantages to taking a partial distribution from an employer plan with the intention of rolling it into an IRA. One is that in some cases it may be difficult for your employer to determine if the distribution is equal to at least 50 percent of the balance to your credit, particularly if your assets in the plan are in the form of stock with a fluctuating value.

Another is that in time, the amount remaining in the plan may grow to a much larger sum than the "more than 50 percent" distributed to you. Because you had taken the early partial distribution, this money would no longer be eligible either for 10-year averaging or for another rollover into an IRA. When distributed to you, it would be taxable as income in the year received.

ROLLOVER OF PROPERTY RECEIVED IN A DISTRIBUTION

A rollover from an employer plan may also include property— most typically, stock in the employer company. Unlike an IRA-to-IRA rollover where the exact property received must be rolled over, you *are* allowed to sell property received from an employer plan—and then to roll it (or a portion of it) into an IRA tax free. In fact, many financial institutions are unwilling to accept the responsibility for being caretaker to your stock in an IRA. Their IRA agreement with you may specify that if you turn over stock, the institution will convert it into cash.

The ability to roll over proceeds from the sale of property greatly widens your options. However, it may complicate the preparation of your tax return. In any event, at this level you should definitely be receiving professional guidance.

Things are still relatively simple if you roll all of the property or all the money you receive from the property's sale into an IRA. In that case, there would be no gain or loss to report on your return for that year.

If your employer gave you a distribution of $100,000 in stock in the company and you sold it within the 60-day period for $120,000 and rolled the entire amount into an IRA, you do not have to report the $20,000 as a gain. However, if you sold the stock for $80,000, you couldn't take the loss.

Procedures become more complicated if you decide to sell property but do not roll over the entire proceeds. In this event, you'll be taxed on the part you do not roll over. Part of that may be a capital gain or loss on the sale, and part or all will be on ordinary income. And as with an all-cash distribution, any portion you keep and do not roll over does not qualify for the favorable 10-year tax treatment.

The fair market value of the portion you do not roll over (after subtracting any nondeductible contributions you may have made) on the date it was distributed to you will be taxed as ordinary income. The difference between the fair market value on the date you received the property and what you obtained when you sold it will be a capital gain or loss.

ANNUITY–TO–IRA ROLLOVER

You may also roll a lump-sum distribution from a tax-sheltered annuity into an IRA. However, you can roll over only the part of the annuity that would normally be taxed, which is the part that does not represent your nondeductible contribution. As with rollovers from employer plans, these rollovers must be completed within 60 days.

The assets later can be rolled into another tax-sheltered annuity—but only if they have not been combined with IRA assets from any other source. And, you are not allowed to roll these assets into an employer plan, only into another annuity.

KEOGH–TO–IRA ROLLOVER

Under some circumstances, a lump-sum distribution may be rolled over from a Keogh plan into an IRA, although few self-employed people would wish to do so. If it is a plan you established, you are not disabled, and you are under age 59½, you must completely terminate your Keogh plan when making the rollover.

If you are age 59½ or older, your Keogh plan can be maintained after you roll the assets into an IRA. But to qualify as a lump-sum distribution, the assets you roll out of the Keogh plan must have accumulated in it for at least five years. If you wish to roll over assets that have accumulated in your Keogh plan for less than five years, you must terminate the entire plan and roll all the assets over.

If you are an employee covered by a Keogh plan and leave the job, you may roll your portion of the Keogh plan into an IRA within 60 days tax free. You can also roll it into another qualified plan if the plan permits it. Some pros and cons of Keogh plans and IRAs are discussed in Chapter 12.

ROLLOVER BY A SURVIVING SPOUSE

A surviving spouse is allowed to roll over an employer's lump-sum distribution into an IRA of her or his own. This could happen either upon the employee's death or because of the termination of the employer's plan after the employee's death.

Under some circumstances, the surviving spouse may be allowed to exclude up to $5,000 of this lump-sum distribution from income during the year of the distribution. This is called the death benefit exclusion, and no part of it can be rolled into an IRA.

The surviving spouse may keep these IRA assets separate from any other IRAs, may mingle them with other IRAs, or may make additional contributions to them. However, under no circumstances can assets received from an employer plan by a surviving spouse be rolled into any other employer plan.

EMPLOYER ROLLOVERS PROS AND CONS IF YOU'RE STILL WORKING

Many circumstances could find you contemplating or receiving a lump-sum distribution of your entire share of an employer's qualified plan while you're still working for that employer. The choices you may have to make include these:

If You Have a Choice, Should You Leave the Money in the Company Plan and Allow It to Grow There Tax-Free for as Long as the Company Allows It?

This will depend largely on how you feel about the company, how well the company plan is doing (and might be expected to do in the future), and whether you have an immediate and pressing need for the money. It might also depend on whether you can roll over the assets to a plan with a new employer immediately—or whether you'll have to put them in an IRA "conduit" instead, possibly not knowing if you'll ever find another employer willing to accept them.

If the employer has terminated your services abruptly or you are leaving because you are dissatisfied, you'll probably want to take the distribution in any event. However, if you're the kind of person who knows that once you get your hands on the money you'll spend it, consider leaving it in the employer plan for at least a while, if the plan permits. This will give you time to consider the alternatives.

Should You Roll the Entire Employer Plan Distribution into an IRA?

If you have many working years ahead and there is no immediate need for this money, you'd be well advised to roll all of it into an IRA even though you may risk losing the favorable tax treatment given to employer plans if you take a lump-sum IRA distribution later. The tax-sheltered earnings in your IRA could more than offset the difference.

If invested at a constant 10 percent rate of return, money would double in the 8th year, triple in the 12th year, quadruple in the 15th year, and quintuple in the 17th year. If you kept it in the IRA for 20 years, it would multiply nearly sevenfold.

At this rate, $100,000 rolled over into an IRA when you are age 45 would have grown to $161,000 in five years, $259,300 in 10 years, $417,700 in 15 years, and $673,000 in 20 years, when you're age 65 and may wish to retire.

Of course, if you have a pressing need for the money, take it. If you've lost a job and have no other financial resources, you may need the distribution to live on. Or, you may conclude that its best use would be to assure a child's education, buy a home, take advantage of an investment opportunity, start your own business, or attain some other personal goal.

You may also have so much assured retirement income from other sources that you may prefer taking the money now. You'll receive the favorable employer plan tax treatment and can do what you wish with the money, including investing in collectibles or other investments barred to IRAs.

Should You Take Part of the Money, Pay Tax on It, and Roll the Remainder Into an IRA?

For most people this would be a poor choice. By taking only part of the distribution, you would lose the employer plan's favorable 10-year averaging tax treatment.

But, there are circumstances where being taxed at the higher rate wouldn't make much difference. If you had little or no income from other sources that year—perhaps because you lost your job with the employer who gave you the distribution—the tax difference might not be significant either.

If You Roll All or Any Portion of the Employer Plan Distribution Into an IRA, Should You Preserve the Option to Roll It Back to Some Other Employer Plan by Always Keeping These Assets Separate from Your Other Assets?

Definitely. Even if you have no intention of putting money into another employer plan now, circumstances could change. One day you might find yourself going to work for an employer who has an excellent plan—and is willing to accept a rollover from your IRA or IRAs.

In setting up this IRA or these IRAs, however, avoid making long-term commitments, at least at the start. If you think you may be rolling these assets back into a new employer plan soon, a money market mutual fund or money market account at a bank or savings institution (where there would be no sponsor penalties if you wanted to move the money) would be your best bet. Avoid buying insurance annuities with big penalties for pulling out in the early years, or long-term savings certificates with early withdrawal penalties that could cut into your principal. You can always move assets to a longer-term IRA later if it becomes apparent you won't be rolling them into another employer plan soon.

EMPLOYER ROLLOVER PROS AND CONS WHEN YOU RETIRE

A different set of factors comes into play if you're given the opportunity to receive a lump-sum distribution from an employer plan when near or at retirement.

Many people will never have the opportunity to make this choice. In the past when people retired, they almost always received retirement benefits in the form of fixed monthly payments for the rest of their lives, with some additional death benefits for their beneficiaries. But this pattern has been changing, especially for middle- and upper-level employees and executives. The demand for lump-sum payments is becoming so insistent—particularly from executives—that nearly every pension plan may have to offer them sooner or later.

The demand for taking pensions in a lump sum stemmed from the creation of IRAs in the Employment Retirement Income Security Act of 1974 (ERISA), which also allowed lump-sum rollovers into IRAs from employer plans. The rationale for this was to allow people to protect themselves. Inflation was eroding the value of fixed payments to retirees. It was reasoned that if you didn't need the lump sum immediately, you could keep compounding it at a relatively high tax-sheltered rate, allowing you to buy a retirement income higher than would be the case otherwise.

Not all financial advisers think this is a good idea, and not all companies allow employees to take a lump-sum distribution. However, the list of those that do is growing.

If you're given this option when you retire, you may have to make these decisions:

Should You Take the Lump-Sum Distribution or Regular Monthly Benefits for the Rest of Your Life?

Again, many factors must be weighed. Are you the sort of person who spends everything you get? If so, don't accept the lump-sum payment unless you are assured of a retirement income from other sources.

Beyond this, are you capable of investing a large sum yourself? Even if you are, would you worry a lot if you had to do so? And, how long can you reasonably be expected to live? Or to continue earning income, if you're still earning or plan to continue in a different line of work? What are your other retirement income sources? Will a spouse or other beneficiary or beneficiaries rely on your retirement income? If so, what death benefits would your beneficiaries receive under the employer plan when you die?

If You Decide to Take the Distribution, Should You Roll All of It into an IRA or Keep It All?

The same factors are involved along with some others, including taxes. If you keep it all, you can use the favorable employer plan tax treatment with 10-year averaging. If you roll everything into the IRA, you'd lose the favorable tax treatment—but, if the money remains in the IRA long enough, you'd come out ahead anyhow. To help you make estimates, some of the fixed-income growth tables in Appendix A enable you to calculate how any sum would grow at various interest rates.

Taxes aside, for many people this choice comes down to what you *want* to do rather than what a financial adviser might think is "best." It's not uncommon for people receiving a large employer distribution at or near retirement—usually more than they've ever owned in a lifetime—to pay the tax and use the remainder for luxuries they could never afford before. In their minds, the pleasure the money buys them more than offsets the loss of additional retirement income—and, if they die soon after taking the money and spending it, they'll have won the game.

On the other hand, if your goal is to build as big a retirement fund as you can, roll everything into an IRA and don't touch it until you have to. Allow the IRA's tax-sheltered leverage to work for you as long as possible. If necessary, exhaust any lower-yielding retirement assets before you begin using your tax-sheltered IRA.

Should You Take Part of the Distribution and Roll the Other Part Over?

Because a distribution at or near retirement would probably involve a relatively large sum, for most people this would be an even less desirable choice than if made when given a distribution early in their working lives. By rolling any part of the distribution into an IRA, you lose the favorable 10-year averaging treatment for what you keep.

All things being equal, it would be better to either keep the entire distribution and pay taxes at the more favorable rate or to roll everything into an IRA and continue sheltering the earnings from taxation.

WEIGHING THE TAX BITE FROM 10–YEAR AVERAGING

Your decision on whether to roll a company plan distribution into an IRA may hinge on how much tax the government would take if you elected not to make the rollover.

For many people, the tax "bite" from 10-year averaging on a distribution from an employer pension plan may be worth accepting. This would be especially true if the distribution is relatively small and you're close to retirement.

The tax you'd pay would be relatively modest. You could reinvest the proceeds without worrying about adding to your taxable income whenever you took money out of the IRA. And no matter what your age, you could do what you wish with this money. If you rolled it into an IRA, after age 70½ you would be required to withdraw at least a minimum amount each year to avoid a big tax penalty.

On the other hand, if it's a large distribution and you anticipate keeping it in a tax-sheltered mode for a relatively long period, you'll probably come out ahead by rolling it over into an IRA. As the size of the distribution increases, the benefit of 10-year averaging decreases.

In weighing the pros and cons of paying tax immediately and gaining full use of the money, you'll also want to consider the rate at which you'd probably pay taxes on the taxable income (if any) from the distribution's proceeds over the years. If you're in a high bracket, you may decide to invest the distribution for tax-free yield. However, even tax-free income would count toward making a portion of your social security benefits subject to income tax if your income is large enough.

To use 10-year averaging, you must have been in the plan at least 5 years before the year of distribution. *Moreover, you are allowed to use it only once after age 59½.* If you think 10-year averaging could be advantageous at some time in the future—if you still have some working years ahead, for instance—this may be a key factor in your decision.

As noted, 10-year averaging allows you to pay tax on a lump-sum distribution as though you had received it in equal amounts over a 10-year period. It assumes that this money is your *only* income during this time. The rate at which tax is applied ranges from as low as 5.5 percent for a few thousand dollars to nearly 40 percent for $1 million.

Table 10–1 shows the effective tax rates for 10-year averaging for a wide range of distributions. The separate 10-year averaging tax is added to your regular tax as computed on your Form 1040 for that year.

(Note: If you participated in an employer plan before 1974, calculations may be more complicated because you may take capital gain treatment for a portion of the distribution that depends on the time you were in the plan before and after

TABLE 10–1 ■ Tax Bite from 10-Year Averaging*

Amount Distributed	Effective Tax Rate (Percent)	Tax Paid	Amount Retained
$ 10,000	5.50%	$ 550	$ 9,450
20,000	5.50	1,100	18,900
25,000	7.22	1,805	23,195
30,000	8.42	2,527	27,473
40,000	10.52	4,207	35,793
50,000	11.82	5,910	44,090
75,000	13.82	10,364	64,636
100,000	14.59	14,594	85,406
250,000	20.65	51,627	198,373
500,000	29.21	146,035	353,965
750,000	35.06	262,939	487,061
1,000,000	38.64	386,391	613,609

*Based on 1985 tax table.
Source: Bercoon + Weiner + Glick + Brook.

1974. Your tax adviser should compute the tax using both methods to determine which would be most advantageous for you.)

On a $20,000 distribution, the tax with 10-year averaging would be computed at a very modest 5.50 percent rate and amount to only $1,100. This would leave you $18,900 to do with as you pleased. A $50,000 distribution would be taxed at an effective 11.82 percent rate. Your tax would be $5,910, and you'd have $44,090 remaining.

A $100,000 distribution would require $14,594 in taxes, leaving you $85,406—actually, still a fairly modest tax if you want the full use of this money immediately. But with a $500,000 distribution, the tax bite would be a painful $146,035. Calculated at an effective 29.21 percent rate, it would leave you with $353,965.

IF IN DOUBT, ROLL IT OVER

If you're not sure what to do with a lump-sum company plan distribution when you receive it, roll it into an IRA. But, be sure to open a new IRA or IRAs. Certainly, at this point, do *not* commingle this money with money in an IRA that already exists.

This way, you can preserve the IRA option while making up your mind. It may also give you time to concentrate on more important immediate matters, such as finding another job if you are given the distribution because you were unexpectedly "terminated." You always have until the date you file your tax return to change your mind, take the money back, list it on your return as a distribution subject to taxation, and use the 10-year averaging procedure. If you receive a lump-sum distribution from an employer plan this year, this gives you until as late as April 15 next year to make your final decision.

Of course, if you open an IRA while still unsure if you wish to keep it, select one that will allow you to withdraw the money later with little or no delay and without paying sponsor penalties or large termination fees. Primarily, this limits your choices to money market savings accounts and money market mutual funds. Certainly, do *not* buy a term certificate of deposit or make other IRA investments that require you to keep money in for a specified period to avoid paying premature withdrawal penalties.

It might be prudent to frankly tell the IRA sponsor what you're doing and obtain assurances that, if you wish, you can close out the IRA with a minimum of delay.

SPOUSE MUST NOW CONSENT TO A LUMP–SUM DISTRIBUTION

As explained in Chapter 8, all qualified employer retirement plans are now required to provide automatic survivor benefits for your spouse unless you elect otherwise—and your spouse must approve the change. In effect, this gives an employee's spouse veto power over a lump-sum distribution from an employer plan for any purpose, including a rollover into an IRA.

This requirement is so new that it is too soon to assess its impact, if any, on rollovers from company plans into IRAs. Of course, if you're not married it won't affect you. And, in most cases, a spouse will presumably be willing to agree to waive the annuity to permit the employee to take a lump-sum distribution that can be rolled over into an IRA.

But this new law is sure to lead to some lively arguments between husbands and wives as well as to some legal tangles, particularly where divorce, separation, or questions concerning the competence of one or the other parties may be involved.

All employer plans must now give participants an opportunity during an election period to elect not to receive the annuity. When you're working for a company, this election period begins on the first day of the plan year in which you reach age 35. If you separate from your job for any reason, it is 90 days from the date on which benefits accrue to you. There is no limit on the number of times you may waive the survivor benefit or revoke the waiver.

However, for a waiver to be effective, the employee's spouse must consent to it in writing and this must be witnessed by a plan representative or notary public. Consent is not required if the participant establishes to the satisfaction of the plan's representative that there is no spouse or that the spouse cannot be located. Any spousal consent to a waiver is effective only for that spouse.

11

Age 59½ and after: Taking Money out of Your IRA

When the IRA program was first opened to everyone who works, the emphasis in virtually everything written about it was on how to put money into IRAs. But as time goes on and more people with IRAs begin reaching their retirement years, there will be growing concern about the rules and procedures for taking money out.

Congress made some major revisions in these rules in 1984. In particular, it greatly changed procedures for calculating the minimum amounts that must be withdrawn each year after mandatory distributions from an IRA begin. These calculations are based on IRS life expectancy tables, which are reproduced in Appendix B of this book.

AGE 59½ AN "IRA MILESTONE"

When you reach age 59½, you are at an important milestone in your IRA program. From this point on, you no longer have to pay the 10 percent tax penalty for taking money out of an IRA.

Between ages 59½ and 70½, you have the greatest flexibility in paying distributions to yourself from your IRA or
IRAs. Each year you may pay yourself as much or as little as
you wish. If you're still earning compensation that qualifies,
you may also continue making contributions to your IRAs—
and, if you can afford them, you should.

Even though you're making some withdrawals, it will pay
to continue contributing even if the money will remain in the
IRA for only a short time. Each contribution reduces your
income tax for that year—and, until you withdraw it, the
money will grow at a tax-sheltered rate, earning substantially
more than in a taxable investment.

For many people, the period after age 59½ includes some
of their peak earnings years when it is easiest to afford maximum contributions. With no federal tax penalty for withdrawing from an IRA after age 59½, the only penalties you
may have to worry about are those that might be levied by
IRA sponsors for withdrawing before specific investments mature—and, with a little planning, some of those penalties are
easy to avoid.

IRAs AS AN INCOME-LEVELING DEVICE

Between ages 59½ and 70½, IRAs can be used as an income-
leveling device. All distributions from your IRA are taxable
as ordinary income in the year received, but proper timing
can minimize the overall tax cost. Try to plan your distributions so your tax bracket doesn't change substantially from
one year to another.

If a source of income is unexpectedly cut off or reduced,
you could make up the difference by paying yourself a distribution from an IRA. Under these circumstances, you may wind
up in no higher tax bracket than if your income remained
stable and you never touched your IRA. On the other hand,
you may not wish to take any distributions during years when
your income is high.

During this period, you may also wish to use your IRAs
for major expenditures you may not be able to handle out of
regular income or savings—a medical emergency, down payment on another home, gift to a child, or whatever.

If maximizing your retirement income is your goal and you are still earning compensation, all things being equal, try to avoid distributing assets from your IRA to yourself until such nonsheltered income investments as savings accounts, bonds, and high-yielding stocks have been exhausted. Normally, the tax-sheltered IRA's earnings will be much higher than aftertax earnings you can get elsewhere with comparable safety.

The one asset you may wish to hold even though it could be liquidated for a relatively large sum is your home, if you own one. The many personal and emotional factors involved with a home often far outweigh dollars-and-cents considerations in making this decision. In any event, before selling your home to raise capital, learn what it will cost to rent or buy a new place to live. You may find that those costs are much higher than you believed.

If you take distributions from your IRAs between ages 59½ and 70½, you are *not* required to file any additional documents with your federal income tax return. However, you are required to list the distributions as part of your income for that year.

PROS AND CONS OF TAKING IT ALL

At any time between ages 59½ and 70½, you may elect to distribute everything in your IRA or IRAs to yourself. If you do, you are still allowed to open another IRA or IRAs before age 70½ if you have income that qualifies.

In deciding whether to take it all, you must weigh many of the same factors that must be weighed by an employee given an opportunity to receive a lump-sum distribution from a qualified employer plan.

First, Consider the Tax Consequences

If it's a big IRA and you take it all, you'll have to pay a big tax bill. If the distribution puts you in the top bracket—currently 50 percent—you'll have to give half of the money to the government by April 15 of the following year. Unless you have a desperate need for the money, try to avoid doing this.

While the lump-sum distribution doesn't qualify for the advantageous 10-year forward averaging treatment available for an employer plan distribution, it does qualify for 4-year averaging (as would any other ordinary income you receive). If you decide you must take a lump-sum distribution, try to do it after several years in which you had relatively little income so 4-year averaging may be of some help.

Next, Look at Yourself

If you're the type of person who is unable to manage or hold onto money, take as little from your IRA as possible. If you need money, arrange for a periodic withdrawal system, either from your IRAs or by using your IRAs to buy an annuity from an insurance company.

What are your other income sources? If your needs are comfortably being met by them, you may wish to delay drawing from your IRA as long as possible while further compounding the tax-sheltered earnings.

How long can you reasonably be expected to live? If you are in poor health and believe that your life span is very limited, you may wish to take much or all of your IRA now and pay the tax—unless you have a beneficiary or beneficiaries you wish to inherit your IRA. If you are in good health and come from a family whose members often live to a very old age, you may wish to make your retirement income from your IRAs last as long as possible.

Just as with someone taking a distribution from an employer plan, much also depends on what *you* want rather than what might shape up on paper as "best." If you have adequate retirement income from other sources and would like to use the money in your IRA for travel or other luxuries you've denied yourself throughout your working life, go ahead and indulge yourself with your IRAs. That may have been your goal all along.

IRA DISTRIBUTIONS AND SOCIAL SECURITY

Now that social security payments are subject to federal income tax if your income exceeds specified levels, the amount you withdraw from your IRA might affect the tax status of your social security benefits.

You may have to pay social security tax on up to half of your benefits if your income plus half of your social security benefits exceeds a base amount. For taxpayers filing individual returns, the base amount is $28,000; for taxpayers filing joint returns, it is $32,000.

In figuring your taxable social security benefits, even income normally exempt from taxation such as interest on municipal bonds is counted.

Example. You are married, with $6,000 of social security income. Your adjusted gross income from interest, dividends, and an employer pension plan is $22,000; you also have $4,000 in interest on municipal bonds, for a total of $26,000. However, your social security benefits are not taxable because with half of your social security benefits ($3,000) added to the $26,000 the total is only $29,000, which is below the $32,000 base amount.

Example. All conditions in the previous example are the same, except that you also have $5,000 income from an IRA, raising your adjusted gross income to $27,000. With your interest on municipal bonds ($4,000) and half of your social security benefits ($3,000) added, the total is now $34,000, which is $2,000 above the base amount. This makes $2,000 of your social security benefits subject to federal income tax.

As you begin taking distributions from your IRA, their impact on the tax status of your social security payments (and on your overall tax situation) will probably vary from year to year depending on your income from all sources and the deductions you are allowed to take.

Between ages 59½ and 70½, when you have the greatest flexibility in deciding how much or how little (if any) you will withdraw from an IRA, it will be easiest to avoid the tax bite on your social security income by concentrating IRA distributions in years when they would be least likely to push your income above the base level. These would be years when your other income would be lower for one reason or another or when your deductions would be significantly higher.

Your tax situation should also be factored into the decisions you must make after you reach age 70½ and must decide how to distribute your IRA or IRAs to yourself for the rest of your life.

AFTER YOU REACH AGE 70½

The idea behind IRAs is to provide money for retirement. Consequently, Congress has decreed that after you reach the year in which you become age 70½ you can no longer contribute to an IRA—and by April 1 of the following year, you *must* start a withdrawal program.

Your choices at this point are to (1) take everything out and pay tax on the entire distribution, (2) use your IRAs to buy an insurance annuity, or (3) begin a regular payout schedule to yourself that provides for substantially nonincreasing payments over a "permissible period." If you fail to take enough out of your IRA each year to meet IRS minimum requirements after the required distributions have begun, you'll have to pay a penalty of one half of the excess amount not distributed.

Taking Everything Out

The major pros and cons were discussed earlier. If you haven't built a large IRA or you've already withdrawn so much that only a small sum remains, you may not have much to lose by taking it all immediately instead of buying a small income far into the future. But, if it's a relatively large sum, you'll probably be better off stretching the payout (and the tax bite) rather than taking it out all at once.

Buying an Insurance Annuity

The IRS gives you the option of ordering the trustee or custodian of your IRA to use the money to buy an annuity contract for you (and, in fact, you can do so at any time after age 59½). You won't be taxed when you receive the contract but will be taxed when you begin receiving payments.

This may be your best course if you don't trust yourself to handle your own affairs. It can also assure that you won't outlive your IRA—although you can now also do this by distributing the IRA to yourself. But if you know you can manage money, you'd probably be better off investing it conservatively and paying yourself out of your IRA rather than buying an annuity. Obviously, when you buy one, some of the money must go for a fee or commission.

Fixed-annuity-type payments are also vulnerable to a loss of buying power to inflation. And, you want to be sure to select the type of annuity best suited for your circumstances. With some annuity plans—a so-called life annuity, for instance—benefits will be paid for as long as you live. But, after you die, no payments are made to your beneficiaries. Other plans will pay your beneficiary for only a relatively short time.

Paying the IRA Out to Yourself in Regular Payments over a Permissible Period

Unless you have a very small IRA or need the money immediately, it would seem prudent to elect a long-term payment program rather than taking all the money and paying tax on it or buying an insurance annuity.

IRS rules covering IRA distributions have been greatly liberalized in this area. Authorized in the Tax Reform Act of 1984, these changes permit the recalculation of your life expectancy as often as annually. Their effect is to make it possible for most people to outlive their IRAs if they wish.

Before 1985, the IRS formula for determining the minimum distribution allowed assumed that after reaching age 70½, men would live another 12.1 years and women would live 15.0 years. In the first year after reaching age 70½, a man was required to withdraw at least 1/12th of the balance in the IRA; in the second year, 1/11th of the balance; and so on. A woman would be required to begin withdrawals with 1/15th of the balance, and the IRS also had tables for what it called the "expected return" multiples for couples with an IRA.

The new rules are similar to those that now apply to distributions from qualified employer retirement plans. Under them, although the payments to yourself must be substantially nonincreasing, they could generally increase if due to investment returns. In other words, under some circumstances the IRA may increase in value by a greater amount than that withdrawn during the year.

The "permissible period" over which you must distribute the entire IRA to yourself is one that does not exceed your life, the lives of you and a designated beneficiary, or a period not longer than the life expectancy of you or of you and the designated beneficiary. The "designated beneficiary" must be someone you have designated to inherit your IRA when you die.

If you elect to pay the IRA out over your lifetime or the lifetimes of you and a designated beneficiary, you must still be careful to pay yourself at least the minimum each year as discussed in the next section. In effect, you have a fair amount of leeway because the IRS allows you to take credits for distributions over the minimum in earlier years (but not for distributions made before the required distributions begin).

When you elect to make your periodic distributions over your life expectancy—or over the life expectancies of you and a designated beneficiary—the "permissible period" can be stretched out through annual recalculations.

Using the IRS life expectancy tables, you are allowed to recalculate your own life expectancy as frequently as annually. If the designated beneficiary is your spouse and you have elected to make your payments over your joint life expectancy, the joint life expectancy of you and your spouse can also be recalculated with these tables as frequently as annually. However, if the designated beneficiary is not your spouse, only your life expectancy may be recalculated.

USING THE IRS MULTIPLES—TABLES FOR INDIVIDUALS

In practice, your tax adviser or IRA sponsor will probably find the proper multiple on the tables and make the required calculation for you. In fact, we strongly recommend seeking professional assistance, particularly if a large IRA is involved. The penalty for not withdrawing enough is severe, and there are still some unanswered questions about this procedure. Nevertheless, after you reach age 70½, for your own protection you should understand how this procedure works.

To use the IRS life expectancy tables, divide the money in your IRA at the first of the year by the appropriate multiple for your age—or by the multiple for the joint life expectancy of you and a designated beneficiary. The result is the minimum you must withdraw from the IRA during the year to avoid the stiff IRS penalty for excess accumulation.

Complete IRS tables for one person and for joint life expectancies of two people are in Appendix B. The tables for individuals can also be used to calculate the minimums that must be withdrawn by beneficiaries who elect to start a regular withdrawal program based on their own life expectancies if begun within one year of the death of the IRA's owner.

(Note: If you do *not* wish to recalculate your individual or joint life expectancy multiple each year or are not allowed to recalculate the multiple, you merely reduce the multiple by one each year. If the multiple is 12.1 this year, it would be 11.1 next year, and so on.)

Table 11–1 is a partial IRS multiple table for individuals, with the multiples for males starting at age 66 and females starting at age 71. You'll note that the multiples for women are higher (and they can stretch out their IRAs that much longer) because their life expectancy is greater.

In this table, the multiple for a 71-year-old male—the age at which required distributions for most males must begin—is 11.6. If you are a man who has not designated a beneficiary and has $100,000 in an IRA, you'd have to withdraw at least $8,621 ($100,000 divided by 11.6) to avoid the penalty.

However, if you wished, you could defer actually withdrawing the money until the end of the year. If you did that and the IRA earned at a 10 percent rate during the year, even after the withdrawal at year-end the balance in the IRA would be larger than at the start of the year—$101,379. Although you withdrew the $8,621 at year-end, during the year the IRA would have earned $10,000.

In the second year, if you wished to recalculate your life expectancy, the new multiple would be 11.0. The minimum you would have to withdraw would be $9,216 ($101,379 divided by 11), and so on.

By recalculating your life expectancy every year, if you wish you can stretch an IRA's payout for as long as you are likely to live. If you're a male, you're not required to distribute everything that remains in an IRA to yourself until you reach age 106; if you're a female, you wouldn't have to distribute every last dime until you are 111 years old.

TABLE 11–1 ■ IRS Life Expectancy Multiples for One
Person *(Multiples for All Ages Are in Appendix B)*

Ages			Ages		
Males	Females	Multiple	Males	Females	Multiple
66	71	14.4	86	91	5.4
67	72	13.8	87	92	5.1
68	73	13.2	88	93	4.8
69	74	12.6	89	94	4.5
70	75	12.1	90	95	4.2
71	76	11.6	91	96	4.0
72	77	11.0	92	97	3.7
73	78	10.5	93	98	3.5
74	79	10.1	94	99	3.3
75	80	9.6	95	100	3.1
76	81	9.1	96	101	2.9
77	82	8.7	97	102	2.7
78	83	8.3	98	103	2.5
79	84	7.8	99	104	2.3
80	85	7.5	100	105	2.1
81	86	7.1	101	106	1.9
82	87	6.7	102	107	1.7
83	88	6.3	103	108	1.5
84	89	6.0	104	109	1.3
85	90	5.7	105	110	1.2
			106	111	1.0

MULTIPLES FOR TWO PEOPLE

If your goal is to stretch out the money in an IRA as far as it can possibly go, you should elect to have a joint multiple with a designated beneficiary. And, the younger the beneficiary, the higher the beginning multiple will be.

Table 11–2 is a small composite section of the IRS joint multiple tables in Appendix B. Looking at it, you'll see that the multiples are much larger. This means the minimum you must withdraw in the earlier years is much smaller, leaving more money in the IRA to continue growing in a tax-sheltered mode. For instance, the joint multiple for a man aged 71 and a woman aged 68 is 19.0, compared with 11.6 for a man of 71 alone and 13.2 for a woman of 68 alone.

Using the earlier example of a $100,000 IRA earning a 10 percent return, with the joint multiple the minimum that

TABLE 11–2 ■ **Composite Sample IRS Joint and Survivor Life Expectancy Table**

Ages						
	Male	71	72	73	74	75
Male	Female	76	77	78	79	80
61	66	20.0	19.8	19.6	19.4	19.2
62	67	19.5	19.2	19.0	18.8	18.7
63	68	19.0	18.7	18.5	18.3	18.1
64	69	18.5	18.2	18.0	17.8	17.6
65	70	18.0	17.8	17.5	17.3	17.1
66	71	17.6	17.3	17.1	16.9	16.6
67	72	17.2	16.9	16.7	16.4	16.2
68	73	16.8	16.5	16.2	16.0	15.7
69	74	16.4	16.1	15.8	15.6	15.3
70	75	16.1	15.8	15.5	15.2	14.9

would have to be withdrawn in the first year would be $5,263 ($100,000 divided by 19.0), compared with $8,621 for a man alone and $6,944 for a woman alone. At the end of the first year the account balance would be $104,737—$100,000 plus $10,000 in interest minus the $5,263 distribution. If the woman is the man's spouse, the multiple recalculated for the second year (male 72, female 69) would be 18.2 on the table. The minimum withdrawal required in the second year would be $104,737 divided by 18.2 = $5,755, and so on.

Remember—you are only allowed to recalculate the joint multiple if the beneficiary is your spouse. For any other beneficiary, you are allowed only to recalculate your own life expectancy with your own multiple on the "one-life" table.

However, if the beneficiary is not your spouse, there would be no point in recalculating until your individual multiple is higher than the joint multiple. And, if the beneficiary you have named is substantially younger than you, that's not likely to happen during your lifetime. For more information on the life expectancy multiples, see Appendix B.

YOU DON'T HAVE TO STRETCH OUT THE PAYMENTS

You are not *required* to use the IRS multiples to stretch payments out as long as they will last. You may establish any other payout schedule that you wish, provided that the payments are not lower than those called for by the multiples in the tables.

You could set up a schedule of monthly or annual payments that would exhaust the IRA at any age between 71 and 106 for males and 111 for females. This will be permissible as long as each payment is more than the minimum specified in the IRS tables for your age.

You could do this by specifying fixed payments that would use up your capital at a varying rate depending on the IRA's earnings, or variable payments that use up the capital in the IRA at a fixed rate irrespective of the rate of return (in which case, of course, you could not be sure exactly how long the IRA would last). Your tax adviser or IRA sponsor can help you draw up a schedule that will meet the minimum withdrawal requirements.

However, even if you decide you want a payout schedule that exceeds the IRS minimum withdrawals, it would be prudent in making your irrevocable election to specify "at least the minimum." This would give you maximum flexibility for adapting to changing conditions later.

DON'T WAIT UNTIL THE LAST MINUTE TO DECIDE

The time to start thinking about the election you will make for distributing your IRA or IRAs to yourself after you reach age 70½ is well beforehand, not at the last minute.

For each IRA you own, Congress apparently intends that this will be an irrevocable decision. You may have to live with the consequences for a long time. The larger your IRA and the greater the proportion of your retirement assets that it represents, the more carefully you must weigh the factors involved—and the more likely that you may need professional advice.

Another reason for thinking about this election early is to be sure your sponsor will allow you to do what you want to do. If you decide you want a distribution schedule that pays you the minimum each year based on recalculating your life expectancy, you may find that your sponsor's rules will not allow you to do this to your satisfaction. Your sponsor may require a more regular schedule or may require that you take all the money out sooner than you'd like.

If so, give yourself plenty of time to check with other sponsors—and to roll over or transfer your IRA to another sponsor if you find one that will allow you to set up a payout program more to your liking. You should also discuss this with your tax adviser well before the time you must act to be sure you understand all the alternatives.

PENALTIES FOR EXCESS ACCUMULATIONS AFTER AGE 70½

To encourage you to use your IRA for retirement, the IRS will assess a big penalty if you don't take enough money out each year after you begin required distributions. If in any year after you reach age 70½ you withdraw less from an IRA than the minimum required by the IRS life expectancy tables, the difference between what you withdrew and the minimum is viewed by the IRS as an *excess accumulation*.

The IRS penalty for an excess accumulation is a substantial 50 percent of the excess. If you were supposed to withdraw at least $10,000 but you withdrew only $6,000, the difference would be $4,000. Your penalty tax for that year would be half of that, or $2,000.

Since 1985, the Minimum Withdrawal Penalty Apparently Applies to Each IRA You Own

Formerly, if you owned more than one IRA, you lumped all of them together to arrive at their total value, and then used the IRS tables to calculate the minimum amount that had to be withdrawn. Irrespective of how much you withdrew (or failed to withdraw) from any one IRA, you were subject to the penalty only if the total you withdrew was not enough in relation to the total value of all of your IRAs.

But now, according to the report of the staff of the Joint Congressional Committee on Taxation, the Tax Reform Act of 1984 requires that the minimum be calculated for each IRA separately. This would mean that no matter how much you have withdrawn from other IRAs, each individual IRA must meet the minimum distribution rules if you are to avoid the penalty.

If you withdraw less than the minimum from any IRA and are subject to the penalty, you must file a Form 5329 with your federal income tax return listing the tax due. However, the government recognizes that it is easy to be misinformed about the minimum contribution by plan sponsors or financial advisers—and how difficult it is for many people to make the right calculations. If you have a good reason for an excess accumulation in an IRA, the government provides an out. You may not have to pay the penalty tax if you can demonstrate that whoever sold you the IRA or advised you gave you the wrong advice—or that you made an honest mistake in using the IRS tables or did not understand them.

If you can demonstrate that your excess accumulation was due to a reasonable error and that you are making additional distributions to correct the situation, the IRS may waive the penalty. The IRS has indicated that it will accept erroneous advice or your own good efforts to understand the instructions as acceptable reasons.

Detail your case in writing. Attach your letter to the Form 5329 when you file your tax return, and pay the penalty tax at that time. If the IRS decides to waive your penalty, it will refund the money.

BACKUP WITHHOLDING ON IRA DISTRIBUTIONS

The IRS backup withholding rules, explained in Chapter 6, apply to distributions from IRAs as well as from all other pension and profit-sharing plans. The key point is that you have the right to elect not to have tax on payments to you withheld. The paying institution is required to notify you of this and to give you an election form to fill out if you decide to exercise that right.

However, even if you elect not to be withheld, the law requires that the institution withhold tax from distributions to you if you have failed to provide the institution with your tax identification number (TIN).

Under the pension withholding rules, if you don't elect not to be withheld, withholding is as follows:

1. Nonperiodic payments, which are withdrawals made on an irregular basis. Withholding is at a rate of 10 percent of the amount distributed. Hence, if you wish to distribute $1,200 to yourself from an IRA and do not elect not to be withheld, the institution or other payer must withhold $120 for federal income tax.

(Note: Even though you take money out of an IRA by making periodic withdrawals, it will be considered a "nonperiodic" distribution if you also have the right to take it all out if you wish, or to vary the amount you take out as you please.)

2. Periodic payments, which are periodic distribution or annuity payments agreed upon in writing. Withholding from these payments is as if they were wages and will depend on your marital status and the number of exemptions you claim.

If you haven't filled out an exemption certificate, withholding will be as though you are a married person with three exemptions. *However, if you have failed to provide the payer with a TIN or have provided an incorrect number, withholding must be at the highest rate—as though you are a single person with no exemptions.*

3. Qualified total distributions, which are withdrawals of the entire IRA. For these, withholding must be at a rate prescribed in tables prepared by the IRS.

DISTRIBUTION CHOICES IF YOU ARE AN IRA BENEFICIARY

Viewed from the perspective of an IRA beneficiary, the rules on taking money out of an IRA or part of an IRA that you inherit give you different options depending on three things: whether the required payments to the IRA owner after the owner reaches age 70½ have already begun, whether you are the deceased owner's "designated beneficiary," and whether you are the deceased owner's spouse.

How you will take these distributions are often complex decisions that may materially affect your own financial situation for the rest of your life. Even if all of the rules were perfectly clear, beneficiaries would be well advised to seek professional counsel to be sure they understand the consequences of their options. But, in fact, there are still questions about some aspects of these rules, which stem from new legislation. Consequently, another reason for seeking professional advice if you inherit an IRA or any part of one is to assure that you are acting on current information.

Whatever your relationship to the deceased owner, it's clear you always have the option of having everything in the IRA distributed to you in a lump sum as soon as that can be arranged and then paying tax on it as ordinary income for the year in which you receive it.

Also, if the required payments to the deceased IRA's owner have already begun after he or she had reached age 70½, whatever your relationship to the deceased, the money must be distributed to you at least as rapidly as the method being used at the time of the participant's death. How much flexibility this gives you will depend on how rapidly the money was being distributed to the participant. Each payment you receive will be taxable as ordinary income in the year you receive it.

If the IRA's owner dies before the required post-70½ payments have begun, the general rule for all beneficiaries is that they have five years in which to distribute the assets in the IRA to themselves. In many cases, this permits easing the tax bite by spreading the distribution over as many as five years.

Additional options are possible if the IRA's owner dies before the required distributions have begun and you are a designated beneficiary of the IRA.

You have the most flexibility if, in addition to being a designated beneficiary, you are also the deceased owner's spouse. If you wish, you can delay taking distributions until the date on which the deceased owner would have reached age 70½. In effect, this puts you in the "shoes" of your deceased spouse. If you don't need the money immediately, depending on the owner's age at the time of death the IRA could continue growing in a tax-sheltered mode for many years.

Beginning on the date the deceased owner would have reached age 70½, if you wish you may then begin a distribution schedule to be paid out during your lifetime or your life expectancy, using the individual IRS expectancy tables to determine the minimums that must be withdrawn. This would allow still more time for tax-sheltered growth in the IRA.

However, as the surviving spouse you are *not* allowed to use the joint multiple device with your own beneficiary to determine the minimum that must be distributed each year. But, you may recalculate your own life expectancy each year after the distributions to you begin.

If you are an IRA's designated beneficiary but are not the spouse of the IRA's owner, you also have the option of distributing the IRA to yourself over your lifetime or your life expectancy as determined by the IRS table for individuals. However, to exercise this option you must begin taking the distributions within one year of the death of the IRA's owner. You are not allowed to delay starting to take distributions until the date the owner would have reached age 70½, as the deceased owner's spouse can do if he or she is also a designated beneficiary.

Another difference if you are a designated beneficiary but are not the deceased owner's spouse is that if you decide to take distributions based on your life expectancy, you are not allowed to recalculate your life expectancy each year as the deceased owner's spouse can do. After the distributions begin, to determine the minimum that must be withdrawn to avoid the still IRS penalty you must lower the beginning multiple by one each year.

In general, if you inherit an IRA, you are not allowed to roll other money into it or to roll it over into any other existing IRA or retirement plan.

Table 11–3 summarizes the options open to people who inherit IRAs or parts of IRAs.

TABLE 11–3 ■ IRA Beneficiary Options at a Glance

All Beneficiaries—If they wish, they can take everything in a lump sum right away and pay tax on it.

If required Distributions to the IRA's owner after age 70½ have already begun—As option to above, all beneficiaries must take distributions "at least as rapidly" as the method being used at the time of the owner's death.

If required distributions to owner after age 70½ have not begun—All beneficiaries have five years in which to distribute assets to themselves. In addition, if you are a "designated beneficiary," the following options are available.

TABLE 11–3 ■ (*concluded*)

*"Designated beneficiary" who is also spouse of the deceased—Designated beneficiaries may delay distributions until date deceased would have reached age 70½. Thereafter, could distribute to yourself over your lifetime of life expectancy. Could recalculate life expectancy as often as annually if desired.

*"Designated beneficiary" who is not spouse of the deceased—You may distribute over your lifetime or life expectancy but must begin distributions within one year of IRA owner's death. Also, not allowed to recalculate life expectancy after distributions begin.

Other Retirement Plans: Keoghs, SEP IRAs, and 401(k)s

In addition to the IRA program and the QVEC plan, which employers may offer as an IRA alternative if they wish, the government allows tax-sheltered contributions to several other retirement plans. These include Keogh plans (which are only for self-employment income), Simplified Employee Pension (SEP) plans, and an increasingly popular plan called the 401(k), which some analysts have called the "super IRAs" of tomorrow.

While these plans differ in some respects, they have one thing in common. It's that under most circumstances if you're participating in one, you are also allowed to have an IRA or IRAs and contribute up to the IRA limits.

KEOGH PLANS FOR THE SELF-EMPLOYED

The best known of these other retirement plans are Keogh plans. These may be opened by anyone who has income from self-employment, whether full or part time.

In recent years, Congress has taken a number of steps aimed at bringing about "parity" between Keogh plans and qualified employer retirement plans. This has involved major changes in both types of plans.

As a result, in design Keogh plans are now the same as qualified plans. In fact, the name *Keogh* itself now has little meaning except to designate a kind of retirement plan for people with self-employment income.

Typically, Keogh plans are maintained by professional people, including doctors, dentists, attorneys, and other professionals with their own practice. They may also be opened by owners of sole proprietorships, business partners, farmers, and other people who work for themselves—independent contractors, writers, artists, composers, free-lance photographers, and so on.

Moonlighting or part-time self-employment income also qualifies. If you make extra money as a free-lance writer or have a small side business, the net profits from these ventures (your "earned income") can be the basis for Keogh plan contributions even though you may also have an employer pension plan and a full-time job.

And, of course, anyone with a Keogh plan may also contribute up to $2,000 or 100 percent of earned income, whichever is less, to an IRA as well.

(Note: If you have a Keogh plan and also intend to use self-employment income as the basis for an IRA contribution, your Keogh contribution must first be subtracted from your total self-employment income. You may then contribute up to the lesser of $2,000 or 100 percent of the sum that remains to an IRA.)

As with an IRA, your Keogh contributions are deducted from your taxable income on your return. Earnings are sheltered from taxation until you begin withdrawing from the Keogh plan, which can begin any time after age 59½ but must begin by April 1 after the year in which you reach 70½. However, unlike an IRA, you may continue making contributions to a Keogh plan as long as you have self-employment income even though you are also making the required withdrawals from the plan after age 70½.

Prohibited transaction rules for both types of plans are similar, and you have the same range of investment options—everything from insured savings accounts and certificates to mutual funds, families of mutual funds, insurance annuities, and self-directed plans.

MANY RECENT CHANGES COMPLICATE KEOGH PLANS

Keogh plans are much more complex than IRAs, and explaining them in detail is beyond the scope of this book. To begin with there are several distinct types of Keogh plans, including profit-sharing plans, money purchase plans, and defined benefit plans, as well as major differences in how these plans work.

In fact, because of some recent changes it is very difficult at this time to state concisely what the present Keogh contribution limits are.

To illustrate—it *is* true that the limit you are allowed to contribute to a Keogh plan for the 1985 tax year and deduct on your tax return is the lesser of $30,000 or 25 percent of earned income. However, in making the 25 percent contribution, *the Keogh contribution itself must first be deducted from earned income.* In practice, this establishes the upper limit for deductible Keogh contributions at 20 percent, not 25.

Example.   You have $100,000 in "earned income." If you contribute 20 percent of that—$20,000—this will leave $80,000 as the figure to which the 25 percent calculation applies. And 25 percent of $80,000 is $20,000. Simple? Of course not!

The situation is further complicated by the fact that for one of the major types of Keogh plans—profit-sharing plans—there is still a statutory limit on contributions of only 15 percent. In fact, the majority of Keogh plans in existence when the current limits were established were this type.

If all you have is a profit-sharing Keogh plan, to take advantage of the full maximum contribution allowed for Keoghs you may need to open a second plan of a different type called a money purchase plan. After doing that you may make the maximum overall Keogh contribution allowed either by contributing to both plans or by "freezing" the profit-sharing plan and making the entire contribution to the new money purchase plan.

Further complicating the situation is the fact that, in many respects, money purchase plans may be less flexible (and hence to many self-employed people, less desirable) than profit-sharing plans. With money purchase plans you are committed to contributing a fixed proportion of your income each year whether you have employees or not; with profit-sharing plans, if you don't have employees you can probably vary the proportion if you wish or even skip a year. And there are other differences a tax professional should explain to you if you are considering opening both types of plans.

Further complicating matters, there will be another increase in maximum deductible contributions to Keogh plans in the 1988 tax year. Beginning January 1, 1988, there will be annual cost-of-living adjustments to the overall contribution limits, with 1986 as the base year. These are to use the formula then in effect for social security cost-of-living increases.

As if that weren't enough, beginning with the 1984 tax year all people with Keogh plans are also allowed to start making voluntary nondeductible contributions in addition to the regular deductible contributions. Formerly, nondeductible contributions were not allowed if you did not have employees in your Keogh plan. The contribution limit for voluntary nondeductible contributions is generally 10 percent of earned self-employment income; but, before making any such contributions into your own plan, check with your tax adviser to be sure you don't overcontribute.

The advantage of making a voluntary, nondeductible contribution to your Keogh plan is the same as making one to an employer plan, if the employer permits it. Although you may not deduct the contribution on your tax return, the earnings or gains are sheltered from taxation. This allows you to earn a market rate of return on a tax-sheltered investment rather than the lower return usually associated with tax shelters.

Keogh plan requirements are also greatly complicated if you have employees and they must be included in the plan. Because of these and many other special characteristics, if you have or are thinking of opening a Keogh plan you should seek out special materials relating to them. As a starting point, consult IRS *Publication 560, Tax Information on Self-Employed Retirement Plans.*

Keogh plans are so complex that before you even open one, you should consult with a professional tax adviser to be sure you understand the obligations you must assume under the plan—

and to help you select the type of Keogh plan (or plans) most appropriate for your circumstances. Some owners of small businesses, for instance, may wish to consider so-called defined-benefit Keogh plans. These are designed to pay you a "benefit" of a specified fixed income when you retire and allow you to make the annual contributions needed to buy that benefit.

IRA–KEOGH PROS AND CONS

If you are self-employed but not in a position to contribute the limit to both an IRA and a Keogh plan in any given year and must decide whether to select one or the other, the differences between these plans may sway your decision.

Without going into how Keogh plans work in detail, for a self-employed person the main advantages of a Keogh plan over an IRA are:

1. Contribution limits are much higher. If you have the income to justify the contributions and can afford them, you can build a much larger fund for retirement or any other purpose than with an IRA. For instance, if you are fortunate enough to earn $100,000 from self-employment after deducting expenses on your Schedule C, contributing $20,000 to a Keogh plan each year at a constant 10 percent return would build a fund worth $134,300 in five years; $350,620 in 10 years; and $1,260,040 in 20 years. If you wished, you could have also been making voluntary contributions and contributing to IRAs during that time.

2. Tax treatment of money withdrawn from Keogh plans may be more favorable than for IRAs. IRA lump-sum distributions are taxed as ordinary income, but Keogh lump-sum distributions can enjoy the same favorable 10-year averaging treatment as qualified employer plans.

3. As with an employer plan, the Keogh lump-sum distribution may be taxed partly as ordinary income and partly as capital gains if that formula is more favorable than 10-year averaging. When the owner of a Keogh plan dies, the beneficiary may also take advantage of a $5,000 death benefit exclusion.

The main disadvantages of a Keogh plan as opposed to an IRA are that if you have full-time employees who have reached age 21 and have been with you for one year or more (three years if they are fully vested immediately), you must include them in your Keogh plan but do not have to include them in an IRA. If there are employees in your Keogh plan, you must contribute at least the same proportion of income for them that you would for yourself, and under some circumstances more. You will also have to meet additional IRS reporting requirements.

While these are the main differences between IRAs and Keogh plans, there are many others. In general, a self-employed person with no employees is better off with a Keogh plan than with an IRA—and, if you can afford it, contribute the limit to both.

IRA, KEOGH DEADLINES NOT THE SAME

Keogh plans and IRAs have different contribution deadlines. A Keogh plan must be opened by the end of the year in which your contributions are to apply. You cannot wait until as late as April 15 of the following year to open the plan, as you can with an IRA. The plan must be set up by December 31.

All that's necessary, however, is that the plan be established. You could open it with a token amount—or even without contributing a cent, if the sponsor allowed that.

Another difference is that with a Keogh plan, if you receive an extension for filing your return, you're allowed to delay making your contribution as late as the extension filing date. With an IRA, even if you get an extension beyond your normal filing date (for most people, April 15), your contributions for the previous year must still be made by April 15.

IF YOUR EMPLOYER HAS A KEOGH PLAN

If your employer has a Keogh plan and you are in it, the employer will make contributions for you just as though you were in a regular employer pension plan. You may also contribute up to the $2,000 maximum each year to your own IRA or IRAs.

Some employers allow employees in their Keogh plans to make additional voluntary contributions up to 10 percent of their income. These voluntary contributions do not affect your

IRA contributions because the voluntary Keogh contributions are not deductible. Your advantage in making them is that all earnings in the plan are sheltered from taxation.

If you are given the option of taking a lump-sum distribution from the Keogh plan, you'll also benefit from the favorable 10-year averaging treatment. If you leave the employer, you may roll the lump-sum distribution tax free into an IRA.

SIMPLIFIED EMPLOYEE PENSION IRAs

If your employer has a Simplified Employee Pension plan, you actually set up an IRA or IRAs on your own but your employer makes the contributions. The employer includes these contributions as income on your W-2 form for that year. However, you can then shelter this income from taxation by deducting the contributions on your tax return.

SEPs were created in the Revenue Act of 1978. The idea was to help smaller businesses provide retirement benefits for employees without much of the red tape and administrative burden associated with regular employer pension plans. But, as often happens, what the government calls simplified is in many respects not simple at all.

In general, an IRA or IRAs you set up under an employer's SEP are governed by the rules covering all other IRAs. You must be given a free choice as to IRA sponsors and the type of IRA you wish to set up.

Once an employer makes the contribution, the employer surrenders all control over the money to the plan's trustee or custodian or to the insurance company, if it's an individual retirement annuity. This gives you the same control you'd have over a regular IRA—and subjects you to the same rules and penalties for rule violations.

One advantage of a SEP IRA is that the employer's contribution limits are much higher than for a regular IRA. They are $30,000 or 15 percent of the employer's compensation to you, whichever is less.

However, the employer is not required to contribute the limit—or even to make any contributions at all in any given year, just so long as everyone is treated alike. Contributions may vary from year to year provided that each person covered by the plan receives the same percentage of income as a contribution. There must be a written allocation formula. If the employer gives a $100,000-a-year employee a $10,000 contribution, which is 10 percent of income, a $20,000 employee must be given a $2,000 contribution, and so on.

Irrespective of what the employer contributes, you are also allowed to contribute up to $2,000 a year (or 100 percent of income) to that or any other IRA or IRAs.

One other difference between SEP IRAs and other IRAs is that if you are still working after you reach age 70½, you are allowed to continue deducting your employer's contributions. However, you are no longer allowed to make your own contributions.

A disadvantage of a SEP is that if an employer offers one, it must be offered to all employees who have reached age 21 and have been employed by the firm for one year. However, employees who are part of a collective bargaining unit or who are nonresident aliens earning no U.S.-source income from the employer may be excluded from consideration.

If you are an employer, you may include yourself in the SEP IRA—but must always contribute for your employees the same proportion of income that you contribute for yourself. The favorable 10-year averaging procedure that can be used with a Keogh plan lump-sum distribution is not available for a SEP, making a Keogh plan a better choice if you are self-employed.

If your employer contributes too much to your SEP IRA, you must withdraw the excess amount before you file your tax return. If you fail to withdraw it, *you* will be liable for the 6 percent excise tax. However, if the employer's contribution was $30,000 or less, you won't have to pay the 10 percent premature distribution tax.

Setting up a SEP IRA usually involves you and your employer both signing Form 5305-SEP, Simplified Employee Pension-Individual Retirement Accounts Contribution Agreement. You keep one copy and your employer keeps the other. This form is not filed with the IRS.

The form includes a question-and-answer section on SEP IRAs. An employer setting up a SEP IRA plan is required to give you a disclosure statement that includes a description of the SEP, requirements concerning employer payments, information on deducting the employer's contribution, and questions and answers about the SEP.

The IRS says that if your employer "selects, recommends, or substantially influences" your choice of IRAs, you must be given a "clearly written explanation" of the terms of those IRAs. And, if they prohibit withdrawals, the Department of Labor may require that you be given still more information. The choice as to where to set up a SEP IRA must always be yours, no matter what your employer may want you to do.

Employer contributions to a SEP IRA for any given tax year may be made as late as three and a half months (by April 15) after the end of the calendar year. If you leave an employer who has a SEP or your employer terminates the plan, you may continue making your own contributions to the former SEP IRA or IRAs.

SEP IRAs AS KEOGH "SUBSTITUTES"

If you are self-employed you may use a SEP IRA instead of a Keogh plan if you wish, although under most circumstances there wouldn't be much point to doing so. You can contribute more to a Keogh plan and may be able to use 10-year averaging on a lump-sum distribution. But, you might consider doing this if you had been eligible to open a Keogh during the year but neglected to do so before the end-of-the-year deadline for opening Keogh plans.

Between the first of the following year and April 15, you'd still have time to open the SEP IRA instead. As a self-employed person with no employees, you're your own employer—and free to contribute up to the lesser of 15 percent of earned income or $30,000 to the SEP IRA of your choice.

401(k) PLANS GROWING—BUT TREASURY SEEKS CHANGES

Growing numbers of employees are covered by what is called a 401(k), an increasingly popular tax shelter written into the Internal Revenue Act of 1978. Some analysts believe that if these plans continue to be structured as they are now, the 410(k) plans could become the "super IRAs" of the future.

However, the elimination of this program was included in the Treasury Department's tax "simplification" proposals in late 1984. Then in 1985, the administration's Tax Reform Program recommended placing an $8,000 ceiling on annual 401(k) contributions, with IRA contributions counting against that ceiling.

At this writing, it remains to be seen what, if anything, Congress will do about these proposals. Some of the country's biggest corporations now have 401(k)s for their employees and presumably would oppose any move to kill the program. If Congress does eliminate the program, which is by no means certain, it's likely money already sheltered in them would be allowed to remain tax sheltered.

The 401(k) plans reduce your compensation from the top and, for tax purposes, treat the reduction as a company contribution to a qualified savings program.

In general, you can put up to 10 percent of your pretax annual compensation into the plan. You pay no taxes on that amount, and the earnings are also sheltered from federal taxes. And so, while your gross income is reduced, your tax bill is too. Some companies even match an employee's contribution.

For example, if your annual compensation is $40,000 and you elect to have your employer contribute $1,200 (3 percent) to the plan, your salary will be reported for your taxable income as $38,800. However, for social security tax purposes, your salary will be reported and taxed at the full $40,000. If you take all of your account balance some years later in a lump-sum distribution, the taxable amount will qualify for 10-year averaging.

This is a particularly good deal if you are earning above the maximum social security level. The "reduction" in your income under this plan will not affect your social security contributions or your eventual social security benefits. Your employer continues to calculate your pension, insurance, and health benefits on the basis of your full salary no matter what the supposed salary "reduction."

Finally, you are also allowed to contribute up to $2,000 to an IRA, assuming you can afford all those contributions.

Unlike IRAs, these plans allow early withdrawal without any tax penalty before age 59½ in case of "hardship," which is up to the employer to define. For a variety of reasons, however, not all employers want to offer the 401(k). There are some complicated rules regarding nondiscrimination in offering these plans to employees. All lower-paid employees must get a prescribed ratio of the benefits of higher-paid employees.

IF ALL YOU'VE EVER HAD IS AN IRA

Beginning in 1982, the basic thrust of the IRA program was changed. It's ironic, but if all you've ever had in the way of a retirement plan is an IRA, those changes and all the related developments that have come since 1982 have left you with little more than you had before.

IRAs were created for you in the first place. They were designed for people who didn't have pension or profit-sharing plans at work. For the most part, this meant people of modest means working for small businesses and mom-and-pop operations that couldn't afford pension plans. Being allowed to set up an IRA gave you your first opportunity to build your own retirement fund. Or, in some cases, instead of offering you a qualified retirement plan, your employer or union set up an IRA for employees instead.

Your only gain under the universal IRA law was the opportunity, starting in 1982, to make somewhat higher contributions. Meanwhile, everyone already covered by an employer plan at work can now make IRA contributions as big as yours— and self-employed people can contribute the full IRA limits even after contributing far more than that to a Keogh plan.

So, in a sense, the people for whom IRAs were created have been sent back to square one. Everyone else who works now enjoys the full benefits of an IRA too—but you enjoy little more than you had before.

Perhaps Congress will do something to correct this situation one day, but don't count on it. The biggest red tape problem with the original IRA law was defining people who were "active participants" in other plans and hence ineligible for IRAs. This created a red tape nightmare Congress is not likely to bring back.

If all you had in the way of retirement benefits before Congress approved the universal IRA was an IRA, the only way to protect yourself now is by contributing all you can afford to an IRA. It's still the greatest tax shelter and retirement tax break around for ordinary people. And, let your representatives in Congress know you're aware of what's happened. If you complain loudly enough, Congress may adopt a formula that allows you to shelter more of your income in an IRA.

Part Three

WHICH
IRAs ARE BEST
FOR YOU?

13

Setting up and
Maintaining an IRA

It's easy to put off opening (or contributing to) an IRA until a few weeks or even days before the deadline, but try not to wait until the last minute.

One reason is that at the last minute, sponsors are also pressed for time. If you visit the sponsor's office at the height of the "IRA season," you'll probably have a longer wait. In the last-minute crush, there's also more chance that an error may be made or that a misunderstanding about the nature or terms of the IRA may arise.

Another reason is that with only a short time in which to act, you could make a mistake. Particularly if you are opening a new IRA, you could rush to seek advice—perhaps from your neighbor, the stockbroker, your cousin the insurance broker, or the friendly banker you chat with on the commuter train—and get advice not really in your best interests.

Naturally, your neighbor, the customer's representative at a securities firm, would suggest buying shares in a front-end load mutual fund on which he or she would earn a commission—or perhaps opening a self-directed account for buying and selling stocks, which raises the happy prospect of many more commissions in the future.

Your cousin the insurance agent would advise buying an insurance annuity, which may cost you a substantial commission. And, the banker would sell you on the virtues of his institution's federally insured IRA plans.

These people would all give you the best advice as they saw it. But, if you had time to investigate mutual funds, you may have found a well-performing no-load fund where you wouldn't have to pay a big commission at the start. Or, if your heart was set on an insurance annuity, comparison shopping might have found a much better deal.

And, you can make a mistake by opening an IRA at just any bank, savings institution, or credit union. The time when all savings plans at these institutions were virtually the same is long gone. These institutions now offer a vast and bewildering array of IRAs. With time to research the market, you may find a significantly higher return or a plan much better suited to your needs.

Before setting up an IRA, try to give yourself time to weigh the options. These may include contributing to your employer's retirement plan if it's allowed or having IRA payroll deductions where you work. Visit, phone, or write local financial institutions, mutual funds, insurance companies, or other IRA sponsors and study their sales literature.

If you must set up an IRA at the last minute, don't tie up your money for a long time. Put it in a money market account, money market mutual fund, or short-term CD. Later, you can move it to some other investment without penalty after you've had time to do some research.

GIVEN A CHOICE, SET UP YOUR IRA CLOSE TO HOME

Whatever investment you select, you'll have to make a choice among sponsors offering that type of investment. All things being equal, if possible set up your IRA or IRAs with sponsors whose offices are convenient to where you live or work.

This should not be your overriding consideration, particularly if no sponsors with the type of investments best suited for you are located near your home or place of business. If you decide that a mutual fund or family of funds is best for you and there are no nearby offices, don't let that stop you. Investors have been dealing successfully with distantly located mutual funds, financial institutions, and other investment sponsors for years by mail, telephone, or wire transfer.

But, if you're fortunate enough to have the choice, there are two reasons why it would be advisable to select a nearby IRA sponsor. First, it's easy for you to go to the sponsor's office yourself to settle misunderstandings if they arise—or to roll the assets out of that IRA at some later date. Second, if you're one of those people who waits until the last minute to make your final IRA contribution (or to make your entire contribution for the tax year, as so many people do), it will be easier—and safer—to meet the April 15 deadline by carrying your contribution to the office yourself if necessary.

If it's the last minute and you're dealing with sponsors hundreds or thousands of miles away, there could be problems. The closer you get to April 15, the more the mails are clogged. And, while telephone and wire transfer instructions are usually reliable, mistakes can happen—especially if the volume of those instructions is unusually heavy.

When you carry a contribution to a sponsor's office, ask for a dated receipt, especially if it's near the deadline. The receipt will prove you made the contribution in the proper tax year even if someone in the sponsor's office makes an error posting your contribution.

SOME QUESTIONS TO ASK

Whatever the type of IRA investment, ask these questions:

What are the fees to get in? An IRA's great advantage is that you can compound the earnings tax deferred until you start withdrawing. To the extent that you must pay fees and commissions, you're losing compounded earning power.

IRA investments with high fees in the early years are especially inappropriate if you plan to retire soon, want the money for some other purpose, or run a high risk of job turnover. You may have to retire and start taking benefits before you've had time to make up those hefty early-year fees. Or, if you lose your job and exhaust your other financial resources, you may have to draw money from your IRA. The hefty sponsor fees would come on top of the 10 percent premature distribution penalty if you are under age 59½ and are not disabled.

How much must you contribute to get in and stay in? Are the minimum investments required higher than you can handle comfortably? Try to be realistic. Don't commit yourself to an IRA that requires contributions so large that you'd have trouble getting the money together. IRAs are a great investment, but don't punish yourself to open or maintain one.

What will it cost to get your money out, perhaps rolling it over into another IRA? Many IRAs charge minimal or no termination fees if you switch to a different IRA, but others may charge stiff fees. All things being equal, don't put your money in an IRA with a high termination fee if you can find a similar investment that doesn't charge one.

How long must you tie up your money? Does the contract require that you keep money in this IRA for a specified period? Does it penalize you for taking money out after you reach age 59½?

This won't be an overriding consideration for everyone. All federally insured banks and savings institutions are required to charge penalties for early withdrawals from CDs if you're below age 59½ and the investment has not matured, and they have the option of charging them after you reach age 59½. That shouldn't discourage you from making these investments if you believe they best suit your needs.

If you're investing for the long term in these institutions, there's no need to be concerned about tying up your money for any reasonable period. But, if you're nearing (or above) age 59½, learn if you can withdraw early without penalty after age 59½. All things being equal, select the institution that allows you to do so.

If you are considering tying up your money for a very long period, such as in a zero-coupon bond, be willing to live with the consequences of that decision. A lot can happen—including changes in your circumstances and in financial markets. Given the inventiveness of IRA marketers, it's also possible that new kinds of IRA investments that will appeal to you will be available in the future.

If it's a fixed-rate investment, how much will you have at the end of a given period of time? This is the key question for any fixed-rate investment. Compounding methods for fixed-rate investments can greatly affect your total return over a long period of time. Be sure you understand how the actual return after a fixed period for any one investment compares with others. For a discussion of this, see Chapter 15.

THE DISCLOSURE STATEMENT

When you set up an IRA, the plan's sponsor is supposed to give you a disclosure statement about your IRA. Read it carefully, especially the sections on fees so you understand what buying and maintaining the IRA will cost. But, be aware that after you have purchased the IRA, sponsors have the right to change fees later after notifying you of the change.

You must be given this statement seven days before the IRA is set up or purchased. As an alternative, the sponsor may give you the statement when you set up the IRA. You then have a seven-day cooling-off period in which to cancel.

With some IRAs, written or oral cancellation or both may be required. Oral notification may be by phone during regular business hours. If your notification is by mail, the regular postmark is used to determine the date. Certified or registered mail uses the date of certification or registration.

If you cancel, you're entitled to a full refund of everything you paid. There should be no charge for commissions, expenses, or changes in market value.

The disclosure statement should discuss the tax requirements, eligibility, and penalties regarding IRAs in general. It is also supposed to provide details about that particular IRA investment including:

- Growth projections of the program's value, if possible to do so.
- Whether and for what period growth projections are guaranteed—and, if not guaranteed, a statement of the earnings rate and terms on which the projection is based.
- Any sales commissions to be charged each year.

- If applicable, the part of each annual contribution used to buy life insurance, which is not deductible, for each year.

Sponsors making growth projections must give illustrations of dollar amounts available at retirement and at specified points during the life of the investment.

In practice, many IRA sponsors do not use the actual interest rate being paid when they make projections. Instead, the IRS allows them to use a sample rate, which can be no higher than the actual rate at the time.

When actual rates are in the 10 percent range, for instance, sponsors may give you a disclosure statement projecting growth at 8 percent. They reason that because they are paying a wide range of rates for different IRAs and these rates change constantly, it would be difficult to revise disclosure statements often enough to keep up with these changes.

Although it may be impractical for sponsors to revise disclosure statements each time rates change, this makes it difficult for people to see how their IRAs would grow. Disclosure statements may also make projections at just a few ages, rather than at your age now.

However, you can make your own estimates of IRA growth by using some of the materials in this book. There are year-by-year projections for growth at selected interest rates in Appendix A. In addition, you can make projections with the effective annual yield tables in Chapter 15.

ESTABLISH A RECORD–KEEPING SYSTEM

If you don't have one already, set up a record-keeping system for your IRA investments. The longer you maintain your IRA or IRAs, the more important this becomes, particularly if you establish a number of IRAs and move them around often. These records should be in addition to your file of IRA statements and other materials from sponsors.

There are at least three good reasons for starting and maintaining complete, easy-to-follow records for your IRAs. These are:

1. To keep track of what and where they are. Over time, unless you have a good record-keeping system, it may become more difficult than you think to keep track of your IRAs. Without a system, you could forget the dates of earlier contributions and overcontribute for one year. Your system should also enable you to see when fixed-term investments are due to expire, at which time they may be renewed automatically unless you direct otherwise.

Although the sponsor may send a renewal notice, usually it won't arrive until shortly before the renewal date. This may not give you the time you need to study your options, and it may not give you any time if you are out of town when it arrives. You should review your IRA records periodically to give yourself plenty of time to weigh alternatives when an investment matures.

2. To keep track of the performance of your IRAs—how much you have invested in each and how far you are ahead (or behind). Periodically, compare returns on your investments with those on comparable investments.

3. To assure that if something happens to you—death, an incapacitating accident, or illness—someone can look at the record and reconstruct the history of your IRAs. This would be especially important if the IRS later raised questions about some aspect of your IRA investments.

Any record-keeping system you feel comfortable with will do. If you don't want to set up your own system, you could use some of the standard investment record-keeping materials sold at stationery stores.

NAMING YOUR BENEFICIARIES

For every IRA you set up, you'll be asked to name a beneficiary or beneficiaries to inherit it if you die.

This decision may be made in the few moments spent looking at the question on the application form and then be forgotten. But it is worth more time and thought, especially since, over a period of time, an IRA could grow to a large sum.

And, as you near age 70½ and the time when the law requires that you stop making IRA contributions and begin withdrawing from it, there's another factor to be considered. It's that if you wish to start a program of regular withdrawals, the minimum that must be withdrawn each year will be determined by a multiple based on your age and the age of your "designated beneficiary." For an explanation of this, see Chapter 11.

Many people mistakenly believe they must name a wife, child, or other close relative as their beneficiary. But you may name anyone you wish—or may name a charity or an institution. You may also submit a list of beneficiaries in order of preference—or you may name your estate.

If you have more than one IRA, you are not required to name the same beneficiary or beneficiaries for all of them. For estate-planning purposes, if you have a large IRA you may wish to split it into two or more IRAs, each with its own beneficiary or beneficiaries.

If the sponsor's form contains only one line for naming a beneficiary, you're not bound by that limitation. You may write in as many beneficiaries as you wish or write them in an order of preference.

It's usually a good idea to have at least a second beneficiary designated to inherit the IRA if the first beneficiary dies. If you have only one living relative and name that person as your beneficiary, if that person dies before you and you don't name another beneficiary, most likely the state in which you live will wind up with your IRA's assets.

This could also happen if you have no will and your only living relative, perhaps your spouse, dies simultaneously with you in an accident or disaster, such as a plane crash. How ironic, if you built a large IRA during your working lifetime— but in the end your efforts went merely to enrich the treasury of the state in which you live simply because you failed to name an alternate beneficiary.

In addition to naming a beneficiary or beneficiaries, you may also specify the method of distribution. Some IRA sponsors request this information. For a discussion of options for beneficiaries, see Chapter 11.

KEEP YOUR BENEFICIARIES UP–TO–DATE

You may change your IRA beneficiaries as often as you wish. Just as you keep track of your IRA investments, remember to change beneficiaries in accordance with changes in your circumstances—and theirs. If a spouse or someone else you have named as a beneficiary dies or becomes incapable of handling his or her affairs, make the change right away— especially if you didn't name a second beneficiary and there's a risk the IRA would be claimed by the state if you die.

You can also change beneficiaries for any other reason. As time goes on, your views about family members or others you named as beneficiaries may change—even toward those you once believed would always be closest to you. For one reason or another, some people may decide they no longer want their children as beneficiaries. There could also be good reasons for not naming your spouse, such as the spouse becoming so incapacitated that he or she could no longer make responsible financial decisions.

As the IRA grows, it would be prudent to seek professional advice to assure that your IRA assets are disposed of as you wish after you die, perhaps correlated as part of a general estate plan. If it is a large IRA, you may be able to reduce the tax consequences by naming a number of beneficiaries rather than leaving everything to one or two.

HOW OLD SHALL YOU SAY YOU ARE?

Needless to say, we strongly urge that you give the sponsor your correct age when you set up an IRA.

But as many accountants, attorneys, and other financial and legal advisers have learned, some people consistently lie about their age, concealing their true age from friends, employers, and members of their family for years. Unfortunately, as these people approach the critical "income tax ages," they are inviting embarrassment and perhaps a delay in receiving social security benefits—and may even be violating income tax regulations.

For instance, you may be known to your family and friends to be 60. But, when your real age reaches 65, you'll want to collect social security benefits. At this point, proof of age will be required—and all will be revealed.

The vanity involved in these deceptions is such that some people delay claiming social security benefits for years for fear of exposing their correct age to their kin—particularly to a spouse who may believe them much younger.

These deceptions are practiced uniformly by men and by women. The practice has increased recently because so many people are entering into second or third marriages today and joining new families. Unlike relatives who knew you when you were a child and can't be fooled, members of these new families will accept any reasonable age you claim to be.

Especially, some people begin concealing their true age after they reach their 40s. It may be to make a more favorable impression on members of the opposite sex—or to deceive employers or business associates who might otherwise view them as "over the hill."

The universal IRA is both compounding problems for people seeking to conceal their true age and inducing other people to consider lying about their age for the first time.

The Form 1040 on which you file your federal tax return does not require that you give your age or date of birth. When you set up an IRA, ordinarily the trustee or custodian will not demand proof of age. All you'll be asked is to provide a birthdate.

Inevitably, some people are tempted to give a birthdate that will make them 59½ or older when actually they are not so they can withdraw money from the IRA later without paying the penalty tax. However, if they keep the assets in that IRA, they'll have to start withdrawing from it when the sponsor's records show they have reached age 70½, even though they may be much younger.

But, people who have been understating their age to their family for years and then open an IRA face other problems. If they understate their age to an IRA sponsor, they'll delay their ability to receive distributions from the IRA without paying the tax penalty. They also risk creating a situation where they would be violating IRS regulations if they don't start a withdrawal program by the year in which they reach the true age of 70½.

It's likely the universal IRA is inducing more people to misstate their age than ever. But because there are so many more opportunities for them to be found out, they are exposing themselves to consequences that may range from embarrassment to chagrin, anger, disappointment, and even social dislocation—not to mention the risk of stiff IRS penalties, disqualification of the entire IRA, and even criminal prosecution if the IRS believes the offense warrants it.

If you conceal your true age from an IRA sponsor, you may get away with it—for a while, at least. The IRS has little control over that situation unless a deception is called to their attention by an accidental disclosure. But, taxpayers who deliberately falsify their age to receive tax benefits are violating one or more IRS Code sections, some with very serious consequences.

THE IRS AND YOUR IRA

Now that IRAs can be opened by everyone who works, deductions for IRA contributions are becoming as commonplace as those for home mortgage interest.

There is little reason for the IRS to challenge your deductions if you contribute to qualified programs and do not over contribute. Normally, your IRA deduction should be automatic.

One area of IRS concentration involves reporting, including proper and adequate withdrawals from an IRA. As discussed in Chapter 6, the IRS is carrying this out through its taxpayer indentification number (TIN) and backup withholding system. Everyone opening an IRA is asked to supply a TIN, and tax will be withheld from your IRA when you take a distribution from it if you do not supply the number.

All IRA custodians are required to send the IRS information forms on every payment from an IRA. This allows cross-referencing to your tax return by IRS computers, just as the IRS cross-references payments to you of interest and dividends by financial institutions and by companies in which you own stock.

The IRS can also be expected to have a monitoring program for reporting correct ages when people receive a payout. If this area becomes a problem, efforts may be made to include a line for your year of birth or birthdate on the Form 1040.

The IRS reporting system is getting more efficient all the time. Although false reporting may go undetected for long periods, the chances of detection are increasing constantly— and ultimately detection may trigger serious consequences.

Our tax system is based on voluntary compliance. Every responsible tax preparer is pledged to support that system, and no responsible preparer will countenance tax cheating if he or she has knowledge of it. Preparers also face severe penalties if they conspire with a client to defraud the government. What many people fail to realize until too late is that when the IRS invokes special penalties, the dollar amounts involved in the offense may not be the main criteria. Rather, the IRS may be more concerned with the flagrancy of the offense and the obviousness of intent to defraud, whether the amount be large or small.

While many millions of items of information on IRAs will be reported to the IRS by IRA sponsors and taxpayers in future years, monitoring this voluminous body of information will become increasingly accurate and routine. New techniques and equipment will simplify the problem.

If you decide to rely on the massive nature of the IRS reporting system to conceal irregularities in your IRA, you are courting big trouble. Despite stories about false and inaccurate tax reporting, the use of social security numbers as tax identification numbers has made the system far more encompassing—and will lead to increased detection of false reporting in the future. If you can build a large sum in an IRA, you'd be foolish to risk losing much of it in taxes and penalties because you broke the rules.

KEEPING UP WITH CHANGES IN IRA RULES

If you're not already aware of this fact, probably the most important thing you will learn from this book is that there is nothing permanent about tax rules and regulations. Our tax system is in a constant state of change. As best you can, try to keep up with the changes to avoid making costly mistakes.

The basic statutes referred to as "the tax laws" are in the Internal Revenue Code. Only Congress can change a law. If there are no reasons for making changes, sections of the tax code may remain unchanged for years.

However, because of the broad coverage of the IRA program and the many financial institutions involved, at least some legislation affecting IRAs will come out of almost every Congress.

In part, these changes will be in response to desires for change from the general population as expressed through their representatives in Congress. Pressure for change will also come from banks, savings institutions, mutual funds, brokerage firms, and insurance companies seeking to expand their IRA authority or to correct what they perceive as cumbersome or unreasonable requirements. And, each president may seek changes in line with the administration's philosophy and goals.

Changes in the basic tax law are just the beginning. After Congress passes a law, the IRS studies it and issues regulations. These are clarifications of and elaborations on its application of the tax code.

Once regulations are issued, interested parties constantly make special requests of the IRS for interpretations of special sets of facts that may not be covered completely in the code or the regulations. These interpretations are called "rulings."

For the most part, the rulings are "private letter rulings" valid only for the parties who requested them. Private letter rulings are published in technical journals and generally read only by professionals with a special interest in tax matters.

But, occasionally the facts have a much broader application than just for the requesting parties and may impact many taxpayers—or, in the case of IRAs, custodians as well. The IRS may then write and release an Official Revenue Ruling, which is its interpretation of how it will view those circumstances for tax purposes. Although official revenue rulings are not absolutely incontestible, they are taken seriously by all professionals and are not challenged without good cause.

Change may also emanate from the courts. Many taxpayers take exception to IRS findings in a tax audit. If a taxpayer feels strongly enough about the issue and is willing to pay the cost, the case can be presented to one of several courts—and may even be heard by the Supreme Court.

These court decisions become precedents for tax professionals in applying the law in subsequent (and even prior) situations. Meanwhile, at its option, the IRS may announce either that it acquiesces in the decision or that it is nonacquiescing—which means it won't be guided by the court's findings in future cases. If this happens, you are on notice that you may have to go to court yourself if you wish to be supported on a similar series of facts.

Consequently, the so-called tax laws are really a complex combination of statutes, Treasury Department regulations, IRS private and general rulings, and court decisions. This results in a constant series of changes, some important and sweeping in nature and others of relatively minor concern to the general public.

If it's a major change affecting most or all IRA owners or potential owners, it will be reported in the news media and money management magazines. Many CPA firms mail newsletters to clients discussing changes of this nature. If the changes benefit banks, savings institutions, securities firms, insurance companies, or other IRA sponsors by liberalizing their services, they will advertise that fact in their promotional campaigns.

Some changes are very technical and will require that your IRA custodian amend your plan. In this case, you'll be sent the amendment for safekeeping with your copy of the plan. You may also be asked to sign a new document if the change requires that you make some kind of decision.

Regular readers of *The Wall Street Journal*, *Barron's*, *Business Week*, and other business periodicals may find references to less far-reaching changes. Otherwise, you could be unaware of many of them. However, while these changes may be of "less significance" to most people, it's always possible one or more will apply to your special circumstances or to some move you are thinking of making.

If you see a tax preparer each year, ask if any changes during the past year apply to you. Get a new IRS *Publication 590* each year to compare how it differs from previous years. For a discussion of *Publication 590*, see the following chapter.

14

Advice
and Information:
Who Needs It—
And Where to Get It

When you walk into a bank, savings institution, credit union, brokerage house office, or insurance agency seeking advice on financial matters, you may assume that the people you're talking to are IRA experts. Many are very knowledgeable and do a good job of answering basic IRA questions. But, if asked questions that go beyond the basics, they may supply you with misinformation. They're not trying to deceive you. It's just that these people don't know everything about IRAs, and they shouldn't be expected to.

Most IRA sponsors have training programs for people who sell IRA investments. Some of these programs are very thorough. Nevertheless, IRA rules and regulations are so complex that even professional tax experts frankly admit they don't know all the answers.

Most people rely on IRA marketers for information on what they can or cannot do. But, however comprehensive their training program, few employees of IRA marketers can be expected to have more than a peripheral education on the tax ramifications stemming from IRAs. It would be unreasonable to expect insurance agents, investment counselors at banks and savings institutions, and customer's representatives at brokerage houses to know all the ins and outs of IRA rules when even the tax professionals don't know them—especially since most of these people have many other responsibilities in addition to providing information about IRAs.

By all means, ask questions. Many of these people have excellent backup research materials in their office. Some can get answers on difficult questions over the phone from IRA experts on special hot lines. And, the best of these people will frankly admit when they are over their heads on some questions and will suggest that you seek professional advice.

But, however sound their sources of information and no matter how hard they try to help, in the last analysis you must seek answers to the most difficult questions on your own. Especially, don't rely entirely on IRA sponsors for advice if a very large sum is involved. Even the IRS won't guarantee that its advice is correct. If that's so, it would be foolish to rely on advice from IRA sponsors if the penalties for making a technical mistake are severe.

By the same token, don't accept all the information you see in IRA promotional materials and advertisements as gospel. Although these materials are usually checked by tax experts, these people can make mistakes, too.

More common, promotional materials may be rendered obsolete by changes in IRA rules or in the law. The longer materials remain in your files, the more likely that at least some of them are out of date.

NEED FOR PROFESSIONAL ADVICE INCREASES WITH TIME

Almost anyone should be able to open an IRA without seeking professional advice, particularly if only a small sum is involved. Even so, if you have a tax adviser, by all means discuss your IRA with him or her. Ask questions on what you don't understand and get the benefit of the adviser's thinking on investments (but don't feel obliged to follow it!).

If you're truly confused about how IRAs work or by your IRA investment options, seek independent professional advice right at the start. By "independent professional advice" we mean the kind you pay for, not that offered by someone with a vested interest in selling you something. People who want to sell you something are professionals too—and many give excellent advice. But, your own best interests demand that you put the greatest reliance on advice from someone with nothing to gain if you take it.

As time goes on, the need for professional advice increases. The larger the sum involved or the greater the proportion of your total assets the IRA represents, the better it would be to obtain expert opinion before proceeding with any important move or change involving your IRA or any part of it.

Also, seek professional advice the closer you get to retirement. If you make a serious mistake in handling an IRA early in your working life and some or all of your IRA is disqualified (or you make a bad investment), you still have time to build other IRAs. But, if you make one with only a few years to go—or are already retired—you won't have time to start over again.

Certainly anyone about to receive a large lump-sum distribution from an employer plan or contemplating any IRA move in which a large sum is involved should get advice from an independent professional *before doing anything*. Similarly, widows or other beneficiaries who have the option of receiving a large distribution from an employer plan or an IRA or taking annuity-type payments instead should seek advice before making a decision.

The experience of independent tax professionals is that most serious mistakes in handling IRAs are made when people act first—and seek advice afterwards. In all too many cases, by then the damage has been done.

FREE INFORMATION FROM THE IRS

Before paying for advice, obtain what free advice is available. This will also make any sessions with an independent professional adviser more productive. The more you already know, the less time your adviser will have to spend explaining IRAs to you—and the smaller your bill for the adviser's services will be.

One free IRS publication everyone with an IRA should have is IRS *Publication 590: Tax Information on Individual Retirement Arrangements.* It is updated every year.

This publication covers IRS rules and regulations pertaining to IRAs in detail. While not as authoritative as the actual IRA regulations, it answers most questions anyone would want to ask. As with many government documents, in trying to cover everything it sometimes fails to adequately distinguish between what is most important and what really doesn't matter much.

Nevertheless, it is comprehensive and covers all major aspects of current IRA rules and regulations. You should obtain a new copy each year and compare it with the old one to see what major changes have been made.

Other free IRS publications that relate to IRAs in one way or another include:

* *No. 448—Estate and Gift Tax*
* *No. 506—Income Averaging*
* *No. 560—Tax Information on Self-Employed Retirement Plans.* Discusses retirement plans for self-employed persons and certain partners in partnerships who are eligible for Keogh plans.
* *No. 575—Pension and Annuity Income.* Explains how to report pension and annuity income on your federal tax return as well as special tax treatment for lump-sum distributions from pensions, stock bonus, or profit-sharing plans.

The most recent editions of these publications can be obtained by visiting any IRS field office or writing the IRS Documents Distribution Center for your state. If there is more than one center for your state, send your order to the one nearest you. The addresses of these field offices are:

Alabama—Caller No. 848, Atlanta, GA 30370
Alaska—P.O. Box 12626, Fresno, CA 93778
Arizona—P.O. Box 12626, Fresno, CA 93778

Arkansas—P.O. Box 2924, Austin, TX 78769
California—P.O. Box 12626, Fresno, CA 93770

Colorado—P.O. Box 2924, Austin, TX 78769
Connecticut—P.O. Box 1040, Methuen, MA 01844

Delaware—P.O. Box 25886, Richmond, VA 23260

District of Columbia—P.O. Box 25886, Richmond, VA 23260

Florida—Caller No. 848, Atlanta, GA 30370

Georgia—Caller No. 848, Atlanta, GA 30370

Hawaii—P.O. Box 12626, Fresno, CA 93778

Illinois—P.O. Box 338, Kansas City, MO 64141

Indiana—P.O. Box 6900, Florence, KY 41042

Iowa—P.O. Box 338, Kansas City, MO 64141

Kansas—P.O. Box 2924, Austin, TX 78769

Kentucky—P.O. Box 6900, Florence, KY 41042

Louisiana—P.O. Box 2924, Austin, TX 78769

Maine—P.O. Box 1040, Methuen, MA 01844

Maryland—P.O. Box 25866, Richmond, VA 23260

Massachusetts—P.O. Box 1040, Methuen, MA 01844

Michigan—P.O. Box 6900, Florence, KY 41042

Minnesota—P.O. Box 338, Kansas City, MO 64141

Mississippi—Caller No. 848, Atlanta, GA 30370

Missouri—P.O. Box 338, Kansas City, MO 64141

Montana—P.O. Box 12626, Fresno, CA 93778

Nebraska—P.O. Box 338, Kansas City, MO 64141

Nevada—P.O. Box 12626, Fresno, CA 93778

New Hampshire—P.O. Box 1040, Methuen, MA 01844

New Jersey—P.O. Box 25866, Richmond, VA 23260

New Mexico—P.O. Box 2924, Austin, TX 78769

New York—
Western New York: P.O. Box 260, Buffalo, NY 14201
Eastern New York (including New York City): P.O. Box 1040, Methuen, MA 01844

North Carolina— Caller No. 848, Atlanta, GA 30370

North Dakota—P.O. Box 338, Kansas City, MO 64141

Ohio—P.O. Box 6900, Florence, KY 41042

Oklahoma—P.O. Box 2924, Austin, TX 78769

Oregon—P.O. Box 12626, Fresno, CA 93778

Pennsylvania—P.O. Box 25866, Richmond, VA 23260

Rhode Island—P.O. Box 1040, Methuen, MA 01844

South Carolina— Caller No. 848, Atlanta, GA 30370

South Dakota—P.O. Box 338, Kansas City, MO 64141

Tennessee—Caller No. 848, Atlanta, GA 30370

Texas—P.O. Box 2924, Austin, TX 78769

Utah—P.O. Box 12626, Fresno, CA 93778

Vermont—P.O. Box 1040, Methuen, MA 01844

Virginia—P.O. Box 25866, Richmond, VA 23260

Washington—P.O. Box 12626, Fresno, CA 93778

West Virginia—P.O. Box 6900, Florence, KY 41042

Wisconsin—P.O. Box 338, Kansas City, MO 64141

Wyoming—P.O. Box, Austin, TX 78769

Foreign Addresses—Taxpayers with mailing addresses in foreign countries should send their requests for forms and publications to: IRS Distribution Center, P.O. Box 25866, Richmond, VA 23260

Puerto Rico—Director's Representative, U.S. Internal Revenue Service, Federal Office Building, Chardon Street, Hato Rey, PR 00918

Virgin Islands—Department of Finance, Tax Division, Charlotte Amalie, St. Thomas, VI 00801

You can also get free advice from IRS personnel. However, these people have heavy workloads, particularly in the months and weeks just before April 15. It's often difficult or impossible to get through on the phone, and people in the office may not be able to devote much time to you.

While IRS information is free, it is *not* guaranteed. If someone working for the IRS gives you information that turns out to be incorrect, the IRS is not responsible if you act on that information and make a costly mistake. Consequently, if a lot of money is involved, you're still better advised to pay for an independent professional opinion.

FREE ADVICE FROM IRA SPONSORS

Most IRA sponsors will be glad to send you free literature on their plans. Obviously, advice from an IRA sponsor must be weighed with the understanding that the sponsor wants you to buy its product. The sponsor's literature will describe the benefits of that product and ignore or play down those of competing products.

However, much general and technical material in sponsor literature can be helpful, and some may go into great detail on some topics. Some sponsors have taken considerable time and expense to do a thorough job of explaining how IRAs work. Sponsor material may also give valuable information on the past performance of that particular IRA investment, which you can then compare with the performance of other IRA investments.

Although this technical material may have been researched with great care, don't rely on it as the final word if you're considering an important move with your IRA or if a large sum is involved. IRA sponsors can make mistakes too—and it's always possible that some material is out of date.

INFORMATION FROM TRADE ASSOCIATIONS

You may also get free information on IRAs from trade associations whose members are IRA sponsors. The leading ones are:

1. The American Bankers Association, 1120 Connecticut Avenue N.W., Washington, D.C. 20036. Information about IRAs offered by commercial banks.

2. Credit Union National Association, *Everybody's Money*, P.O. Box 431, Madison, Wis., 53701. Information about IRAs offered by credit unions; free with self-addressed, stamped envelope.

3. Investment Company Institute, 1600 M Street N.W., Washington, D.C., 20036. The institute provides information on all types of mutual funds. It has a free booklet, free membership list, and other free brochures. In addition to including the names, addresses, and toll-free phone numbers of members, the list categorizes them by type of funds. These include aggressive growth funds, balanced funds, bond funds, growth funds, growth and income funds, income funds, money market funds, and options funds.

If you're interested in a particular type of mutual fund, the institute will provide specialized lists, such as those that invest only in small companies or in such specialized areas as gold, energy, and technology.

4. No-Load Mutual Fund Association, 11 Penn Plaza, New York, N.Y., 10001. For $2 the association will send you its latest directory of more than 300 no-load funds. The funds are grouped by investment objective. The booklet gives investment requirements, services, addresses, and toll-free telephone numbers for the funds.

5. U.S. League of Savings Institutions, 111 E. Wacker, Chicago, Ill., 60601.

ADVICE FROM THE NEWS MEDIA

Obviously, IRA advice in newspapers and magazines and on television and radio news and information programs is more objective than that from IRA sponsors and trade associations. But, in technical respects, it may be less reliable. This is particularly true if the story or article must compress a lot of information into a short time period or space, requiring that important details or qualifications be omitted.

Materials from most IRA sponsors and all major trade associations have been checked by attorneys and other professionals who work closely with IRS rules and regulations. But, articles and commentaries in the news media usually reflect the research of the writers, many of whom must work under tight deadlines and rely on outside sources of information.

The most reliable information is from writers, commentators, and publications specializing in business, finance, or money management. Publications such as *Money, Changing Times, U.S. News and World Report, Business Week,* and *The Wall Street Journal* have knowledgeable staff writers and researchers preparing this material. On the whole, material in magazines is probably a little more reliable than that in newspapers simply because magazines may have more time in which to check facts. The least reliable stories are those in daily newspapers or on television or radio reporting a major new development the moment it has been announced, before there has been time to double-check the details and analyze the announcement's implications.

As a rule IRA advice on television and radio is most reliable when given by network business news or money management specialists or by experienced business reporters with local stations. The least reliable information is from general news reporters for local stations, who often must present very complex material they haven't had time to learn much about.

While news stories, articles, and commentaries can broaden your understanding of IRAs and keep you abreast of major changes in the law, they're no substitute for professional advice related to your unique circumstances.

Also, some articles, stories, and commentaries about IRA investments are colored by what might be called the "what's new" syndrome. The people who prepare this material are constantly seeking something new to write about, or at least new approaches to old topics. Sometimes they get so carried away with looking for new material that they lose perspective.

WHEN YOU MAY NEED INDEPENDENT PROFESSIONAL ADVICE

When your IRA or IRAs begin representing a substantial portion of your assets or when you're nearing retirement, it might

pay to have an independent professional adviser review your
IRA program every few years. The situation can be likened
to a checkup with your physician or dentist. Often, a professional can anticipate a problem before it comes to a head—
and, in the long run, save you money and grief.

Beyond this, consider seeking independent professional
advice about your IRA or IRAs under any of these circumstances:

• You're not sure if you qualify for an IRA or for a
  spousal IRA.
• You're uncertain about how to start an IRA or what
  IRA investment is best for you at this point.
• You can't decide whether you'll be better off making
  deductible contributions to your company retirement
  or profit-sharing plan or setting up your own IRA.
• You're uncertain as to what long-term investment
  goals are most appropriate for your temperament or
  circumstances.
• You're trying to relate your IRA to a total financial
  planning and retirement program.
• You're considering a rollover or transfer of a large
  sum.
• You're about to begin a program of withdrawals
  from an IRA or IRAs. (Will they be qualified withdrawals? Are they financially sound? Is the timing
  right? Most people should seek advice at this crucial
  period.)
• You're planning a will or trust agreements involving
  an IRA.
• Your logical heir has a physical or mental disability,
  and you want to be sure the funds are managed pru-
  dently when you die.
• You're getting married or divorced.
• Your economic circumstances have changed significantly—for better or for worse.
• The IRA plan you are in is amended in a way you
  don't understand.
• Congress makes changes in the IRA law.
• You are uncertain of the consequences of any action
  you are thinking of taking with an IRA.

WHO PROVIDES INDEPENDENT PROFESSIONAL ADVICE?

Independent professional advice on IRAs is provided by certified public accountants (CPAs), lawyers, and financial advisers and planners.

Certified public accountants may be consulted for all tax-related questions, financial and investment decisions, possible state and inheritance tax consequences, anything related to such other plans as qualified employer plans, and rollover possibilities, mechanics, and options. CPAs also have the most experience in tax return preparation and can relate best to the tax return treatment of investment transactions, including IRA transactions.

Many noncertified accountants are also well qualified. When selecting any accountants, inquire if they belong to national accounting groups, are licensed to practice in your state, and are enrolled agents. The latter means they may represent taxpayers in dealing with the IRS—if your return is selected for an audit, for example—and that they have demonstrated by examination that they qualify to practice in the tax area.

Some lawyers can do most of the things CPAs do and sometimes more, but try to select one who deals regularly in tax matters. Many lawyers who have other areas of specialization do not get involved in matters closely related to IRAs and taxes.

However, you need a knowledgeable lawyer for preparing wills, trusts, prenuptial agreements, and other documents in which IRAs might figure. No other professionals are qualified to handle those things. A lawyer should also be consulted if you have questions about your IRA beneficiaries or beneficiary statement.

State or local CPA or bar associations will furnish you with several names from which to select if you do not have a lawyer or CPA. However, don't select any of these people if you don't feel comfortable with them. As with other kinds of services, a referral from a satisfied client may be your best source for finding a lawyer, CPA, or financial adviser. If you don't know any, your friends, relatives, neighbors, or a co-worker may be able to help.

Many financial planners are thoroughly trained and are registered, but anyone can call himself or herself anything.

Financial planners are known by any of a number of names. These include investment analysts, estate planners, investment or financial consultants, securities analysts, tax-shelter consultants, investment representatives, and various combinations of these. The best are qualified to do many of the things lawyers and CPAs can do, but most will recommend that you consult a lawyer or CPA for matters not specifically covered by their areas of expertise.

Before consulting any independent professional adviser, don't hesitate to check credentials and get some references. Ask the advisers about their membership in professional organizations, their practice, and their areas of expertise. Any honest, competent professional will be glad to explain exactly what he or she does or does not do.

Be wary of any professional who claims he or she can do anything and everything. Also, the more money involved, the less you should rely on one person for all of your advice.

GETTING THE MOST FOR YOUR MONEY

When you seek professional advice about an IRA (or anything else), you'll save money if you phone and make an appointment rather than dropping in unannounced. When you call, tell the adviser how you got his or her name, what you'll want to discuss, and what type of questions you'll have. In most cases, the adviser should be able to tell you how long you'll need to meet and should be able to estimate the fee fairly closely.

When you go to the meeting, have your questions written out in advance so you'll be sure to touch on everything that concerns you. Be on time. Don't make small talk about irrelevant matters because the clock will be running. It will cost you as much to discuss the weather as it will to ask the most complicated technical questions.

In general, fees charged by attorneys are highest. They range from a low of $50 to $60 an hour up to $125 or more, with the biggest fees charged in large metropolitan areas. Fees charged by CPAs are slightly less than those for lawyers, while fees charged by noncertified accountants are generally less then those charged by CPAs by 10 to 50 percent.

Financial planners may charge in a variety of ways, including hourly, a fixed fee, or a percentage of the value of the portfolio they manage. Some who call themselves "planners" are paid for selling a product to you. You should be wary of advice from those people.

Many independent financial planners cannot deal economically with you unless a fairly large sum is involved. The fee they would have to charge to give advice on how to handle a small sum would simply not be worth it to you. Usually, you should approach one with the idea of not just discussing your IRA but of relating your IRA to all of your other assets.

ADVICE THAT ALWAYS NEEDS A SECOND OPINION

Wherever you go for information, here is some advice that should automatically cause you to seek at least a second informed opinion—particularly if the advice is from someone you don't know very well:

- I'll be your executor or trustee under your will or trusts.
- Long term, the (stock market) (bond market) (any other market) will be your best deal.
- With an (annuity) (insured savings certificate) (anything else) you'll never have to worry.
- Go to any (bank) (savings and loan association) (credit union) because they're all the same.
- Put your money here and forget it until you're ready to retire.
- Sign here and we'll take care of everything.
- You *must* act now to take advantage of this opportunity.
- Tell us where your IRA money is now, and we'll show you how you can get a much higher return.
- This is a little-known investment for IRAs and pays a lot higher than savings accounts, money market funds, annuities, and other things most people put their IRA money into.
- Forget everything you've heard until now about where to put your IRA money.

Does some of this advice sound familiar? Of course it does. Many of these same words and phrases were inducing people to make questionable investment decisions long before IRAs were invented.

15

Weighing Your IRA Investment Options

Congress opened the IRA program to everyone who works at a time of great change in savings and investment markets. Most important:

1. Savings rates at banks and savings institutions were in the process of being deregulated—a process that is now virtually complete. These institutions now have an almost free hand in creating savings plans. This allows them to offer types of IRAs that were not possible before.

2. Distinctions between types of traditional financial institutions are being blurred by consolidations, the creation of new financial conglomerates, and the breakdown of many historical barriers between institutions. To cite a conspicuous example, mutual funds and brokerage houses now compete directly with banks and thrift institutions for household savings through money market mutual funds, which did not even exist until the 1970s.

Since the early 1930s, financial institutions in the United States had been structured along fairly rigid lines. Banks met a community's commercial lending needs, savings institutions (savings and loan associations and mutual savings banks) supplied money for housing, insurance companies stuck to selling insurance, and brokerage houses and mutual funds dealt in more risky investments. But in the 1970s, computerization and the new electronics technology brought about an increased blending of these functions—a process speeded by mergers of different types of firms.

The trend is toward new and ever-larger "baskets" of financial services at the same office. The companies and financial conglomerates offering these baskets of services see IRAs as a way to attract many new customers—and hope that in time these IRA customers will begin buying many of the other services they offer too.

The other side of the deregulation coin is that the more people get paid for their savings, the more borrowers must pay for loans to buy homes, cars, farm equipment, or whatever. It's at least conceivable that one day this could contribute to political pressure to reimpose some controls and lower the rates paid to savers, just as the low ceilings on many savings accounts in the 1970s resulted in pressure to begin removing savings rate controls.

Meanwhile, IRA sponsors—primarily banks, savings institutions, mutual funds, securities firms, and life insurance companies—are competing vigorously for your IRA dollars with good reason. The inflation of the 1970s and early 1980s induced people to start shifting their savings out of long-term investments into shorter-term investments or investments where money is available on demand. Although the inflation rate has eased since then, many savers and investors remain "gun-shy" about tying up money for long periods.

Sponsors see IRAs as a fast-growing source of more stable capital, and the battle for IRA dollars can be expected to intensify in the years ahead.

YOUR CHOICES ARE NOW MORE COMPLICATED

Because of these developments, IRA investors have a far wider choice of investments than ever. In addition, the intensified competition tends to keep returns to IRA investors high.

On the other hand, even to make the simplest kind of IRA investment today—namely, a federally insured account or certificate at a bank or savings institution—you face some complex investment choices.

In the past, these choices were made mostly by wealthier investors—or by the managers of financial institutions where people invest or deposit their money. These institutions are called financial "intermediaries," meaning they are the middlemen between people with relatively small sums to invest and the larger markets where this money would be invested.

But now you must make your own decisions about such things as whether interest rates will rise or fall—which, in turn, depends on such things as the state of the economy, the government's fiscal and monetary policies, and the state of mind (always nervous and unpredictable) of professional money managers and investors. In effect, even at banks, savings institutions, and credit unions you now have the option of reducing interest rate risk by selecting variable-rate or market-rate, payable-on-demand savings instruments. However, in reducing interest rate risk in this fashion, you also give up the chance of "locking in" a higher rate if interest rates fall.

UNDERSTANDING "INTEREST RATE RISK"

The risk in buying a stock is obvious. If the price of the stock goes down and you have to sell, you'd suffer a loss.

Many investments carry another kind of risk—interest rate risk. If you don't know much about financial markets, this risk may not be apparent to you. But, it's very real and could cost you plenty if interest rates go against you. (The other side of that coin is that if interest rates move in a direction favorable to you, you could sell your investment before it matures for more than you paid for it.)

For instance, all government notes and bonds are "safe" in that when they mature, the government will redeem them at face value—and, if you want your money out before they mature, you may sell them in the open market. One great advantage of U.S. government securities is that there is always an active market for them, and you can always find a buyer at some price reasonably near the current "market."

However, the longer the bond's date to maturity, the greater the risk that, if you had to sell during a period when interest rates were higher than when you originally purchased the bond, you'd have to lose some of your principal. And, if interest rates have risen sharply, the loss could be substantial.

If you buy a long-term, $1,000 bond that pays 8 percent interest when it is issued and if market rates for comparable bonds then soar to 12 percent, to sell the bond you'd have to accept a price that would yield the buyer around 12 percent, not 8 percent. That would lower the price by about one third, to about $667. (Of course, if you bought a bond at 12 percent and rates then dropped to 8 percent, you could sell it for about $1,500—a substantial gain.)

The point is that even U.S. government bonds, about the safest investment you can make, are not risk free. On the contrary, extreme swings in interest rates can result in drastic changes in their market value—what someone would pay for them today, not the price when they mature. This risk applies to all interest rate related investments.

Allied to this, if you tie up your money for a long period at a low rate and interest rates then rise substantially, even if you wait until the investment matures and get all of your money back, you would have lost the opportunity to reinvest the money at a higher rate during the interim.

One way to look at interest rate risk is as the market equivalent of the penalty you ordinarily pay if you withdraw from a fixed-term CD at a bank or savings institution before it matures. The main difference is that the CD penalty is a "one-way street" on which you always lose, whereas with market instruments you could sell your investment for more than you paid for it if interest rates fall. However, your potential capital loss from interest rate risk is usually much greater than could be suffered through an early withdrawal penalty.

IRA investments that carry interest rate risk include any investments where your return is quoted in terms of interest rate yield. These include government and corporate bonds and notes, zero-coupon securities, preferred stock, "Ginnie Maes" (securities of the Government National Mortgage Association), and mutual funds that invest in any of these. Even though usually not negotiable to the extent that you would be locked into below-market rates if interest rates rise and you could only get out by paying a penalty, they also include bank and savings institution CDs.

Virtually all high-yielding common stocks, such as those issued by utilities, also have interest rate risk. When rates are falling, generally their prices rise; when rates are rising, generally their prices fall.

FACTORS TO WEIGH IN SELECTING IRAs

Most people planning an IRA program should probably play it safe, particularly if they intend to use IRAs to help finance their retirement. Unless you're assured of substantial retirement income from other sources, it would be prudent not to take chances.

When your IRA gets big enough you can always consider diversifying by putting some money into investments that promise more gain although carrying more risk. But, for the first few years anyhow, it might be better to err on the side of being too safe rather than making investments that could result in you losing some capital.

If your IRAs will be one of your most important sources of retirement income, you'll want to continue being conservative in selecting IRA investments. On the other hand, if you're assured of a comfortable retirement income from other sources, you can afford to take more risks. In fact, if you have a generous company plan and substantial personal investments, it would be appropriate to use your IRAs for highly speculative ventures (assuming you have the temperament for them).

On a safety scale, the safest IRA investments are U.S. government securities, followed by federally insured accounts and certificates at banks, savings institutions, and credit unions. Money market mutual funds and the types of securities in which they invest have relatively little market risk but are not insured. Mutual funds that invest partially or entirely in common stocks promise higher gains than investments that assure the return of your principal, but they also carry the risk of the loss of principal. At the top of the risk scale are self-directed plans where you make all of your own decisions in buying and selling stock but lack the downside protection afforded by the diversified portfolios you can get through stock mutual funds. Many oil and gas, real estate, and other limited partnerships also carry a high degree of risk.

GENERAL INVESTMENT STRATEGIES

There is no magic formula for assuring the maximum investment success with an IRA. As with any other investment, investors must match investments to their preferences and capabilities.

The basic IRA investment choices are to invest for income or to invest for growth. There is no general consensus among financial advisers as to which is the best strategy. Even if there were, there is no guarantee that it would be the right strategy.

The argument in favor of investing for income—in savings certificates, money market funds, bonds, annuities, utility stocks, and other high-dividend-paying stocks—is that you are making the most efficient use of IRAs because all interest and dividends are compounded tax free until withdrawn.

Some analysts don't like using IRAs to buy stocks for long-term appreciation because when stocks are in an IRA they do not enjoy the favorable long-term capital gains treatment. No matter how long the period over which the gains are established, you must pay tax at the ordinary income rate when you begin withdrawing from your IRA. These experts argue that when you make stock market investments it should be with non-IRA money, so you can take full advantage of capital gains provisions.

The basic argument favoring investment for growth is that income investments don't give you enough protection against inflation in the future—and that the only way to enjoy this protection is by going into mutual funds that invest in stocks or buying stocks yourself through a self-directed plan. In addition, because you are not concerned with capital gains and losses in an IRA, you may have much more latitude in buying and selling decisions in a self-directed common stock plan than buying and selling stocks otherwise.

Whatever strategy you select—and there's no reason why you can't diversify by using both strategies to some degree—building a substantial IRA fund will probably depend more on following some of the elementary IRA-handling suggestions in this book rather than tying all of your fortunes to any specific investment strategy. In particular, so long as you invest regularly, invest early each year, and continue bettering the consumer price index, you should be on the way toward carrying out a successful IRA program.

GUIDELINES FOR IRA INVESTORS

IRA investors range from people with little or no experience or understanding of financial markets to top-level executives served by high-paid professional advisers who use the most sophisticated investment techniques. But, whatever your investment know-how, here are some IRA investment guidelines that will never get you in trouble:

Don't Invest In Anything You Don't Fully Understand. This Applies to the Simplest IRA Investments as Well as the Most Complicated.

Do you really understand what a floating-rate savings certificate is? Or, how the index it is tied to works? Do you know what a mutual fund is, or how it works? Do you understand the terms of an insurance annuity being suggested to you as an IRA investment—and the basis on which its return to you will be established?

If you don't know the answers to these or other questions about your IRAs, it's not difficult to get most of them. Usually you'll find the answers in literature prepared by IRA sponsors or in their disclosure statements. Read the literature and ask questions. Don't put yourself in the position of being vulnerable to an unpleasant surprise simply because you failed to understand how a particular investment works—or what the fees or penalties would be if you decided to get out of that investment before the end of an agreed-upon period.

Understanding how an investment works also means understanding what the IRA sponsor will do with your money— that is, how the sponsor plans to invest the money so as to be able to pay you and make a profit besides. And, of course, it also involves understanding the risks in that investment.

No matter what an IRA sponsor tells you, every investment carries risk of one kind or another. The risk of investing directly in stocks or mutual funds that invest in stocks is that stock prices can go down—possibly very far down—as well as up. The risk of investments with a fixed rate of return—

particularly, those that require you to tie up money for a long period—is that a rise in interest rates could lower their market value, and serious inflation could erode their real buying power. The risk in money market mutual funds, money market savings accounts, and other short-term instruments is that yields can drop quickly and sharply, greatly reducing your investment return almost overnight.

Don't Invest in Anything You Don't Feel Comfortable With.

Understanding an investment and feeling comfortable with it are two different things. You may fully understand the risk involved in a stock mutual fund or self-directed stock fund— and you may also have so much retirement income assured from other sources that, in your financial circumstances, you could easily afford those risks. But, if you couldn't sleep nights because you worry about the price of your stocks (or the stocks in your mutual fund) going down a few points, avoid these investments.

For one thing, it isn't worth the aggravation. IRAs are supposed to help ease your money worries, not add to them. If you build a large IRA (or roll a large sum into an IRA from an employer pension plan) and the money is in stocks or a stock mutual fund, relatively small fluctuations in market prices could vary the value of your IRA by thousands of dollars a day. This is in the nature of the investment and is no cause for alarm. But, if paper losses would overly concern or depress you—and a steep and prolonged market break could result in substantial paper losses—seek IRA investments that assure the value of your principal.

Another reason for avoiding these investments if you do not have the temperament for them is that when you begin making decisions on the basis of fear, more often than not these will be bad investment decisions.

As a Rule (but not Always!) the Higher the Return on an Investment, the Greater the Risk.

There are some glaring exceptions to this. Most notable, low-yielding passbook savings accounts are no safer than other savings instruments at banks and savings institutions. But, on the whole, any time you are promised greater-than-usual profits or earnings it is at the cost of some additional degree of risk. If higher returns are available in IRAs that invest in second mortgages, for instance, that's because there is more risk in buying second mortgages then in many other IRA investments.

The Younger You Are, the More Time You Have to Correct Mistakes.

If you make an investment mistake or two, there's time to rectify it. Also, you have long-term trends in investments like the stock market working for you. If you're investing in the stock market (or a mutual fund that invests in common stocks) for only a few years, you may have to liquidate your investment during a down cycle in the market. Over a long term, however, the odds are weighted more and more in your favor.

On the other hand, the younger you are, the longer you have the power of tax-sheltered compounding working for you. In light of the tremendous growth than can be achieved over the years in even the safest IRA investments, the risks young people assume when they put IRA money in investments where they may suffer a loss may be greater than appears at first glance.

The Closer You Get to Retirement, the More Cautious You Should Be.

As you near retirement, investment mistakes could have more serious consequences. In general, money in riskier investments should be moved to safer ones. But, even when you retire, it could also be a mistake to overdo the emphasis on safety. With longer life expectancy and many people opting for early retirement, you may have another 20 or 25 years during which your IRA investments would be working for you. If you understand and feel comfortable with investments in stocks or stock mutual funds, it would be a mistake to pull out of these investments entirely just because of your age. Keep some IRA money in them as a hedge against inflation.

In General, Be Wary of Investment Concepts that Haven't Had Time to Establish a Track Record.

The expansion of the IRA program is inspiring new investment ideas that sound great at first but may have hidden risks or disadvantages that become more obvious as time goes on. It takes a while for investments to demonstrate how they would perform through varying business cycles. Don't allow anyone to make investment experiments with your IRA dollars.

IRA INVESTMENTS TO AVOID

Any investment that already shelters income from taxation is a bad IRA investment. These include all municipal bonds and tax-free money funds. These investments are already tax sheltered. You gain nothing by putting them in an IRA to begin with. Because of their tax-sheltered status, they usually pay a below-market rate. You can almost always earn a higher market rate with nonsheltered investments. In addition, even the lower earnings from municipal bonds, tax-free money funds, and the like would be taxable to you as ordinary income when you begin withdrawing money from your IRA.

Similarly, because they shelter earnings from taxation, IRAs are not appropriate for tax-deferred annuities. If you wish to invest in these annuities, they should be purchased on their own merits in addition to, not as a substitute for, an IRA.

IRAs AT BANKS AND SAVINGS INSTITUTIONS

Safety and convenience are the reasons why, despite the many other investments now available, roughly two out of three people with IRAs still have them in the form of savings accounts and certificates at banks, savings institutions, and credit unions.

Selecting a savings account at these institutions used to be relatively simple. All accounts had ceilings fixed by federal regulations, and all institutions offered the same savings plans. And, because they all wanted to be competitive, virtually all paid the same (the ceiling) rate.

However, the savings rate deregulation that began in 1978 and is now virtually complete has changed that. Today, savings products are no longer standard. Each institution's savings plans differ in at least some respects from those of other institutions—perhaps in major respects—and some institutions have hundreds of plans.

On virtually all accounts an institution may pay any interest rate it wishes, and the rate may be either fixed or floating. If it is a floating rate that changes periodically, the rate may be tied to any index beyond the institution's control.

Institutions can also establish "tiers" of rates and need not even pay the same rate for the same savings instrument at all of their offices. They can also compound rates in any way they wish, which sometimes makes a significant difference in your return.

As competition for IRA investments has intensified, some banks and savings institutions have expanded the kinds of IRAs they offer by joining forces with mutual funds, brokerage houses, and insurance companies. As one aspect of financial deregulation, some of these institutions have discount brokerage operations where you can buy mutual funds shares or establish a self-directed IRA in which you can buy and sell stocks, zero-coupon bonds, and the like.

It's probable that as the IRA program grows and financial deregulation continues to blur distinctions between financial institutions, more banks and savings institutions will begin offering types of IRAs usually associated with other kinds of institutions. But, despite this trend, savings accounts and certificates remain their basic IRA product.

Savings Account Pros and Cons

Safety at these institutions is in the form of federal savings insurance provided by agencies of the U.S. government—and, for some institutions in a few states, by state or private insuring agencies. The federal insurance ceiling is $100,000 for accounts in the same institution. (Ceilings of the state-based agencies vary but, after some state-based insurance systems ran into trouble in 1985, it's likely efforts will be made to phase these systems into the federal system.)

For IRAs and Keogh plans, the statutory federal savings insurance ceiling is *in addition to* that for other accounts you may have in the same institution. You may have up to $100,000 in any combination of IRA and Keogh accounts in the same institution as well as another $100,000 in nonretirement accounts and be insured for all of it.

In recent years, a number of insured institutions have failed, and others have been kept afloat only with the aid of the federal deposit insurance agencies. There have been suggestions that depositors would suffer losses if the resources of these agencies were exhausted. However, it is unlikely that any Congress or president would allow this to happen, and both houses of Congress have reaffirmed that the "full faith and credit" of the U.S. government stands behind federally insured deposits.

Savings above the insured ceiling may be another story. If an institution with accounts covered by federal deposit insurance must be liquidated—(and, typically, the regulators do all they can to avoid the last-resort step of liquidation)—you will be paid off up to the insurance ceiling along with all other depositors. However, everything in your IRA above the insurance ceiling could be at risk. You may get some or all of that money back eventually. But, it could take time—perhaps several years—before the affairs of the liquidated institution could be settled. And, while the affairs of the institution are being settled, money remaining in your IRA would not earn interest.

If your IRA gets so large that its value nears the insurance ceiling, it would be prudent to stop contributing there and to open an IRA elsewhere. You can have IRAs in as many institutions with federal savings insurance as you wish. Accounts in each institution are protected to the limit.

Deposit insurance at commercial banks and state-chartered savings banks is provided by the Federal Deposit Insurance Corporation; at savings and loan associations and federal savings banks, by the Federal Savings and Loan Insurance Corporation; and at credit unions, by the National Credit Union Administration.

Another major advantage of setting up an IRA at a savings institution, bank, or credit union is convenience. Most people live or work near one or more depository institution offices or can get to them easily.

Other advantages are that there are usually no fees, or at most minimal fees, for opening, maintaining, or closing IRAs—although since deregulation there has been a trend toward establishing fees—and that most people understand what these institutions are and what they do with your money.

If you buy a fixed-rate CD, you'll also know exactly what it will be worth when it matures, a big help in making long-term plans. With many other IRA investments, it is not possible to know exactly what the IRA will be worth in the future.

But, there are also disadvantages. In exchange for the safety of federal deposit insurance, typically your return is not as great as you would earn (or hope to earn) on noninsured IRAs. And, of course, you do not have the opportunity for substantial capital appreciation that goes with such high-risk investments as the stock market.

Another disadvantage is that with most existing savings instruments at banks and thrift institutions, you may have to pay a penalty if you withdraw money before the instrument matures.

These penalties should be of less concern for owners of IRAs than for other depositors. Presumably, people with IRAs are investing for the long term. It's not likely you'd be forced to make early withdrawals from your IRA account simply to meet day-to-day living expenses.

Nevertheless, these penalties may discourage you from moving funds to another IRA. This could be to take advantage of a higher return elsewhere, because you're moving, or for any other reason. In some cases, the penalties mandated by federal regulatory authorities could cut into your principal and lower your IRA's value. (However, as noted, losses you could suffer in other investments through interest rate risk are potentially much greater.)

If you are age 59½ or older, banks and thrift institutions may waive the penalty for pulling out of a retirement savings certificate before maturity—if they wish.

The option is all on their side. If you are near (or above) age 59½ and there is a possibility you may wish to withdraw principal from an IRA savings certificate before it matures, learn what the institution's policy is before buying the certificate. All things being equal, set up your IRA or IRAs in institutions that will give you the option of withdrawing without penalty after age 59½.

Penalties not All the Same

There is a lot of confusion about penalties levied for withdrawing money prematurely, beginning with who is responsible for them. The penalty is required by government regulations but is paid to the institution.

More confusion arises over the fact that, depending on when the account was opened or renewed, different penalties may apply—and institutions may assess more stringent penalties than the minimum if they wish.

Currently, the *minimum* penalties are as follows:

- Accounts opened or renewed on or after October 1, 1983—the loss of 31 days' simple interest for certificates maturing in more than one year.
- Accounts opened or renewed between June 2, 1980 and October 1, 1983—the loss of three months' interest if the certificate's term is less than one year, and six months' interest if the term is one year or more.
- Accounts opened or renewed before June 2, 1980—the loss of three months' interest, with the interest rate for the remainder of the term reduced to the institution's passbook rate.

People usually start thinking about cashing in CDs early when interest rates are rising, and they can get higher rates elsewhere. Institutions are required to specify the penalty they will assess for early withdrawal in their savings agreement with you.

When opening an IRA (or any other account) at a depository institution, do not assume that the early withdrawal penalty will be the minimum. The minimum penalties required beginning October 1, 1983 are markedly less stringent than some earlier penalties. In addition, because of deregulation, institutions must pay more to attract savings. Consequently, a number of institutions assess penalties higher than the minimums.

And, read renewal notices for your maturing CDs carefully. When the account is renewed, institutions can change the penalty or make other important changes, which must be explained in the renewal notice.

What Are Market Rates?

For depositors, the chief benefit of deregulation is that banks and savings institutions are now paying "market rates" on virtually all accounts. Market rates are interest rates generally in line with those paid on comparable money market instruments. Because deposits at most banks and savings institutions have federal savings insurance, the most comparable instruments in terms of safety are U.S. government securities.

One characteristic of market rates is that they change constantly. These changes result from changes in the supply and demand for money, as well as from the expectations of major participants in the money markets. Another is that while they move generally in tandem, for comparable savings instruments rates are not always the same—and indeed, in an ever-changing free market, it would be impossible for them to be the same.

This means that in today's deregulated savings market, the market rate for any given savings instrument can be anywhere in a small range of rates rather than one rate offered by all institutions.

Another basic fact about money markets is that, historically, short-term interest rates (meaning rates on instruments that mature in a relatively short time) are usually lower than long-term rates. That's on the theory that the longer you allow someone to use your money, the more you should be paid for it.

There have been a few times when short-term interest rates were higher than long-term rates. But usually, if you're willing to commit your money for the long term, you should expect to be paid more than for money committed for only a short time or that can be withdrawn at any time without penalty.

Consequently, at any moment there are several "tiers" of savings interest rates. One may be a range of short-term rates, for maturities up to one year. Another may be a range for intermediate-term instruments, with maturities from one to three or four years. Another may be a range for long-term instruments, with maturities up to 10 years or more.

Many institutions create still other tiers by paying higher rates for larger deposits.

Which Way Will Interest Rates Go?

The kind of account (or other investment, for that matter) you select for your IRA may depend on whether you think interest rates will go up or down during the term of the account.

If you think interest rates will fall, invest in a fixed-rate certificate. This will "lock in" today's presumably high rate for the full term. With this option, you'll also know exactly what the certificate will be worth when it matures.

But, if you think rates will rise, buy a variable-rate certificate. Presumably this will be paying an even higher rate as it nears the end of the term than it was in the beginning.

For most people, the problem is that trying to decide what interest rates will do is like trying to decide whether a flipped coin will come up heads or tails. There's no way be sure.

Interest rate movements are determined by a host of complex and unpredictable factors. These include the state of the economy, demand for money and credit, federal spending policies, Federal Reserve policies, economic and financial developments in other parts of the world, and such unpredictable contingencies as wars, natural disasters, and financial panics.

Many economists themselves have poor records in forecasting interest rate movements, and current moods in money markets can be misleading. They can change from euphoria to gloom overnight on the basis of new statistics or the presumed stance of the Federal Reserve's Board of Governors.

This being the case, be wary of concentrating too great a proportion of your IRAs in investments that will do best if interest rates move in one direction. Unless you have very strong convictions about what rates will do, consider hedging your bets.

You could put half of your IRA money in a fixed-rate CD that would be the best choice if interest rates fall during its term. Put the other half in a floating-rate CD that would be the best choice if rates rise.

Then, sit back and see how they compare. You won't come out as well as if you had put all of your money on the right choice. But, you'll come out better than if you'd put it all on the wrong one.

Kinds of Savings Accounts

Because of deregulation, many thousands of varieties of accounts and certificates are being offered by banks and savings institutions. These accounts are marketed under a bewildering array of names.

But, despite the many variations, there are only a few general types of accounts. Of these only two—time deposits and money market accounts—are most likely to be used by people with IRAs.

(Note: About the time IRAs were made "universal," all federally insured banks and savings institutions were allowed to offer special 18-month "IRA/Keogh Retirement Accounts" that lacked many of the restrictions that then applied to most other accounts. But, as part of the general deregulation of savings rates, in late 1983 authority for these special certificates was revoked as no longer necessary.)

Deregulation is creating the greatest variety of savings plans in the area of time deposits. In addition to fixed-rate and floating-rate CDs, some institutions allow you to select any term you wish. This is useful if you need the money at a specific date—the date you plan to retire, for instance—or wish the term to end on the same date other IRA investments mature so you can combine those funds.

Other varieties include:

Add-on CDs.   Some institutions allow you to make additional deposits to existing CDs. If yours does, be sure you know if the addition extends the term of the CD or if the term remains the same. If the term is not extended, the institution may have a date during the term after which you are not allowed to make additions. Also, when you make additions, will it be at the original rate or at a different rate?

Discounted CDs.   Usually, when you buy a CD you pay face value for it. But, if it wishes, an institution can sell you a CD on a discounted basis. The price you pay will be below the CD's face value, and the CD will then mature at face value. (This is how U.S. Savings Bonds and original issue Treasury bills are sold.)

The ultimate discounted CDs are *zero-coupon CDs,* which are patterned after zero-coupon bonds. The CD is for a long period of time, so you can buy it at a huge discount. You don't have to worry about how to reinvest your interest, and you know exactly what your investment will be worth at some date far in the future. For more on the pros and cons of zero-coupon investments, see the discussion in the section on brokerage house IRAs.

Earnings-based accounts.   These are so new that, at this writing, only a few institutions have offered them. However, they're worth discussing because they are so different.

With an earnings-based account, part of your interest will be determined by the profitability of specific investments the institution will make with your money. Typically, you'll be guaranteed a "floor" rate slightly below the market—8 percent, perhaps, when other CDs are earning about 10 percent.

No matter what happens, the institution promises to pay you at least 8 percent. But, if the investments turn out well you'll be paid an above-market rate based on their earnings.

In many ways, earnings-based accounts are similar to limited partnerships. The major differences are that earnings-based accounts guarantee a "floor" rate and are covered by federal deposit insurance, features which limited partnerships lack. (In exchange for this degree of safety, your potential overall return is usually somewhat lower than with a limited partnership.)

The first earnings-based accounts involved investments in real estate developments and were offered by savings institutions. If these are successful, it's likely more will follow.

Many people will find it difficult or impossible to judge the value of these investments. People who buy these CDs run a risk that they will never earn more than the floor rate. Unless you are a sophisticated investor or have personal knowledge of the investments to be made, you'd probably be better off putting your money in a more conventional account that pays a rate higher than the floor on the earnings-based account,

On the other hand, if you're knowledgeable about the investments to be made, believe they are sound, and are willing to accept the lower floor rate if your judgment is wrong, then go ahead.

Money Market Deposit Accounts (MMDAs)

Not all banks and savings institutions offer MMDAs as IRAs, but these accounts can serve a number of purposes for IRA investors. One is as a "cash-equivalent" account, which is why Congress mandated the creation of these accounts in the first place. They were designed to be directly competitive with money market mutual funds.

There are no penalties for withdrawals from MMDAs, which typically pay interest rates slightly below U.S. Treasury bill rates and less than what institutions are paying for fixed-term CDs. But, while the rate is lower than for fixed-term investments, they are a good place for IRA money if you're not sure what longer-term commitment you wish to make or if you simply wish to avoid a longer-term commitment at the time.

They are also useful as a temporary "parking place" for rollovers from company pension plans or from other IRAs.

Institutions can link the interest rates they pay on their MMDAs to an index if they wish, but most institutions establish their own rates. The rate they intend to pay can be announced and guaranteed for no more than 30 days in advance. If they wish, they could guarantee the rate for only 24 hours and change the rate daily, but typically they change the rate once a week, on the same day of the week.

MMDAs opened as IRAs are not required to have minimum balances, but institutions may establish minimums if they wish.

Because these accounts are called money market accounts, there is some confusion between them and money market mutual funds. Whatever the promotional names given to them by the institution, money market accounts are savings accounts; money market mutual funds are mutual funds that invest in money market instruments.

Long-Distance Banking

Financial deregulation is spurring the use of long-distance banking as banks and savings institutions try to attract deposits from (and make loans to) customers outside their primary market areas.

It wouldn't pay to buy a $2,000 CD at a distant institution for a few cents extra interest. Making deposits at a distant institution involves expenses—postage, if you're willing to accept the delay of several days before your deposit is credited, and more if you move the money by wire transfer or overnight delivery.

When dealing with a distant institution you lose one of the main advantages of this type of investment—that of doing business with an institution convenient to where you live or work. But, if you have a large IRA and the rate offered is significantly higher than you can obtain locally, you may conclude that the loss of this advantage is worth it.

If the institution is out of state, check with your attorney to be sure it won't complicate matters for your heirs if you die. And, be sure you understand if—and how—the institution's deposits are insured.

One problem with long-distance banking is that although the institution you select may be paying the highest rate when you open the account, it may no longer be paying a relatively high rate when your CD matures. You would then have to make a long-distance IRA rollover or transfer to move the money to another sponsor.

How Compounding Affects IRA Growth

Because of deregulation, there are now many more differences in how banks and savings institutions compound money in their accounts. Compounding differences don't create significant differences in dollar terms at first unless a very large sum is involved. But, as time goes on, the dollar differences grow.

Table 15–1 shows how $2,000 contributed to an IRA at the start of each year would grow at different frequencies of compounding if earning a constant 10 percent return. After one year, the difference between an IRA compounded annually and one compounded daily is only $13 and, after five years, $261. IRAs compounded with other frequencies fall somewhere in between. But, after 10 years, the difference is $1,357; after 20 years, $10,743; and after 30 years, $51,254.

Table 15–2 shows how a $100,000 lump-sum deposit, presumably a rollover from an employer pension plan, would grow with no additions. In five years the daily compounded IRA would be $3,780 larger; in 10 years, $12,317 larger; in 15 years, $30,105 larger; and, in 20 years, $65,411 larger.

All other things being reasonably equal, the longer you plan to maintain your IRA in an investment of this type, the more it pays to select the IRA that compounds most frequently. You may not find any institutions that compound daily. But, even if one compounds quarterly or monthly, over time your total return will be significantly more than for one that compounds annually.

Comparing Rates and Yields: When Lower May Be Higher

Deregulation makes it more difficult to compare the CD rates paid by banks and savings institutions. Yet, because there now are more differences in how these institutions figure the interest they pay, it's important to be able to make these comparisons.

If you're going to buy a fixed-rate CD or one with rate changes known in advance, the simplest and best way to compare them is to ask each institution how much your CD will be worth when it matures. (The CDs should be for the same term, of course!)

Whatever the maturity, also ask for the *effective annual yield*. In describing the return on your savings, this number means most.

TABLE 15–1 ■ **How Money Grows with Different Compounding Methods** *(10 Percent Interest— Assumes $2,000 Invested at Start of Each Year)*

Years	Annual	Semiannual	Quarterly	Monthly	Daily	Advantage Daily over Annual
1	$ 2,200	$ 2,205	$ 2,208	$ 2,209	$ 2,213	$ 13
2	4,620	4,636	4,644	4,650	4,663	43
3	7,282	7,316	7,334	7,347	7,373	91
4	10,210	10,271	10,303	10,325	10,373	163
5	13,431	13,529	13,580	13,616	13,692	261
6	16,974	17,121	17,198	17,251	17,366	392
7	20,872	21,080	21,191	21,267	21,431	559
8	25,159	25,446	25,598	25,703	25,930	771
9	29,875	30,259	30,463	30,604	30,909	1,034
10	35,062	35,566	35,833	36,018	36,419	1,357
11	40,769	41,416	41,761	41,999	42,516	1,747
12	47,045	47,867	48,304	48,607	49,264	2,219
13	53,950	54,978	55,526	55,906	56,731	2,781
14	61,545	62,818	63,498	63,969	64,995	3,450
15	69,899	71,462	72,298	72,877	74,140	4,241
16	79,089	80,992	82,011	82,718	84,260	5,171
17	89,198	91,498	92,732	93,589	95,459	6,261
18	100,318	103,802	104,566	105,598	107,853	7,535
19	112,550	115,853	117,629	118,865	121,569	9,019
20	126,005	129,933	132,048	133,522	136,748	10,743
21	140,806	145,456	147,964	149,713	153,545	12,739
22	157,086	162,570	165,532	167,599	172,134	15,048
23	174,995	181,438	184,924	187,358	192,705	17,710
24	194,694	202,241	206,329	209,186	215,470	20,776
25	216,364	225,175	229,956	233,300	340,663	24,299
26	240,200	250,461	256,036	259,940	268,543	28,343
27	266,420	278,338	284,824	289,368	299,397	32,977
28	295,262	309,072	316,599	321,878	333,540	38,278
29	326,988	342,957	351,674	357,793	371,326	44,338
30	361,887	380,315	390,390	397,468	413,141	51,254
31	400,276	421,502	433,125	441,297	459,415	59,139
32	442,503	466,911	480,296	489,716	510,625	68,122
33	488,954	516,974	532,364	543,206	567,296	78,342
34	540,049	572,169	589,838	602,296	630,011	89,962
35	596,254	633,021	653,278	667,574	699,415	103,161
36	658,079	700,110	723,304	739,687	776,220	118,141
37	726,087	774,076	800,599	819,352	861,217	135,130
38	800,896	855,624	885,919	907,358	955,278	154,382
39	883,186	945,530	980,096	1,004,580	1,059,371	176,185
40	973,704	1,044,651	1,084,049	1,111,982	1,174,566	200,862

TABLE 15–2 ■ **Growth of $100,000 with Different Compounding Methods** *(10 Percent Interest)*

Years	Annual	Semi annual	Quarterly	Monthly	Daily	Advantage Daily over Annual
1	$110,000	$110,250	$110,381	$110,471	$110,512	$ 512
2	121,000	121,551	121,840	122,039	122,128	1,128
3	133,100	134,009	134,489	134,818	134,965	1,865
4	146,410	147,745	148,450	148,936	149,152	2,742
5	161,051	162,889	163,889	164,531	164,831	3,780
6	177,156	179,585	180,872	181,760	182,157	5,001
7	194,872	197,993	199,649	200,792	201,304	6,432
8	214,359	218,287	220,375	221,218	222,464	8,105
9	235,795	240,661	243,252	245,045	245,849	10,054
10	295,374	265,329	268,505	270,705	271,691	12,317
11	285,312	292,525	296,379	299,051	300,250	14,938
12	313,843	322,508	327,147	330,366	331,811	17,968
13	345,227	355,565	361,109	364,959	366,689	21,462
14	379,750	392,011	398,596	403,175	405,234	25,484
15	417,725	432,192	439,976	445,393	447,830	30,105
16	459,497	476,491	485,651	492,032	494,904	35,407
17	505,447	525,331	536,067	543,554	546,926	41,479
18	555,992	579,177	591,718	600,472	604,416	48,424
19	611,591	638,543	653,145	663,349	667,949	56,358
20	672,750	703,993	720,950	732,810	738,161	65,411

Your actual return is not determined by the stated (nominal) interest rate alone. It is also determined by the frequency (if any) at which money is compounded.

Each time interest is compounded, the next calculation is made with a bigger principal because the interest earned has been added to the original principal. You are earning interest on interest, and the more frequent the compounding, the higher the effective annual yield.

Your effective annual yield on an IRA compounded once a year at a nominal 8 percent interest rate is just that—8 percent. But, it would rise to 8.16 percent if the money is compounded twice a year, 8.24 percent if compounded quarterly, 8.30 percent if compounded monthly, and 8.44 percent if compounded daily.

(Note: There are differences in how institutions define "daily" compounding. Some use a formula that divides each year into 365 equal parts or compounding periods. Others use a formula that divides each year into 360 equal parts. The 360-day formula produces a slightly higher yield. In this book, all tables showing "daily compounding" are based on the higher-yielding 360-day method.)

Table 15–3 summarizes effective annual yields compounded annually, semiannually, quarterly, monthly, and daily for money on deposit for one, two, and three years. You can see that the higher the interest rate, the more likely that an apparently "lower" rate with more frequent compounding will actually earn a better return than a higher rate with less frequent compounding. After one year, for instance, at 10 percent, the effective annual yield with daily compounding (10.66 percent) is higher than 10.50 percent compounded annually, and so on.

Just as more frequent compounding increases the effective annual yield for money that remains on deposit for one year, the yield becomes progressively higher if money remains on deposit for more than a year. At 8 percent compounded annually for just one year, for example, the annual yield is 8 percent. But, this rises to 8.32 percent after two years and 8.66 percent after three years.

To be directly comparable, yields must be for the same period. If not, comparisons could be misleading. A higher yield quoted on the basis of a longer period may actually work out to a lower yield than one quoted for a CD with a shorter term.

If the CD's term is less than one year, the effective annual yield is still an accurate way to compare CDs *of the same term*—comparing one six-month CD with another, for instance. However, obviously it's virtually certain you won't be able to earn this return for the entire year. When the CD matures, it's virtually certain to be renewed at a different rate because of changes in money markets.

"Simple" Interest: When More May Be Less

A different kind of calculation is required when "simple interest" extends beyond one year. This means interest is *never*

TABLE 15–3 ■ Effective Annual Yields with Different Frequency of Compounding *(Percent)*

Interest Rate	Annual	IRA Maturing in One Year Semi annual	Quarterly	Monthly	Daily
5.00%	5.00%	5.06%	5.09%	5.12%	5.20%
5.50	5.50	5.58	5.61	5.64	5.73
6.00	6.00	6.09	6.14	6.17	6.27
6.50	6.50	6.61	6.66	6.70	6.81
7.00	7.00	7.12	7.19	7.23	7.35
7.50	7.50	7.64	7.71	7.76	7.90
8.00	8.00	8.16	8.24	8.30	8.44
8.50	8.50	8.68	8.77	8.84	9.00
9.00	9.00	9.20	9.31	9.38	9.55
9.50	9.50	9.73	9.84	9.92	10.11
10.00	10.00	10.25	10.38	10.47	10.66
10.50	10.50	10.78	10.92	11.02	11.23
11.00	11.00	11.30	11.46	11.57	11.79
11.50	11.50	11.83	12.01	12.13	12.36
12.00	12.00	12.36	12.55	12.68	12.93
12.50	12.50	12.89	13.10	13.24	13.51
13.00	13.00	13.42	13.65	13.80	14.08
13.50	13.50	13.96	14.20	14.37	14.67
14.00	14.00	14.49	14.75	14.93	15.24
14.50	14.50	15.03	15.31	15.50	15.83
15.00	15.00	15.56	15.87	16.08	16.42

		IRA Maturing in Two Years			
5.00%	5.12%	5.19%	5.22%	5.25%	5.33%
5.50	5.65	5.73	5.77	5.80	5.90
6.00	6.18	6.28	6.32	6.36	6.47
6.50	6.71	6.82	6.88	6.92	7.04
7.00	7.24	7.38	7.44	7.49	7.62
7.50	7.78	7.93	8.01	8.06	8.21
8.00	8.32	8.49	8.58	8.64	8.80
8.50	8.86	9.06	9.16	9.23	9.40
9.00	9.41	9.63	9.74	9.82	10.01
9.50	9.95	10.20	10.33	10.42	10.62
10.00	10.50	10.78	10.92	11.02	11.23
10.50	11.05	11.36	11.52	11.63	11.86
11.00	11.60	11.94	12.12	12.24	12.49
11.50	12.16	12.53	12.73	12.86	13.13
12.00	12.72	13.12	13.34	13.49	13.77
12.50	13.28	13.72	13.96	14.12	14.42
13.00	13.84	14.32	14.58	14.76	15.07
13.50	14.41	14.93	15.21	15.40	15.74
14.00	14.98	15.54	15.84	16.05	16.40
14.50	15.55	16.15	16.48	16.71	17.08
15.00	16.12	16.77	17.12	17.37	17.77

TABLE 15–3 ■ (concluded)

Interest Rate	Annual	Semi annual	Quarterly	Monthly	Daily
IRA Maturing in Three Years					
5.00%	5.25%	5.32%	5.36%	5.38%	5.47%
5.50	5.81	5.89	5.94	5.96	6.07
6.00	6.37	6.47	6.52	6.56	6.67
6.50	6.93	7.05	7.11	7.16	7.29
7.00	7.50	7.64	7.71	7.76	7.90
7.50	8.08	8.24	8.32	8.38	8.54
8.00	8.66	8.84	8.94	9.01	9.18
8.50	9.24	9.46	9.57	9.64	9.83
9.00	9.83	10.08	10.20	10.29	10.49
9.50	10.43	10.70	10.84	10.94	11.17
10.00	11.03	11.34	11.50	11.61	11.84
10.50	11.64	11.98	12.16	12.28	12.54
11.00	12.25	12.63	12.83	12.96	13.24
11.50	12.87	13.29	13.50	13.66	13.95
12.00	13.50	13.95	14.19	14.36	14.68
12.50	14.13	14.62	14.89	15.07	15.42
13.00	14.76	15.30	15.59	15.80	16.16
13.50	15.40	15.99	16.31	16.53	16.92
14.00	16.05	16.69	17.04	17.28	17.68
14.50	16.70	17.40	17.77	18.03	18.47
15.00	17.36	18.11	18.52	18.80	19.26

compounded no matter how long you must keep the money on deposit.

When an institution advertises a simple rate for a period of more than one year, your equivalent effective annual yield will always be less than the advertised rate. That's because, in making the calculation, the size of your deposit never increases as it would after every compounding period if interest were compounded.

If you earned 8 percent compounded annually for three years in an IRA opened with a $1,000 deposit, the $1,000 would earn $80 in the first year (8 percent of $1,000), leaving a year-end balance of $1,080. This would earn $86.40 in the second year (8 percent of $1,080), bringing the balance to $1,166.40. In the third year it would earn $93.31 (8 percent of $1,166.40), giving you a balance of $1,259.71 after three years.

But, with simple interest you would earn $80 each year ($1,000 × 8 percent), for a total of $240 in interest and a closing balance of $1,240.

How misleading simple interest quotations can be under some circumstances can be seen in Table 15–4. It shows the equivalent effective annual yields after from one to eight years for simple interest rates ranging from 5 to 15 percent.

Using this method of calculating interest, you can see that if an institution offers to pay "12 percent" for four years, you can do just as well with an investment that pays 10.30 percent and is compounded annually. If the institution offered to pay "12 percent" for eight years, you could do as well with an investment that was compounded annually and paid only 8.78 percent.

To protect yourself, read the fine print in advertisements and promotional mailings. Be especially wary if the interest rate promised in big, black type is substantially higher than what other institutions are paying for IRAs.

Multiple Rate IRAs

As a promotional device, some institutions advertise IRAs that have two interest rates—a high initial rate effective for a limited period and a lower rate for the remainder of the CD's term.

Again, the key number is the effective annual yield. The Federal Reserve Board has said in a policy statement that in these advertisements, there should be a "conspicuous statement" of the average annual effective yield for the multiple rate. If you don't see it in the advertisement or don't understand what the ad says, ask someone at the institution to tell you the real yield, so you know exactly what you're buying and can compare the return on this IRA with others.

If IRA customers are offered a high initial rate and a lower rate for the remainder of the term, the Fed's policy statement also said that both rates should be displayed in equal type size, and the ad should make clear the length of time the different rates apply.

TABLE 15–4 ■ Equivalent Effective Annual Yields for Simple Interest Rates with No Compounding *(Percent)*

Simple Interest Rate	Equivalent Effective Annual Yield After							
1 Year	*2 Years*	*3 Years*	*4 Years*	*5 Years*	*6 Years*	*7 Years*	*8 Years*
5.00%	4.88%	4.77%	4.66%	4.56%	4.47%	4.38	4.30
5.50	5.36	5.22	5.10	4.98	4.87	4.76	4.66
6.00	5.83	5.67	5.53	5.39	5.26	5.14	5.02
6.50	6.30	6.12	5.95	5.79	5.64	5.50	5.37
7.00	6.77	6.56	6.37	6.19	6.02	5.86	5.72
7.50	7.24	7.00	6.78	6.58	6.39	6.21	6.05
8.00	7.70	7.43	7.19	6.96	6.75	6.56	6.38
8.50	8.17	7.87	7.59	7.34	7.11	6.90	6.70
9.00	8.63	8.29	7.99	7.71	7.46	7.23	7.01
9.50	9.09	8.72	8.39	8.08	7.81	7.55	7.32
10.00	9.54	9.14	8.78	8.45	8.15	7.88	7.62
10.50	10.00	9.56	9.16	8.81	8.48	8.19	7.92
11.00	10.45	9.97	9.54	9.16	8.81	8.50	8.21
11.50	10.91	10.38	9.92	9.51	9.14	8.80	8.50
12.00	11.36	10.79	10.30	9.86	9.46	9.10	8.78
12.50	11.80	11.20	10.67	10.20	9.78	9.40	9.05
13.00	12.25	11.60	11.04	10.53	10.09	9.69	9.32
13.50	12.69	12.00	11.40	10.87	10.39	9.97	9.59
14.00	13.14	12.40	11.76	11.20	10.70	10.25	9.85
14.50	13.58	12.79	12.12	11.52	11.00	10.53	10.10
15.00	14.02	13.19	12.47	11.84	11.29	10.80	10.36

MUTUAL FUND IRAs

Mutual funds (which, according to the Investment Company Institute, hold about 12 percent of all money in IRAs) pool money from thousands of people and invest it in a broad range of investments selected by professional money managers. About half of the money in mutual fund IRAs is in equity (common stock) funds, about one third is in money market funds, and the remainder is in bond and income funds.

The mutual fund industry's strength in the battle for IRA dollars is its broad spectrum of investments. These range from the most conservative—in the form of funds that invest only in U.S. government securities—to the most aggresssive, which take risks in hopes of achieving superior capital gains. They also include money market mutual funds, which invest directly in money market instruments.

Minimum contributions to set up an IRA at most mutual funds range from $25 to $500, although some requirements are higher or lower. As a rule, subsequent contributions can be for smaller amounts, perhaps $50 or $100. Some funds also arrange to have withdrawals made automatically from your checking account and placed directly into the fund's IRA.

A major advantage of mutual funds is that they can provide a broad degree of diversification for a small investment. If you invest in a common stock fund, for $2,000 or less you can buy a stake in 50 or 60 companies—or, if it is a balanced fund, in a combination of stock and bonds. Your mutual fund investments can be spread over a broad range of industries— or, if you wish, concentrated in the field where you think the possibility of gain is greatest.

Some funds invest only in high-tech or health care stocks, for instance. Others concentrate investments in special fields such as precious metals or energy.

Families of mutual funds, which are groups of funds operated by the same investment company, believe they offer a great advantage by giving investors the ability to shift from one type of investment to another without being concerned about breaking IRS rollover and transfer rules. Typically, investors in a family of funds can transfer assets with just a phone call or by filling out a few forms. Some fund families charge a minimal fee to switch, and others allow you to move for free.

However, some families prefer that you don't move money around too much. Because constant fund switching by large numbers of investors greatly complicates planning for the managers of the investment portfolios, these funds place limits on how often you are allowed to switch.

Load and No-Load Funds

If you've dealt with mutual funds before, you know that in addition to differing in their investment goals there are two basic types of funds insofar as costs are concerned—load funds and no-load funds.

Every mutual fund has a management group that makes the fund's buying and selling decisions. This group charges management fees that vary between one half and 1 percent of the fund's total assets annually.

In addition, *load funds* have sales organizations. Buyers of shares in load funds are charged a sales commission, which until recently was almost always 8.5 percent of the amount invested. This is compensation for the registered stockbroker's representative, financial planner, or insurance agent who helps you select that fund.

The *no-load* funds don't charge sales commissions. For years, the no-load funds rarely if ever advertised, except in a few financial journals. However, the more than 300 no-load funds, including 21 families of no-load funds, are now much easier to find. Many advertise in local newspapers and on local radio and television stations.

Many investors have done well in load funds. With a load fund, you also get the personal service of the man or woman who helps you select that IRA investment.

On the other hand, over the years there has been no great difference in performance records of load mutual funds in general as compared with no-load funds. Between mid-1974 and mid-1984, the no-load funds in the *Forbes* stock fund composite had an average annual total return of 17.6 percent, slightly more than the 17.2 percent reported for load funds.

All things being equal, you'll probably be better off buying a no-load fund that invests all of your annual IRA contributions rather than paying a big commission to a load fund. As demonstrated in Chapter 4, commissions can greatly reduce your overall investment return. The only way you could come out ahead would be if the investment for which you paid a commission performed substantially better than noncommission investments.

Load and No-Load Distinctions Blurring

Until recently, distinguishing between load and no-load mutual funds was fairly simple. Load funds charged sales fees of up to 8.5 percent, while the no-load funds didn't charge any commissions. But, this picture is becoming clouded by changes at both ends of this spectrum, and distinctions between some load and no-load funds are blurring.

Some funds now charge commissions in the 3 percent range; others don't charge when you invest but charge when you take money out. With some funds, the sooner you take money out, the higher the redemption fee.

There are now also 12(b)1 funds, which refers to a Securities and Exchange Commission rule. These deduct the fund's sales expenses from its assets, reducing the value of the shares accordingly. Although some 12(b)1 funds may be called "no-load," actually all of the fund's shareholders are paying the commissions for each sale (and older shareholders who may have paid a commission of as much as 8.5 percent are now paying this commission, too).

Some of these funds also have a "back-end" load in the form of a redemption fee. One major brokerage house charges 5 percent of the lesser of cost or market value for redemptions in the first year, with a sliding scale down to zero after five years.

Read the Fund's Prospectus

Every mutual fund states its financial objective in its prospectus. Before you can invest in a mutual fund, the fund must give you a copy of its prospectus.

Some or most of it may be difficult reading, but it will be worth your while to try to read it anyway. Especially, study the fund's objectives to be sure its goals are compatible with yours. If you are near or in retirement, for instance, and this IRA will be your main source of retirement income, be sure the fund is not committed to making relatively speculative investments that pay little or no dividends and may not reap major capital gains for years.

Then, look at the specific investments in the fund's portfolio to see what is being done with investors' money. The prospectus should also disclose the fees charged by the management group. If it is a 12 (b)1 fund that deducts sales charges from the fund's assets, this will also be disclosed in the prospectus.

As long as you continue to hold shares in the fund, keep the prospectus, as well as any new prospectus the fund sends you and the periodic quarterly reports on how the fund is doing. If the fund's managers change the fund's goals or objectives, they must state that in a new or amended prospectus. Also, by comparing portfolios from one quarterly report to another you can see which investments the fund has been buying—or selling.

The prospectus also gives you the fund's investment record over the years. To compare that fund's performance with other funds, consult some of the references described later in this section.

Mutual Fund Performance

On the whole, mutual funds that invest wholly or partly in the stock market have performed well over the years. There have been periods, however, when poorly timed purchases and sales would not have done well, and there are always periods when stocks in general do poorly.

This suggests that purchases of shares in mutual funds that invest in the stock market should be made for the long haul. They would not be appropriate for anyone in or very near retirement who may wish to begin withdrawing from the fund soon, unless the bulk of their retirement income was coming from other sources. And, even in periods when funds as a whole are thriving, there are always some funds that substantially lag the market.

If you've never invested in a mutual fund before and are given an opportunity to do so, perhaps in a payroll deduction IRA plan at work, remember that the value of your investment can go down as well as up. In even the best-managed funds, values usually drop if there is a sharp drop in the overall stock market. These are not always little dips in price; they can be substantial. If you're going to invest in a mutual fund, you must be prepared to live with that—and be able to sleep at night even if your fund's value has fallen since you bought it.

How well your mutual fund IRA will do depends on the timing of your investments, how long you invest the money, and how well that fund does.

The Investment Company Institute, the trade group for the mutual fund industry, reports that the most conservative common stock funds—those that invest for both growth and income—would have grown to $412,471 by 1983 if you invested $2,000 at the start of each year for the previous 30 years. The funds in this study were load funds, and all contributions were subject to an 8.5 percent commission. This is an annual rate of return over the 30-year time span of about 11.1 percent.

In its 1984 mutual fund issue (August 27), *Forbes* magazine reported that its stock fund composite had an average annual total return for 1974–84 of 17.5 percent, its balanced fund composite had a return of 13.9 percent, and its bond and preferred stock fund composite had a return of 10.2 percent. These compare with 14.9 percent for Standard & Poor's 500 stock average.

Fund Families and Types of Funds

Some mutual fund families have more than 20 individual funds, including stock funds, bond funds, and mixed funds of one type or another. But basically, the essential elements of a mutual fund family are a money market mutual fund, a common stock fund, and an income fund.

The money market fund is for liquidity, for taking advantage of high short-term yields, and for parking funds between investments. Common stock funds are usually for the growth of capital through the stock market. An income fund consisting of bonds, preferred stocks, or other high-yielding stocks such as utilities can be used to lock in current yields for income and to achieve capital gains when interest rates are falling. Of course, during periods when interest rates are rising, the values of the shares in these funds will fall.

Although many people associate mutual funds with investments in common stocks, they are also especially appropriate for the purchase of corporate bonds by small investors. A small investor must pay a premium price to buy an odd lot—and may find the bonds difficult to sell even at a large discount if the bonds must be sold before they mature.

Other basic mutual fund types include growth income funds, which seek to combine income and long-term growth; balanced funds, which seek to balance growth-oriented stocks with income-producing bonds and preferred stocks; specialty funds that specialize in the securities of particular industries or types of securities; and municipal bond funds, which are inappropriate for IRA investments because their income is already tax exempt.

A few mutual funds now take money only through IRAs, Keogh plans, or other tax-deferred retirement accounts. These are post-IRA versions of so-called tax-qualified mutual funds designed especially for tax-sheltered investors. Formerly, these funds were used only by pension funds, universities, and other tax-sheltered entities.

The reasoning behind these "IRAs only" funds is that, with no tax consequences for investors to worry about, the fund's managers can trade the fund's holdings as the market dictates. In particular, they claim they are more likely to take short-term profits, whereas managers of regular stock funds may be reluctant to generate many short-term gains that would have to be passed on to shareholders. So far, however, there is no conclusive evidence to demonstrate that as a group, these funds are significantly outperforming other mutual funds.

Money Market Mutual Funds

Money market mutual funds are virtually a cash equivalent. When interest rates are high, they can be used as a basic IRA investment; and, at any time they can be used to park money between IRA rollovers.

There is no penalty for taking money out of money market mutual funds, which invest in money market instruments. Primarily, these are U.S. Treasury obligations, certificates of deposit issued by commercial banks and other financial institutions, and commercial paper or corporate IOUs issued by private corporations.

Maturities of these instruments are short term. Consequently, the yield on a money market fund is directly related to the volatile changes in short-term money markets. Historically, rates on short-term instruments are usually lowest in the investment spectrum. But, in the inflationary environment of the late 1970s and early 1980s, they were sometimes higher than other rates, providing very generous money fund returns.

Money market funds are relatively new and, for a while, enjoyed remarkable growth. They developed because, in the 1970s, there were ceilings on the interest rates banks and savings institutions could pay, but free-market rates on money market instruments were much higher.

The first money market mutual fund was organized in 1972. By 1982, their balances averaged more than $230 billion. But, this growth came to a halt at the end of 1982 when, as part of the savings deregulation process, Congress mandated the creation of money market deposit accounts at banks and savings institutions.

However, the money funds are now firmly established as an investment alternative. They are especially appropriate and convenient when used in conjunction with other mutual funds or as a cash parking place for investors in stock and bond markets.

Many money market funds are operated independently, and most are no-load. In addition, all families of mutual funds include a money market fund.

Money market mutual funds are not covered by federal savings insurance nor by the Securities Investor Protection Corporation program, which covers investments in securities held by brokerage houses. If a money market mutual fund runs into trouble, all your investment is at risk.

To date, the industry's safety record has been excellent. Investor safeguards include regulation by the Securities and Exchange Commission, annual audits by independent certified public accountants, and the fact that all assets are held by an independent custodian bank.

There have been some controversial efforts to rate money market mutual funds by safety. These concerns have also led to the creation of a number of money market funds that invest only in U.S. government securities. If you want the highest degree of safety in a money fund, invest in one of these—but in exchange for safety, of course, these funds pay a slightly lower yield.

Switching Strategies

Investing in a family of funds gives you a wide range of options. You may pursue a single investment objective—or hedge your bets by splitting your IRA contributions into two or more funds. It also gives you a degree of diversification not possible if you are investing as little as $2,000 a year or less in a self-directed plan at a brokerage house.

Investments can be changed either according to changes in your own circumstances or changes in the marketplace. If you inherit a big chunk of money and no longer need to rely on your IRA for a substantial part of your retirement income, you can switch to funds that seek maximum capital gains by investing in small, fast-growing companies. But, if you're nearing retirement and are concerned about safety, you could switch to a money fund heavily invested in government securities—or, if you believe interest rates will remain reasonably stable or come down, to a bond or other income fund.

You can switch to adapt to market changes. If the stock market is sluggish or declining but interest rates are high, you could keep most or all of your investment in the family's money market fund. But, if interest rates fall and the stock market takes off, assets could be shifted out of the money fund and into a growth-oriented common stock fund.

In real life, of course, things don't work that simply. To be successful in switching your mutual fund investments, you or someone advising you must know when markets are turning—when interest rates are indeed peaking or hitting bottom and when major turns are taking place in the stock market. If you make a mistake in judgment, you can wind up losing money by switching from one fund to another—or at any rate not making nearly as much.

Being allowed to switch mutual fund investments won't make you any smarter than you were before. If you've been successful in the past at calling turns in interest rates and tops and bottoms in the stock market, you'll probably be successful at switching from one mutual fund to another. But, if you haven't been able to call turns in interest rates or stock market tops and bottoms before, you're not likely to do any better by shuffling assets around in a mutual fund family. The versatility of a family of mutual funds gives you great flexibility, but you must have the financial sophistication and know-how to exploit it. Otherwise, you may frankly be better off sticking to the one or two funds in the family that offer investments you understand and feel comfortable with, even if you are forgoing the chance for bigger gains.

The difficulty of calling market turns and interest rate peaks and troughs has given rise to a type of financial adviser called a market timing service. In the past, they worked primarily for institutional and other large investors. Some now perform this service for individual investors, including people with IRAs, and others sell switching information.

However, there is no conclusive evidence that the timers are any better at spotting tops and bottoms of the stock market than are individual investors or the portfolio managers of mutual funds.

In a sense, frequent fund switching contradicts some of the rationale for investing in a mutual fund in the first place. This rationale is that many people don't have the time, interest, or training to study all the information needed to make investments—and that mutual fund decisions are made by professionals who make it their full-time job.

While the ability to switch from one fund to another in the same family gives you a lot of versatility, it won't assure investment success. For most people, the ability to switch funds will probably be more valuable in adjusting to changes in their own circumstances—the need for safer and more conservative investments as they approach retirement, for instance—than in trying to "play" financial markets.

And, if you open an IRA at a mutual fund family with the intention of switching funds one day, be sure you understand the family's switching rules. Some allow unlimited switching, but others have restrictions. Typically, some allow only one telephone transfer per month. Others may require written

instructions before you can switch, and there may also be
minimum investment requirements that would prevent you
from switching under some circumstances.

Learning More about Mutual Funds

While past performance is no guarantee of future success,
before investing in a mutual fund or family of funds you may
wish to do some research and make some comparisons.

Any fund that consistently lags in performance should be
avoided. You should also avoid being carried away by recent
performances that are unusually spectacular. This often means
the stocks in the fund have gone up about as far as they're
going to go. In the case of a very new fund, it could mean only
that it made some spectacular gains beginning at a very low
base—gains that can never be repeated proportionately as the
fund grows.

Your best bet is a fund with strong performance over a
long period of time, such as 10 years. (Even this can be misleading if the money managers who guided the fund during
those 10 years have left and the portfolio is under new direction.) In general, be cautious about any fund that has not been
in business long enough to establish a sustained track record.

To obtain this kind of information, if you have a stockbroker with reference materials, ask to see the latest reports
from Wiesenberger Investment Companies Service, Johnson's
Investment Company Charts, or Lipper Analytical Services.
You may also be able to find one or more of these reference
sources in a public library or a university library, if you have
access to one.

In addition, every August *Forbes* magazine publishes an
annual report on mutual funds that grades them for performance in up and down markets.

Two industry trade associations can provide general information on mutual funds, including their addresses and investment goals. These are The Investment Company Institute,
1600 M Street N.W., Washington, D.C., 20036; and the No-
Load Mutual Fund Association Inc., 11 Pennsylvania Plaza,
Suite 2204, New York, N.Y., 10001. For more on the information these trade groups can provide, see Chapter 14 of this
book.

Donoghue's Mutual Fund Almanac, published by the Don-oghue Organization, Box 540, Holliston, Mass., 01746, has performance records on 850 mutual funds and is published annually for $23.

Monthly performance comparisons of more than 500 mutual funds are available from *United Mutual Fund Selector,* a service of United Business Service Company, 212 Newbury St., Boston, Mass., 02116. The service is twice monthly, and the comparisons are in the first issue of each month.

The Individual Investor's Guide to No-Load Mutual Funds, by Gerald W. Perritt, Ph.D., and L. Kay Shannon, is published by the American Association of Individual Investors, 612 N. Michigan Avenue, Chicago, Ill., 60611. It provides detailed information on 292 no-load mutual funds and lists investment advisory services that specialize in mutual fund evaluation and selection. Individual copies are $16.

Self-Directed Accounts, Zeros, and Other Brokerage House IRAs

Brokerage houses are among the most aggressive marketers of IRA programs, and their share of the market is growing. From about 9 percent of all IRA money at the end of 1983, it rose to about 12 percent at the end of 1984.

As more people who opened their first IRAs when the program was greatly expanded in 1982 build their IRAs to near the $10,000 level, it's likely the proportion of brokerage house IRAs will continue to rise. Fees and commissions can seriously crimp the earning power of a small IRA invested with a brokerage house, but they become less of a constraint when the balance in the account reaches five figures.

You'll find the biggest selection of IRA investment options at the large brokerage houses. And, large or small, any brokerage house that wishes can set up a self-directed plan through which you can buy and sell stocks, bonds, or other securities for your own IRA.

You can also buy load mutual funds through a broker. Some will sell you an insurance annuity IRA plan or a CD issued by a federally insured bank or savings institution. Many of the large brokerage houses also have their own families of mutual funds in which you can switch just as with other mutual fund families.

Typically, it costs a little less to take the mutual fund approach with a big brokerage house than to establish a self-directed plan. In April 1985, Merrill Lynch was charging $15 to establish its mutual fund account, compared with $30 for a self-directed account. Both the mutual fund and the self-directed account also required an annual custodial fee of two tenths of 1 percent of the assets in the account, with a minimum fee of $20 and a maximum of $100. In addition, the firm charges a final custodial fee of $50 when the account is closed. These charges, typical for the industry, are in addition to the normal brokerage commissions and sales charges for most IRA investments.

Self-Directed IRAs

The type of IRA most associated with brokerage houses is the self-directed account, which works much like a regular brokerage account.

With a self-directed IRA, legally your IRA is in the possession of a qualified custodian or trustee, usually a bank or savings institution. But, you make all the decisions, giving you far more flexibility in controlling investments than with any other type of IRA. You decide how much risk you're willing to assume and direct the brokerage house to buy or sell investments, just as you would for your own account. In addition to the traditional stocks and bond, these may include corporate bond unit trusts, limited partnerships in real estate and oil and gas ventures, zero-coupon bonds, or any other investments not prohibited for IRAs by law.

Generally speaking, self-directed accounts are appropriate primarily for more sophisticated investors. And, while a self-directed account gives you the greatest latitude in making investments, the fees and commissions for buying and selling securities or making other investments make this one of the most expensive ways to go.

Most brokers put any cash that flows into the account— from dividends or interest, for instance—into a money market mutual fund until it's reinvested. These amounts will be small in the beginning, but over time they can substantially increase your overall return. Don't sign up for a self-directed IRA without this feature.

Because you're dealing with the same trustee, a self-directed IRA allows you to switch funds from one investment to another at any time without a tax penalty. But, while you may trade pretty much as you wish in a self-directed account, you're not allowed to sell stocks short. Because IRS rules prohibit using IRA assets as a pledge or collateral for a loan, most brokerage houses interpret this to mean that margin trading in a self-directed IRA is prohibited. Even if you find one that interprets it otherwise, don't start trading on margin until you've checked it out with your own tax adviser.

Some brokerage houses establish limitations to prevent customers from taking high-risk speculations with IRA money. And, although brokers' accounts are the only way to make certain investments—options, for instance—most brokers limit IRA investors to writing covered calls—that is, buying stocks and simultaneously selling calls on them. This mechanism provides a way to increase the income on a stock, but you'd have to give up some profits if the stock's price rises sharply and the stock is called away from you. In any event, if you don't already know how options work, you shouldn't start learning in an IRA.

Is a Self-Directed Account Right for You?

The great advantage of a self-directed IRA is its flexibility. You have more investment options than with any other type of IRA. And, while current law prohibits IRA investments in "hard" assets, a self-directed account can be used to buy stock in companies in the hard-asset field—in gold and silver mines, for instance. But, consistent success with a self-directed IRA requires one and preferably both of the following:

If you intend to rely primarily on your own judgment to make investment decisions, particularly if they involve buying and selling common stock, you should have already established a successful track record as an investor. If you've been consistently successful at making your own investment decisions in the past, it's likely you'll continue doing so with IRA investments. But, if you have no experience in the types of self-directed IRA investments you're thinking of making or if your past record in making these investments has been poor, the chances of you suddenly blossoming into an investment wizard with your IRA are not good— and the higher cost of a self-directed account makes the odds against you even greater.

Be honest with yourself. If you've been a successful investor, you probably have a pretty good idea of how profitable your investments have been. In fact, the more successful you've been, the more likely it is you know fairly precisely how far ahead of the game you are. When your stocks are going up, it's satisfying to sit down at the end of each week to figure out how well you're doing. But, when they're going down, it's amazing how long you can put off seeing just how bad the news really is.

If you have any doubts, before setting up a self-directed IRA in which you'd buy and sell common stocks, go over your investment records and tax returns for the last 5 or 10 years. Is your current portfolio of stocks worth more than you paid for it? And, in past years, have your capital gains been greater than your losses? If you can't answer yes to both questions, you shouldn't risk your IRA money in the stock market unless your retirement income is already amply secured.

On the other hand, if your retirement income *is* already amply secured—if you're so well off or have a guaranteed retirement income so large that you wouldn't worry if markets turned against you and you lost part or all of your IRA—go ahead and "play craps" with these tax-sheltered dollars. Who knows? You might score spectacular gains.

If you do not have the knowledge and experience to make your own investment decisions, you should at least have a competent broker or investment counselor to make these decisions for you.   Ideally, this should be someone with a proven record in giving you sound investment advice in the past. It would not be prudent to set up a self-directed IRA if the investment decisions are to be made by someone who hasn't already demonstrated competence to you unless that person comes with high recommendations from a knowledgeable investor you know and trust.

There are thousands of highly competent customer's representatives at brokerage houses, but don't allow investment decisions involving your retirement money to be made by a stranger. As in any other business, some customer's representatives are better than others. Not all have the experience or knowledge required to make investment decisions for you or would take enough interest in your account. Unfortunately, at some investment houses, accounts with small balances get very little attention. Customers who don't trade often are known as "orphans." And, just as with insurance agents and savings counselors at banks and thrift institutions, it would be unrealistic to assume that all customer's representatives at brokerage houses are familiar with the intricacies of IRA rules and regulations.

When Does a Self-Directed Account Pay?

If you're considering buying and selling stock through a self-directed account at a brokerage house, you must decide at what point it would pay. If all you have to invest at the start is $2,000 or less, the fees—particularly the commissions on each transaction—would probably eat up much or all of your profits, if any. On the purchase or sale of 100 shares of a $20 stock, the commission at the typical full-service brokerage house would be about 3 percent, or $60.

You can substantially reduce those commissions by dealing with a discount broker. But, to do this you should be the sort of investor who has been dealing with a discount broker already—someone who doesn't need a broker's guidance on what to buy or sell and who does his or her own research on stocks and other investments. If you feel you must sit down and discuss your investment program and goals with your broker—and you'd want to rely on your broker's research facilities—you should continue dealing with a full-service brokerage firm.

Fees at discount brokerage firms vary widely. A 100-share purchase or sale of a $20 stock at a discount firm would cost anywhere from about $25 to $45. Also, comparing discount broker fees is difficult because, looking at their rate charts, it's not easy to see at a glance which broker really has the best deal for your trading patterns.

Most brokers work on a sliding scale. The broker who charges the lowest commission on a relatively large block of stock may not charge the lowest for a small block. Nevertheless, if you're an independent-minded investor accustomed to going it alone, the discount broker can save you a lot of money.

Realistically, whether you're dealing with a full-line brokerage house or with a discount broker, most advisers suggest having at least about $10,000 in your IRA before you start trading in common stocks.

With only a few thousand dollars to invest, you're limited to buying and selling stocks in odd lots, where transaction costs are higher—or to buying and selling very low-priced stocks, where investment risks are often greater. Some brokerage houses won't even buy a stock selling below a certain price out of concern that the risks for their clients would be too great.

Until your IRA gets big enough, you can build your capital with bank or savings institution CDs or a money market fund. When it gets large enough, switch to a self-directed IRA and begin building your IRA stock portfolio.

Even with $10,000 or so to invest, you will not be able to buy enough different stocks to provide the diversification some advisers recommend. But, if the stocks in your IRA are in addition to other stocks you own, this may not be a problem.

Zero-Coupon Bonds

If any one investment has become particularly associated with IRAs and other tax-deferred programs, it would be the zero-coupon bond—and particularly, zeros backed by U.S. Treasury securities. In February 1985, the government recognized the growing popularity of zeros by making it possible for investors to hold shares of certain new U.S. Treasury notes and bonds directly.

While they are not for everyone, zeros are particularly appropriate for IRAs, Keoghs, and other tax benefit investment plans. They are also being marketed as unit trusts, which are portfolios of fixed-income securities—and some financial institutions are issuing zero-coupon certificates of deposit.

Zero-coupon bonds were originally designed chiefly for tax-exempt institutions and foreign investors with no U.S. tax obligations. But, at about the time the IRA program was opened to everyone who works, the market for zeros was greatly broadened.

These bonds are called "zeros" because they pay no interest. Instead, they are sold at a deep discount from face value.

Part of the appeal of zeros is that they allow investors to lock in interest rates for virtually any period of time up to 20 or 30 years and to do so with very small investments. At around a 12 percent yield, for instance, a $100 investment would grow to $1,000 in 20 years; a $2,000 investment would grow to $20,000.

(Note: To see some year-by-year estimates of how zeros grow, turn to the B tables in Appendix A of this book, which show what money grows to at various rates of return if left untouched. That is exactly what you are buying in a zero—pure compounded growth.)

If zeros were taxable investments, the IRS would require you to pay tax on the invisible interest each year even though you didn't receive it. This lessens the desirability of zeros as a taxable investment. But, if they are in an IRA, these invisible gains are sheltered from taxation.

The first fund composed entirely of zero bonds was successfully offered to the IRA market by Paine Webber, Jackson & Curtis Inc. But, the zero market really took off in 1982 when Merrill Lynch introduced its Treasury income growth receipts investments, called TIGRS. Salomon Brothers then began issuing CATS, or certificates of accrual on Treasury securities, and other securities firms followed with their own versions.

When you buy one of these, you are not actually buying the Treasury security itself. You buy a receipt entitling you to a share of the income and value of a Treasury security held in escrow for you. Originally, these securities had semiannual interest coupons attached to them, but the securities firms that bought them stripped these coupons off and sold interests in the coupon and the principal.

Because of the safety of government securities and the many advantages of zeros, which allow people to invest in Treasury securities for very small sums, demand for these receipts was enormous. By early 1985, at least $45 billion in Treasury securities had been stripped and resold by securities firms under various names.

At first, the government opposed this trend and claimed the securities firms were defacing the bonds. But, once it was established that imputed interest on the stripped bonds would be taxed each year, the government's attitude changed—and, in 1985, the government jumped into the market itself by making it possible for investors to hold a share of the stripped notes and bonds directly.

It did this through its STRIPS program, an acronym for Separate Trading of Registered Interest and Principal of Securities. In effect, these are zero-coupon U.S. Treasury securities. Institutions buy bonds and notes that are eligible for STRIPS and present them to a Federal Reserve bank for stripping of the coupons. From this point on, it is a book-entry deal.

Brokerage firms, banks, and other institutions responded quickly to this new kind of government security. In the first two weeks after they were offered, more than $1.9 billion in strips were created. Some observers believe they will eventually displace other zero-coupon securities backed by U.S. government obligations, although an aftermarket in these other securities will continue.

Because they have direct government backing and avoid complicated trust arrangements, STRIPS yield a little less than other government-backed zero securities. If they do wind up displacing other government-backed zero securities, they may also make it more difficult to sell these other securities in the aftermarket. While buyers will be found, it could be at some discount from the price paid for STRIPS of similar face value and maturity.

One major advantage of all zero securities is that you know exactly what your investment will be worth 5, 10, or 20 years down the road, whenever it matures. In that sense, they are just like the U.S. government EE bonds you buy at a discount.

Another advantage is that there are no interest payments during the life of the security so you don't have to worry about how to invest the interest. Other bonds pay interest every six months, which must be reinvested at the rates then prevailing. These rates could be lower—and, whatever the rates, it would be difficult for small investors to put small sums into high-yielding, long-term securities.

But there are some disadvantages, too. One is that zeros carry a high degree of interest rate risk. Particularly in the early years, because they are issued at such a deep discount from face value, their price could drop sharply in the after-market if interest rates in general rise. (On the other hand, their prices would rise if interest rates fall.)

Zeros should not be purchased unless you are prepared to hold them until maturity. Otherwise, a zero may be difficult to sell at a reasonable price before it matures. If you decide there's something else you want to do with the money, you may have problems getting out of this investment without taking a substantial capital loss. Consequently, a zero bond may not be the best IRA investment for older people who may need the money before the bond matures. It could also cause problems for your heirs if you died before the bond matured and they wanted to liquidate the investment.

With all zeros, there is a sales charge, which varies from issuer to issuer. Here you may also face the problem of hidden brokerage fees that could be built into the price you pay. Some brokerage houses charge more than others, reducing your yield. The important figure to you is the net yield, and you should be sure you understand what that is. When buying zeros, ask for the yield to maturity, so you can compare it with the return then available on other IRA investments.

Finally, if it is a corporate bond, look at the financial strength of the issuer. Will the issuer be in a position to pay off the bonds when they mature in 10 or 20 years? Most likely it will—but, if it won't, your zero bond will have become a very poor investment. With regular coupon bonds, at least you would have earned interest every six months until the com-pany defaulted, but with a zero you earn nothing until ma-turity. Buying zero bonds through a fund with a diversified portfolio will reduce that risk, but it is there nonetheless.

Zeros are creating a lot of excitement but, while they have some characteristics that make them appropriate for many long-term IRA investors, basically they are another play on interest rates. You buy them in hopes interest rates will go down, allowing you to lock in a high yield for well into the future.

If you guess right, you'll do well. But, if interest rates remain at roughly the same level over the period you hold the zero bond, you'd have come out ahead buying a coupon bond (which normally pays a slightly higher yield) and reinvesting the coupons at current rates, assuming you could do so. And, you'd come out far behind if interest rates rise.

Limited Partnership IRAs

Brokerage accounts are also being structured to offer limited partnership IRAs in oil and gas, real estate, and other business ventures. These IRA partnerships are designed to produce income rather than to produce tax write-offs, traditionally the great attraction for these deals.

Primarily, limited partnership IRAs are for sophisticated investors or for investors who can afford sophisticated financial advice. To participate in one you may have to meet certain income and net worth requirements, which can vary depending on the state in which you live. If you are not already making investments of this kind, it would be unwise to start making them in an IRA unless you can afford to take losses.

A "limited partnership" is an agreement between a general partner who presumably has the knowledge and expertise to operate the venture and a group of "limited partners" who put up most of the money. Until fairly recently, many deals of this type required investments of at least $10,000 or more in each unit. But now, many partnership units are available through some brokerage houses at the $2,000 level and sometimes less, making them possible for IRAs.

The main advantage of limited partnership IRAs is that they give you the opportunity to invest in a venture you probably couldn't afford on your own. Through a limited partnership you can participate directly in specific oil and gas, real estate, or other ventures without any responsibility for their operations. At the same time, your liability is limited to your investment. If the venture runs into trouble, you cannot be assessed for more money.

An oil and gas income IRA involves producing properties with proven reserves. There is no high-risk drilling venture to worry about; the cash flow usually begins quickly, often in the first year. But, if you don't know much about these investment programs yourself, check the deal out with someone who does before committing your IRA funds.

Through limited partnerships, IRA investments can also be made in income-producing real estate. These can involve office buildings, apartment complexes, and shopping malls as well as the financing of properties. In fact, any income-oriented limited partnership, including those that lease computers, boxcars, or other equipment, could be structured as an IRA.

The disadvantages of limited partnerships as IRAs include relatively high fees—often from 7 to 10 percent of your investment—and relatively high risk. The returns are not guaranteed; they're simply what the promoter hopes to earn. Expected returns from oil and gas partnerships, for instance, could be lowered substantially if the price of oil in world markets continues to drop; returns on real estate investments may not be realized if real estate values fall, if too many real estate syndicates bid real estate prices to unrealistic levels, or if buyers of the properties owned by your partnership are unable to meet the mortgage payments. And, all IRA limited partnerships must forgo the tax advantages usually associated with these investments.

The main thing to look for in checking a limited partnership proposal is that the company running the show has been in business for a reasonable time and has a successful investment record. And, returns expected on limited partnerships should be better than those available on long-term bonds. Otherwise, there would be no point to assuming the added risk.

Other Self-Directed IRAs

Through a self-directed IRA you can also play the interest rate game with corporate and government bonds and, until you build an IRA of considerable size, with bond funds.

IRA sponsors are also adapting such other financial instruments as securities guaranteed by the Government National Mortgage Association. These are mortgage-backed securities with a monthly cash flow, representing monthly payments on home mortgages. While not direct obligations of the U.S. government, they are backed by the full faith and credit of the government.

The sponsors of the "Ginnie Mae" unit trusts see them as an investment alternative for people who were settling for low interest in return for safety—and are now seeking a higher return. Monthly interest and principal payments are automatically reinvested, if you wish. The fund's trustee will redeem units at any time, with the price determined by any principal repayments as well as the market price of the securities in the portfolio. If interest rates have gone up since you bought the units, the market price will be lower; if they have gone down, the price will be higher.

The price of the units includes a sales charge, typically about 3.5 percent. In the past, these securities have been totally repaid in about 12 years. However, some will be longer lived than others. If the underlying mortgages are government subsidized, the mortgages are likely to last for the full term. Otherwise, you may receive an early prepayment of much of the principal.

Self-directed IRAs have also been set up to invest in second mortgages and deeds of trust. These earn a high return but carry a relatively high degree of risk. Some investors in these IRAs suffered losses when home buyers were unable to meet payments on their loans. Unless you are a seasoned investor in this field and can afford higher risk, these and other riskier IRA investments should be avoided.

Brokered CDs

Federally insured CDs issued by banks and savings institutions can also be purchased at some brokerage houses. Typically, the brokerage house buys a jumbo CD from a federally insured bank or savings institution and then breaks it up and sells it to individuals. Each buyer's portion is covered up to the $100,000 limit by federal deposit insurance.

While not all brokerage houses offering retail CDs will do so, many will buy your CD back before it matures. Unlike the CDs you buy at a bank or savings institution, there are no penalties for early withdrawal. However, you'll have to sell the CD back at the current market price, which is determined by the current level of interest rate.

This means that to cash in your brokered CD early, you must assume the interest rate risk. If interest rates have gone up since you bought the CD, you'll get a lower price when you sell it than you paid for it; you could suffer a capital loss much greater than the penalty you would have paid had it been a

CD with a bank or savings institution. But, if interest rates have fallen, you'll get a higher price than you paid.

SIPC Insurance Coverage at Brokerage Houses

Accounts at brokerage houses that are registered with the Securities and Exchange Commission are insured by the Securities Investor Protection Corporation (SIPC). This insurance covers up to $500,000, including up to no more than $100,000 in cash.

There are some significant differences between SIPC insurance and the insurance of deposits at banks and savings institutions.

One is that when it comes to the maximum $100,000 in cash covered by SIPC insurance, the coverage is supposed to apply only to funds held for the purpose of purchasing securities. If you are using the broker as a repository for money you don't plan to reinvest in stocks, technically this money is not covered by SIPC insurance.

Another difference is that SIPC insurance and federal deposit insurance don't work in the same way. When a bank or savings institution must be closed, the goal of the insuring agencies is to move as quickly as possible to pay off insured depositors. While in some cases the SIPC has been able to arrange for the quick transfer of customer accounts to other brokerage firms, in others customers have had to wait months before being paid off or having their securities returned to them.

If your stocks began declining in price while frozen in the account, you would be unable to sell them.

Even if you are investing with a discount brokerage firm owned by a bank or savings institution or working through it, those funds are covered by SIPC insurance, not federal deposit insurance from the FDIC or FSLIC.

INSURANCE COMPANY IRAs

The life insurance industry holds a little more than 10 percent of all money in IRAs, a proportion that has remained fairly steady since the IRA program was opened to everyone who works. While some insurance companies have taken an aggressive approach toward marketing IRAs, others have maintained a relatively low profile, even during the busy "IRA season."

The industry's basic IRA product is the flexible annuity, which may be either fixed or variable. You decide how much and when you wish to contribute to the plan. With a fixed annuity, you're guaranteed a maximum opening rate for the first year or two, and then a minimum return every year or six months thereafter.

Typically, the written guaranteed minimum return over a long term is very low, such as 4 percent. The company may pay you more than this minimum if justified by the results of its investments. In recent years, almost invariably insurance companies have paid more than the minimum, making their IRAs competitive with other kinds of IRAs.

With variable annuities, you may be given a choice of several investments, including different kinds of mutual funds.

Just as with a family of mutual funds, you're dealing with the same trustee and can switch from one fund to another without a rollover or transfer. Typically, an insurance company group will include one or more common stock funds, a money market fund, and a bond or fixed-income fund.

Whatever the type of IRA you open with an insurance company, when you're ready to start withdrawing from it, the company hopes you'll buy an annuity that will pay you a set income while you are retired. However, you're not obliged to buy an annuity. If you wish, you can withdraw all of the money as a lump-sum distribution or transfer or roll it over into another IRA.

Costs May Vary Greatly

While the variable annuities marketed by insurance companies permit switching, they often provide fewer types of funds from which to choose than mutual fund families do and may charge higher management fees.

Charges and fees can vary greatly. Most life insurance is sold by agents who work on commission. Most IRA annuities are too, although some are marketed by brokerage houses.

The traditional way of charging a life insurance commission is to assess the fee at the beginning, a so-called front-load plan. However, in marketing their IRA products many insurance companies have adopted back-load charges, which will be assessed if you withdraw the money before a specified period of time has elapsed, usually up to 10 years.

Typically, these back-load fee schedules range from 6 to 10 percent of the IRA's value. One major company charges a 7 percent withdrawal fee for the 1st to the 4th year and thereafter drops the charge by 1 percent for all future years to the 10th year, when it is 1 percent. There is no withdrawal charge after that, and withdrawal fee schedules are less stringent if you are age 60 or above.

Insurance IRA Pros and Cons

With IRA annuities you'll get safety and stability—and, if you shop around, reasonable earnings rates. The trade-off is that during its accumulation period (the time during which you are making contributions and the IRA is building in value) the average rate earned on these IRAs may be slightly lower than the rates paid by some other sponsors.

Of all major types of IRAs, those sold by insurance companies are probably the most difficult to research and compare. There is a great variety in the way these plans work from one company to another, and there are no central sources you can consult to weigh the relative merits of one insurance company's IRA against others. And, if it's not a mutual fund plan, you cannot keep track of how well or poorly your investment is doing by reading *The Wall Street Journal, Barron's,* or the business pages of a large daily newspaper, as you can with mutual funds and stocks and bonds.

Spokespersons for the insurance industry believe one of the advantages of their IRA is the personal service of the insurance agent who markets it and who, in many cases, will come to your home to discuss and explain the product. So far it is the only major type of IRA sold in this manner.

On the other hand, the person who provides personal services and sells you the IRA must be paid for his or her efforts, and this will come out of your capital.

Until Congress greatly liberalized the payout rules for IRAs after people reach age 70½, if you decided to buy an insurance company annuity for your retirement, an insurance company

IRA was also the only way you could select a payout option that would assure that you'll never outlive your income from that IRA.

The trouble with fixed-annuity-type payments during your retirement years is that their buying power can be eaten away by inflation. Even at the low 4 percent inflation rate that prevailed between 1982–84, a dollar's buying power would be cut by one third in a decade. The $1,200-a-month pension you retire with today would be worth only $800 a month in today's buying power 10 years from now.

Of course, if it's a lifetime annuity and you live long enough, selecting an annuity would prove a wise choice. But, if you don't live long after retiring, it will not have been the best choice—and, as is discussed later in this chapter, with some annuities your heirs could wind up with nothing.

If you've been successful in handling and investing money during your working lifetime, there wouldn't seem much reason for turning assets over to an insurance company to manage when you're ready to retire. Because the insurance company must take some of your capital as its fee, you should be able to equal or exceed an annuity's return with investments of comparable safety. You'll also be assured that if you die soon after you retire, the assets remaining in the IRA will go to your beneficiaries.

It's easy to compare what an insurance annuity would pay you with what your IRA would earn on its own. Ask a few companies and agents how much annuity income the money in your IRA could buy. Then, see how much your IRA would earn each month and each year in such other investments as banks or saving institution CDs, high-yielding mutual funds, or self-directed portfolios of Treasury or corporate bonds or high-yielding stocks.

Unless the income from the insurance company is substantially higher, you'll probably come out ahead with one of these alternative investments. Until you reach age 70½, you don't even have to touch the principal of these other investments if you elect not to—and, if something happens to you, your heirs will inherit all of it.

On the other hand, retirement income from an insurance annuity does have the advantage of being guaranteed, and you don't have to worry about any loss of retirement income due to the ups and downs of the economy. An insurance annuity would be also appropriate if you don't trust your ability to handle and invest the money in your IRA in the future— or if you have other sources of retirement income and wish to diversify.

On the whole, the life insurance industry has an impressive history of safety over a long period. But, particularly if you have a large IRA or will depend on the annuity for a substantial part of your retirement income, be as sure as you can of the soundness of the insurance company.

If you wish to do your own research into the comparative merits of life insurance companies in general, A. M. Best & Co., a publishing house specializing in the insurance industry, has manuals that provide a great deal of information ranging from the size of individual companies to the specific securities held by each firm. Many of the Best manuals are available at public libraries or through major insurance agencies. A Best rating of A or better would be an acceptable safety level.

Rules Similar to Those for Other IRAs

The IRS rules governing IRA annuities are similar to those for other IRAs. The annuity must be issued in your name as the owner, and either you or your beneficiaries if you die are the only ones to receive the benefits.

The amount in your account must be fully vested at all times, and the contract must provide that you cannot transfer it to anyone else. If you're given any refunded premiums, you must use them to pay for future premiums or to buy more benefits. This must be done before the end of the calendar year in which you receive the refund.

You may have a spousal IRA if you have a nonworking spouse, and distribution rules after age 70½ are the same as for other IRAs.

Until November 6, 1978, the IRS allowed IRAs to be set up by buying an endowment contract from a life insurance company. An endowment contract is an annuity that also gives you life insurance coverage.

However, if you have one of these older IRA endowments you are not allowed to deduct any portion of the premium that goes for life insurance, which means your immediate tax savings will be less than with other IRAs. If the total yearly premiums on all of your endowment contracts are more than $2,000, the endowment contracts will not be treated as an IRA. Each year the insurance company must give you a statement showing how much of your premiums went for life insurance and cannot be deducted.

To qualify as an IRA, the premiums on any insurance contract written since November 6, 1978 must be flexible. The company may establish minimum contributions, but you must have the right to make contributions whenever you wish—or, if you choose, not to make any contributions. Congress mandated this to assure that if people did not have income that qualified for an IRA because of a change in their circumstances, they would not be required to continue making payments on the investment. If you have an IRA insurance contract issued before November 6, 1978, that does not have flexible payments, you may exchange it for one that does.

As with other IRAs, when you buy an IRA annuity you must be given a disclosure statement. The disclosure statements prepared by insurance companies are often difficult to understand. If you don't get clear answers to your questions, take the disclosure statement to someone who can explain it to you. Especially be sure you know what the fees to get in or out of the IRA will be, how much the company is actually guaranteeing to pay, how the company will be investing your money, and how the payout provisions work.

Also, how will the return on your investment be calculated? Annual compounding will result in a lower total return than quarterly or daily compounding. And, will it be calculated before or after fees or charges are subtracted? If it is after charges are subtracted, the actual yield on your total investment would be less than the stated rate of return. These little differences can make a big difference in what your IRA will be worth over a long period of time.

Buying Retirement Income with an Annuity

If you conclude that you'd prefer buying retirement income with an IRA annuity rather than investing the money yourself, whether you've built the IRA with an insurance company or in some other investment, take time to do some shopping around.

Even though you may have accumulated your IRA with an insurance company, you're not obliged to buy your annuity from that company. When you're ready to retire, you can take the money and buy the annuity from some other insurance company, if you wish.

Some annuities guarantee a certain payment for life, and others guarantee payments for a specified period, but terms can vary greatly. Even if you make identical payments to them, all companies do not pay the same income.

In addition, some companies set the amount they'll pay regularly and won't change that amount under any circumstances. This leaves you vulnerable to the impact of inflation on a fixed-retirement income.

Ironically, it was to prevent just this that Congress created IRAs. Fixed-income retirement plans were losing purchasing power so fast that Congress acted to give people a way to protect their retirement purchasing power by investing money themselves. Unless you're convinced that the inflation rate is going to fall to zero and that actual price deflation is likely for some time to come, a fixed-payment IRA retirement annuity would seem a questionable investment. Other insurance companies have more flexible programs and will adjust your payments upward if their profits rise.

In addition to rate differences, there are also big differences in payout programs. Under some, if you die after you start receiving income from the annuities, your heirs won't get a dime. What the insurance people call a "life-only" policy pays you only to the date of your death. No matter when you die, no more payments are made.

A "life and period certain" contract is a little more complicated. It will pay you to the date of your death, whether it is 1 or 30 or 40 years, assuming you could live that long. But, it also contains a provision guaranteeing your heirs these payments for a specified period of time.

The longer this guarantee, the smaller the periodic income payment. The most common agreement is for 10 years certain, but it could be for 3, 5, 20 years, or any other period.

If you outlive the specified period, you could very well come out ahead. But, if you die before the period is over, results could be very different. The insurance company would be obligated only to continue payments to your heirs to the end of the specified period, and then payments would stop.

To use a worst-case scenario, if you bought a "life and period certain" IRA annuity and the "period certain" was 10 years, if you died after 10 years your heirs would receive nothing no matter what the investment results of the money contributed to the IRA over the years.

Many other types of annuities are also on the market. If you're married, you'll probably want some type of a joint and survivor annuity, which will pay income as long as either you or your spouse lives. This is the type of annuity now required by law for employer retirement plans unless the spouse waives this option in writing.

If you don't like the choices offered by one insurance company, see what the others have. Be sure the annuity you buy is right for you—and for anyone who may depend on you for support during your retirement years.

Insurance in Connection with IRAs

Although you are not allowed to buy an insurance policy as an IRA, you may obtain insurance along with an IRA if the premiums are paid separately and are paid by you, not by the IRA's trustee.

In addition, hundreds of banks and savings institutions now offer free life and/or disability insurance in a form generally known as "IRA completion insurance." This insurance pays you or your beneficiary what would have been accumulated in the IRA if your contributions had continued.

Most of these free programs are created by insurance companies, brokers, or service organizations and are sold to the banks and savings institutions that offer them. If the institutions pay for these policies, the cost is limited by IRS regulations covering the value of premiums that can be given in connection with IRA deposits. These limits are $10 for deposits of up to $5,000 and $20 for deposits of more than $5,000.

Otherwise, your enrollment in a group insurance plan offered in connection with an IRA would not be considered a prohibited transaction if the premiums are paid by you, not out of the plan's funds.

INDIVIDUAL RETIREMENT BONDS

If you bought some of these bonds before the government stopped selling them, you should consider redeeming them and rolling over the proceeds into some other kind of IRA.

Sales of individual retirement bonds were halted by the Treasury Department in May 1982. The department decided that sales were so low that it was no longer worth the effort.

In the Tax Reform Act of 1984, Congress allowed holders of these bonds to redeem them irrespective of whether or not they have reached age 59½.

If you redeem your bonds, you have 60 days in which to roll the proceeds over into another IRA or other IRAs. If you do not roll the money over, you must take it into your income for that year. And, if you are under age 59½ and are not disabled, you'll have to pay the 10 percent premature distribution penalty.

These bonds were authorized in 1974 by the same law that created IRAs. While they are risk free, they are also one of the least desirable IRA investments. Although the rate they paid was increased periodically over the years, it was only 9 percent when sales were discontinued, less than for almost any other kind of IRA investment at the time.

In addition to the low rate, they have other disadvantages. IRA bonds stop paying interest on the first day of the month in which you reach age 70½. If you don't redeem the bonds and roll the proceeds into another IRA by the end of that year, you'll be liable for tax on the whole sum in that year. Consequently, unless you're willing to pay tax on the entire sum, you must be prepared to redeem these bonds and make a rollover when you reach age 70½.

If you die before you reach age 70½, IRA bonds stop paying interest on the first day of the month you would have reached age 70½ or the fifth anniversary of your death, whichever is first.

You're not paid any interest on these bonds until you cash them in. Interest is compounded semiannually. The bonds mature on the semiannual interest accrual date that falls just before the date on which you reach age 70½ (or on that date, if both are the same).

To redeem bonds, either bring them to a Federal Reserve Bank or branch yourself or mail them to the Bureau of Public Debt, Division of Securities Operations, Payment and Reissue Section, Room 531-D, 13th and C Street S.W., Washington, D.C., 20226. When redeeming bonds by mail, write a covering letter requesting the payment. Then sign the back of the bond and have your signature certified by an officer of a bank or savings and loan association. To give yourself a record of the mailing, it would be best to send your bond and letter by registered or certified mail.

While you cannot redeem these bonds at banks and savings institutions, these institutions may be able to help you handle redemption requests. Especially, you should have no trouble getting help if you plan to roll the redemption proceeds into that institution's IRA.

COLLECTIBLES

Although investors have not been allowed to purchase tangibles and collectibles as IRA investments since 1982, there's always a slight possibility Congress will repeal this provision of the law. If you put tangibles into an IRA before 1982 they are not affected by the ban. But, you may not deduct contributions for any purchased after 1981.

The rationale used by Congress for eliminating collectibles and tangibles as permissible IRA investments is that these investments don't encourage savings or capital formation. When people put IRA money in financial institutions it is loaned out to businesses and consumers, stimulating the economy and creating more jobs. But, when you buy a collectible, the money usually goes to a dealer who can do anything he or she wants with it, including putting it in a box and burying it in the back yard.

If collectors and dealers could persuade Congress to allow collectibles in IRAs again, how would they rate as IRA investments?

Generally speaking, collectibles do well when inflation is rising and people want them as an inflation hedge. But, when the inflation rate falls, many investors desert this market and prices weaken. Many investors who bought at the peak of the collectible boom in the early 1980s suffered big losses.

To be successful you must be very knowledgeable about the field in which you are buying. Nobody knows more about any category of collectible than a serious collector. If you're not an expert yourself, you'll always be at a disadvantage in making buying and selling price decisions. If someone else makes these decisions for you, you must pay for the service.

If your collectibles soar in value while in your IRA, you would have to pay tax on the gain as ordinary income when you take them out of your IRA—which you must start doing soon after you reach 70½, just as with any other IRA. At this point, you would have to start selling them off whether you wanted to or not. Also, collectibles and antiques don't pay dividends or interest. By putting collectibles in an IRA you give up the tax shelter you could have received on interest- or dividend-paying investments. For the novice collector, there is also a risk of being defrauded by counterfeits or other deceptive practices. Finally, collectibles should be purchased for the long haul. There is often a big spread between a dealer's selling price and the wholesale buying price. It may take years before you could resell a collectible at a meaningful profit.

If Congress does allow IRA investments in collectibles again, it's likely the rules for making them would be at least as stringent as before they were banned.

Under the old rules, you had to direct your investments through a trustee in a self-directed IRA. Many trustees who handled the more traditional investments were unwilling to undertake the responsibility of handling IRAs made up of collectibles. Those that did charged extra fees.

More important to many serious collectors, you could not take personal possession of the collectibles in your IRA, even temporarily. They had to remain in the possession of the trustee or of a custodian appointed by the trustee, which involved more fees.

The mechanics of getting the collectible to the trustee were also up to you. The dealer held the collectible for you, and you sent the money to the trustee along with an order to invest. You were not allowed to pay the dealer directly.

You could sell from the account at any time. But, in addition to incurring sales charges, you were responsible for making all sales arrangements, just as you were responsible for buying arrangements. If the buyer wanted to see the asset, it would have to be at the facilities of the trustee or the custodian. To complete the sale, the transaction had to be between the buyer and the trustee because payment to you would be a premature distribution.

16

Conclusion

Although it has been several years since Congress opened the IRA program to everyone who works, relatively speaking the program is still little more than in its infancy.

Even if the number of people now contributing to IRAs remains fairly constant, the money now invested in IRAs would grow at a mushrooming rate similar to that illustrated by some of the tables in this book. But, it's likely the number of participants will increase—and that, sooner or later, Congress will raise the IRA contribution limits again.

It won't be long before IRAs hold a significant store of the nation's savings capital. And, as IRAs begin providing more people with retirement income, they may become recognized as the "fourth leg" in retirement finances, as distinct from social security, private and public pension plans, and income from other assets.

The IRA program will be around for a long time. The sooner you understand its opportunities (and its limitations), the more effectively you can use it. Hopefully, this book has contributed to that understanding.

Appendix A:
IRA Growth Tables

These tables will enable you to make your own estimates of what IRAs would grow to at various rates of return. With them, you can project the growth of any IRA into the future whether you're making regular additional contributions each year or not. The tables can be used for many purposes: projecting the growth of IRAs you already own, comparing the growth of your IRAs with other IRAs, and helping you decide whether to roll a lump sum distribution from an employer plan into an IRA.

WHAT YOU CAN DO WITH THESE TABLES

There are two sets of tables available. Both allow year-by-year IRA growth estimates for up to 40 years at annual rates of return. The first set of tables included in this appendix—the A tables—is for estimating how IRAs would grow with fixed annual contributions. The tables provide examples showing how IRAs with annual contributions of $1,000, $2,000, and $4,000 would grow, allowing year-by-year growth estimates for up to 40 years at annual rates of return ranging from 6 percent to 20 percent (whole numbers only).

The second set—the B tables—allows you to estimate how IRAs would grow if you made no more contributions.

You can stop making contributions to an IRA for many reasons. Perhaps you can't afford more contributions, or you want to start contributing to another IRA or IRAs instead. Or maybe you are going to drop out of the work force, or roll over a large sum from an employer retirement plan and never contribute more to it.

By using the A and B tables in combination, you can estimate:

- What your IRA would grow to if you changed the fixed amount you contributed each year, or began contributing a fixed amount for the first time.
- What your IRA would grow to with fixed contributions if the rate of return changes.

You can also make these estimates with calculators alone by various methods. However, you will probably find that using the multiples on these tables in combination with a calculator will be quicker, especially if you are trying to project an IRA's growth far into the future.

THESE RESULTS ARE ESTIMATES ONLY

The results you'll achieve with these tables are *estimates only*, as are all other examples in this book.

The key numbers in the tables are *basic multipliers* for terms ranging from 1 to 40 years. To simplify your calculations, these basic multipliers have been reduced to three digits after the decimal point. Consequently, results of calculations made with the basic multipliers will differ slightly from those made by computers or calculators that base calculations on more than three digits. However, even with a large sum over a long period of years, differences would be relatively minor. Moreover, even calculations made with more precise calculating methods are at best only rough estimates as to the results you would actually achieve investing in an IRA.

One reason is that the longer the time involved, the greater the likelihood of changes in interest rate levels and IRA contribution limits that will tend to make today's estimates of IRA growth obsolete. If inflation rates rise to substantially higher levels, for instance, IRA contribution limits would probably increase accordingly to keep pace with higher salary levels.

Another reason is that these projections—those in the tables in this book, as well as those made by IRA sponsors in advertisements and promotional literature—are based on idealized conditions almost never achieved in real life.

The tables assume that to achieve the stated results, all contributions will be made at exactly the start of the year. Tables in promotional literature and advertisements of most IRA sponsors usually make the same assumption.

Although many IRA investors may concentrate investments near the beginning of the year, however, it is highly unlikely—and in many cases impossible—that they will make their total IRA investments at *exactly* the start of the year. January 1 is a legal holiday (New Year's Day), and if it falls on a weekend there may be other days when financial institutions are closed and financial markets are not operating.

In real life, IRA investments will be spread out during the year or even into the following year for most of us. Many people wait until the last minute to make their IRA contributions, while many others with IRAs make regular payroll contributions during the year and into the following year, complicating their actual rate of return with compounding.

Consequently, although the calculating methods used to estimate IRA growth in this book are slightly less precise than those used by the computers that create many of the growth tables in IRA promotional literature, no method can pinpoint exactly how an IRA will grow for most people. But all these methods give a reasonable estimate of what your IRA would grow to over the specified period of time.

USING THE A TABLES—IRAs WITH FIXED ANNUAL CONTRIBUTIONS

Each of the A tables, which are for calculating the future worth of IRAs with fixed annual contributions, has five columns. The first indicates the plan years completed. The second, and most important, column lists the basic multiplier for each of the 40 plan years. The multiplier is what $1 would grow to at that rate of return and for that period of time. If you multiply any other number by it, it will show what the other number would grow to at that rate of return for that period of time. The other three columns show how $1,000, $2,000 (the maximum individual contribution), or $4,000 (the maximum a working couple could contribute) would grow at the designated rate of return. These last three columns can be used to make quick, "at a glance" estimates of how an IRA would grow with those fixed contributions; in many cases this may be all the information you'll need.

If you were contributing the maximum $2,250 to a spousal IRA earning 10 percent and planned to retire in 20 years, for instance, you could quickly see on the 10 percent A table that in 20 years your IRA would grow to about $140,000 ($141,755). Or if you and your spouse were contributing $2,000 each at a 12 percent return and wanted to estimate what your IRAs would grow to in nine years, the 12 percent A table would show the answer to be about $65,000 ($66,192).

For other than the numbers in the last four columns on the tables, use the basic multiplier, which shows the growth of $1. Here are some examples:

Problem: What would an IRA grow to if you contributed $1,250 a year for 17 years at an average 10 percent return?

Answer: Turn to the 10 percent A table and find the multiplier for 17 years, which is 44.599. Then multiply that by the amount contributed each year: 44.599 × $1,250 = $55,749.

Problem: What would an IRA grow to if you contributed $1,600 a year for 12 years at an 8 percent return?

Answer: Turn to the 8 percent A table. The multiplier for 12 years is 20.495 × $1,600 = $32,792.

NOTE: If you are making investment estimates in round numbers, you may be able to take mathematical shortcuts by using one of the numbers in the tables of examples rather than by finding the multiplier and multiplying the estimates out. For instance, to estimate how regular contributions of $500 would grow, just divide the $1,000 examples in half. Or to estimate how a working couple's combined contributions of $3,000 would grow, multiply the $1,000 example by three, and so on.

The $1,000 column is especially useful in taking shortcuts. Dividing those numbers by 10—which simply involves putting a decimal point in front of the last digit—shows how $100 would grow.

USING THE B TABLES—IRA GROWTH WITH NO ADDITIONS

Each of the B tables, which are for estimating the future worth of an IRA if no further contributions are made, has three columns. The first shows the plan years completed; the second gives the basic multiplier for each year. The other column shows how $1,000 would grow at the designated rate of return.

As with the A tables, to estimate what any sum would grow to at a given rate, multiply the sum by the basic multiplier for the desired period of years.

Problem: You build an IRA up to $16,320 and then stop making contributions at age 38 because you prefer contributing to a company plan at work. At a 10 percent return, what will the IRA be worth in 27 years when you are age 65?

Answer: Turn to the B 10 percent table. The multiple for 27 years is 13.109 × $16,320 = $213,939.

Problem: You receive a $126,580 rollover from an employer plan at age 59. If invested at an average 12 percent return, what will your IRA be worth in six years when you are 65?

Answer: Turn to the B 12 percent table. The multiplier for 6 years is 1.973 × $126,580 = $249,742.

Problem: You build an IRA worth $3,650 and then quit work at age 26 to marry and have a family. Invested at an average 10 percent return, what will the IRA be worth in 39 years when you are age 65?

Answer: Turn to the B 10 percent table. The 39-year multiplier is 41.144 × $3,650 = $150,176.

HOW TO ESTIMATE GROWTH IF THE AMOUNT CONTRIBUTED CHANGES

By using both sets of tables, you can make a two-step estimate of what your IRA would grow to if you changed the fixed amount contributed each year (or began making fixed contributions each year.)

To do this, first go to the appropriate B table—the table showing what an IRA would grow to with no further additions. Use the multiplier on this table to estimate what the total in the IRA at the time you changed the amount contributed regularly (or began contributing the same amount regularly) would grow to with no further additions.

Then turn to the appropriate A table. Use that multiplier to estimate what the new fixed contributions would grow to over the same time period. Then add the two results together.

Problem: After you've built an IRA worth $204,760, Congress changes the law and increases the maximum annual contribution to $3,000. You plan to retire in six years. What will your IRA be worth if you can invest it at a 10 percent return while contributing the new limit of $3,000 each year?

Answer: First turn to the 10 percent B table. The multiplier for six years is 1.771 × $204,760 = $362,630.

Then turn to the 10 percent A table. The six-year multiplier is 8.487 × $3,000 = $25,461.

$362,630 + $25,461 = $388,091.

Problem: Contributing to an IRA on an irregular basis, you have accumulated $73,525. You can now afford to contribute $2,000 each year for 10 years until you retire. If you can invest it at 8 percent, what will the IRA be worth then?

Answer: Turn to the 8 percent B table. The 10-year multiplier is 2.158 × $73,525 = $158,667.

Then turn to the 8 percent A table, which shows that in 10 years $2,000 will grow to $31,290.

$158,667 + $31,290 = $189,957.

HOW TO ESTIMATE IRA GROWTH IF THE RATE OF RETURN CHANGES

The same two-step procedure can be used if you're making fixed contributions and the rate of return changes.

In this case you'd first turn to the appropriate B table to estimate what the IRA would grow to at the new rate with no more additions. Then turn to the A table to see what the regular additions would grow to at the new rate.

> *Problem:* You have accumulated $130,678 in an IRA and reinvest it at a new return of 12 percent. If you are contributing $2,000 each year, what will the IRA be worth in eight years?
>
> *Answer:* First turn to the 12 percent B table. The eight-year multiplier is 2.475 × $130,678 = $323,428.
>
> Then turn to the 12 percent A table, which shows that in eight years regular $2,000 contributions would grow to $27,550.
>
> $323,428 + $27,550 = $350,978.

◼ 6% A: How IRA Would Grow at Constant 6 Percent

Return *To estimate what any sum invested regularly at this return would grow to for any period of from 1 to 40 years, multiply that sum by the basic multiplier, which shows what $1 would grow to. The table assumes that each investment is made at the start of each year.*

Plan Years Completed	Basic Multiplier ($1)	$1,000	$2,000 (Single IRA Maximum)	$4,000
			Examples	
1	1.060	$ 1,060	$ 2,120	$ 4,240
2	2.183	2,183	4,366	8,732
3	3.374	3,374	6,748	13,496
4	4.637	4,637	9,274	18,584
5	5.975	5,975	11,950	23,900
6	7.393	7,393	14,786	29,572
7	8.897	8,897	17,794	35,588
8	10.491	10,491	20,982	41,964
9	12.180	12,180	24,360	48,720
10	13.971	13,971	27,942	55,884
11	15.869	15,869	31,738	63,476
12	17.882	17,882	35,764	71,528
13	20.015	20,015	40,030	80,060
14	22.276	22,276	44,552	89,104
15	24.672	24,672	49,344	98,688
16	27.212	27,212	54,424	108,848
17	29.905	29,905	59,810	119,620
18	32.760	32,760	65,520	131,040
19	35.785	35,785	71,570	143,140
20	38.992	38,992	77,984	155,968
21	42.392	42,392	84,784	169,568
22	45.995	45,995	91,990	183,980
23	49.815	49,815	99,630	199,260
24	53.864	53,864	107,728	215,456
25	58.156	58,156	116,312	232,634
26	62.705	62,705	125,410	250,820
27	67.528	67,528	135,056	270,112
28	72.639	72,639	145,278	290,556
29	78.058	78,058	156,116	312,232
30	83.801	83,801	167,602	335,204
31	89.889	89,889	179,778	359,556
32	96.343	96,343	192,686	385,372
33	103.183	103,183	206,366	412,732
34	110.434	110,434	220,868	441,736
35	118.120	118,120	236,240	472,480
36	126.268	126,268	252,536	505,072
37	134.904	134,904	269,808	539,616
38	144.058	144,058	288,116	576,232
39	153.762	153,762	307,524	615,048
40	164.047	164,047	328,094	656,188

■ 8% A: How IRA Would Grow at Constant 8 Percent

Return To estimate what any sum invested regularly at this return would grow to for any period of from 1 to 40 years, multiply that sum by the basic multiplier, which shows what $1 would grow to. The table assumes that each investment is made at the start of each year.

Plan Years Completed	Basic Multiplier ($1)	$1,000	Examples $2,000 (Single IRA Maximum)	$4,000
1	1.080	$ 1,080	$ 2,160	$ 4,320
2	2.246	2,246	4,492	8,984
3	3.506	3,506	7,012	14,024
4	4.866	4,866	9,732	19,464
5	6.335	6,335	12,670	25,340
6	7.922	7,922	15,844	31,688
7	9.636	9,636	19,272	38,544
8	11.487	11,487	22,974	45,948
9	13.846	13,846	26,972	53,944
10	15.645	15,645	31,290	62,580
11	17.977	17,977	35,954	71,908
12	20.495	20,495	40,990	81,980
13	23.214	23,214	46,428	92,856
14	26.152	26,152	52,304	104,608
15	29.324	29,324	58,648	117,296
16	32.750	32,750	65,500	131,000
17	36.450	36,450	72,900	145,800
18	40.446	40,446	80,892	161,784
19	44.761	44,761	89,522	179,044
20	49.422	49,422	98,844	197,688
21	54.456	54,456	108,912	217,824
22	59.893	59,893	119,786	239,572
23	65.764	65,764	131,528	263,056
24	72.105	72,105	144,210	288,420
25	78.954	78,954	157,908	315,816
26	86.350	86,350	172,700	345,400
27	94.388	94,388	188,676	377,352
28	102.965	102,965	205,930	411,860
29	112.283	112,283	224,566	449,132
30	122.345	122,345	244,690	489,380
31	133.213	133,213	266,426	532,852
32	144.950	144,950	289,900	579,800
33	157.626	157,626	315,252	630,504
34	171.316	171,316	342,632	685,264
35	186.102	186,102	372,204	744,408
36	202.070	202,070	404,140	808,280
37	219.315	219,315	438,630	877,260
38	237.941	237,941	475,882	951,764
39	258.056	258,056	516,112	1,032,224
40	279.780	279,780	559,560	1,119,120

■ 10% A: How IRA Would Grow at Constant 10 Percent

Return To estimate what any sum invested regularly at this return would grow to for any period of from 1 to 40 years, multiply that sum by the basic multiplier, which shows what $1 would grow to. The table assumes that each investment is made at the start of each year.

Plan Years Completed	Basic Multiplier ($1)	$1,000	$2,000 (Single IRA Maximum)	$4,000
			Examples	
1	1.100	$ 1,100	$ 2,200	$ 4,400
2	2.310	2,310	4,620	9,240
3	3.641	3,641	7,282	14,564
4	5.105	5,105	10,210	20,420
5	6.715	6,715	13,430	26,860
6	8.487	8,487	16,974	33,948
7	10.435	10,435	20,870	41,740
8	12.579	12,579	25,158	50,316
9	14.937	14,937	29,874	59,748
10	17.531	17,531	35,062	70,124
11	20.384	20,384	40,768	81,536
12	23.522	23,522	47,044	94,088
13	26.974	26,974	53,948	107,896
14	30.772	30,772	61,544	123,088
15	34.949	34,949	69,898	139,796
16	39.544	39,544	79,088	158,176
17	44.599	44,599	89,198	178,396
18	50.159	50,159	100,318	200,636
19	56.275	56,275	112,550	225,100
20	63.002	63,002	126,004	252,008
21	70.402	70,402	140,804	281,608
22	78.543	78,543	157,086	314,172
23	87.497	87,497	174,994	349,988
24	97.347	97,347	194,694	389,388
25	108.181	108,181	216,362	432,724
26	120.099	120,099	240,198	480,396
27	133.209	133,209	266,418	532,836
28	147.630	147,630	295,260	590,520
29	163.494	163,494	326,988	653,976
30	180.943	180,943	361,886	723,772
31	200.137	200,137	400,274	800,548
32	221.251	221,251	442,502	885,004
33	244.476	244,476	488,952	977,904
34	270.024	270,024	540,048	1,080,096
35	298.126	298,126	596,252	1,192,504
36	329.039	329,039	658,078	1,316,156
37	363.043	363,043	726,086	1,452,172
38	400.447	400,447	800,894	1,601,788
39	441.592	441,592	883,184	1,766,368
40	486.851	486,851	973,702	1,947,404

■ 12% A: How IRA Would Grow at Constant 12 Percent

Return *To estimate what any sum invested regularly at this return would grow to for any period of from 1 to 40 years, multiply that sum by the basic multiplier, which shows what $1 would grow to. The table assumes that each investment is made at the start of each year.*

Plan Years Completed	Basic Multiplier ($1)	$1,000	$2,000 (Single IRA Maximum)	$4,000
			Examples	
1	1.120	$ 1,120	$ 2,240	$ 4,480
2	2.374	2,374	4,748	9,496
3	3.779	3,779	7,558	15,116
4	5.352	5,352	10,704	21,408
5	7.115	7,115	14,230	28,460
6	9.089	9,089	18,178	36,356
7	11.299	11,299	22,598	45,196
8	13.775	13,775	27,550	55,100
9	16.548	16,548	33,096	66,192
10	19.654	19,654	39,308	78,616
11	23.133	23,133	46,266	92,532
12	27.029	27,029	54,058	108,116
13	31.392	31,392	62,748	125,568
14	36.279	36,279	72,558	145,116
15	41.753	41,753	83,506	167,012
16	47.883	47,883	95,766	191,532
17	54.749	54,749	109,498	218,996
18	62.439	62,439	124,878	249,756
19	71.052	71,052	142,104	284,208
20	80.698	80,698	161,396	322,792
21	91.502	91,502	183,004	366,008
22	103.602	103,602	207,204	414,408
23	117.115	117,115	234,310	468,620
24	132.333	132,333	264,666	529,332
25	149.333	149,333	298,666	597,332
26	168.374	168,374	336,748	673,496
27	189.698	189,698	379,396	758,792
28	213.582	213,582	427,164	854,328
29	240.332	240,332	480,664	961,328
30	270.292	270,292	540,584	1,081,168
31	303.847	303,847	607,694	1,215,338
32	341.429	341,429	682,858	1,365,716
33	383.520	383,520	767,040	1,534,080
34	430.663	430,663	861,326	1,722,652
35	483.463	483,463	966,926	1,933,852
36	542.598	542,598	1,085,196	2,170,392
37	608.830	608,830	1,217,660	2,435,320
38	683.010	683,010	1,366,020	2,732,040
39	766.091	766,091	1,532,182	3,064,364
40	859.142	859,142	1,718,284	3,436,568

■ 14% A: How IRA Would Grow at Constant 14 Percent

Return *To estimate what any sum invested regularly at this return would grow to for any period of from 1 to 40 years, multiply that sum by the basic multiplier, which shows what $1 would grow to. The table assumes that each investment is made at the start of each year.*

Plan Years Completed	Basic Multiplier ($1)	$1,000	$2,000 (Single IRA Maximum)	$4,000
			Examples	
1	1.140	$ 1,140	$ 2,280	$ 4,560
2	2.439	2,439	4,878	9,756
3	3.921	3,921	7,842	15,684
4	5.610	5,610	11,220	22,440
5	7.535	7,535	15,070	30,140
6	9.730	9,730	19,460	38,920
7	12.232	12,232	24,464	48,928
8	15.085	15,085	30,170	60,340
9	18.337	18,337	36,647	73,348
10	22.044	22,044	44,088	88,176
11	26.270	26,270	52,540	105,080
12	31.088	31,088	62,176	124,352
13	36.581	36,581	73,162	146,324
14	42.842	42,842	85,684	171,368
15	49.980	49,980	99,960	199,920
16	58.117	58,117	116,234	232,468
17	67.394	67,394	134,788	269,576
18	77.969	77,969	155,938	311,876
19	90.024	90,024	180,048	360,096
20	103.768	103,768	207,536	415,072
21	119.435	119,435	238,870	477,740
22	137.297	137,297	274,594	549,188
23	157.658	157,658	315,316	630,632
24	180.870	180,870	361,740	723,480
25	207.332	207,332	414,664	829,328
26	237.499	237,499	474,998	949,996
27	271.889	271,889	543,778	1,087,556
28	311.093	311,093	622,186	1,244,372
29	355.786	355,786	711,572	1,423,144
30	406.737	406,737	813,474	1,626,948
31	464.820	464,820	929,640	1,859,280
32	531.035	531,035	1,062,070	2,124,140
33	606.519	606,519	1,213,038	2,426,076
34	692.572	692,572	1,385,144	2,770,288
35	790.672	790,672	1,581,344	3,162,688
36	902.507	902,507	1,805,014	3,610,028
37	1029.998	1,029,998	2,059,996	4,119,992
38	1175.337	1,175,337	2,350,675	4,701,348
39	1341.025	1,341,025	2,682,050	5,364,100
40	1529.908	1,529,908	3,059,816	6,119,632

■ 16% A: How IRA Would Grow at Constant 16 Percent

Return *To estimate what any sum invested regularly at this return would grow to for any period of from 1 to 40 years, multiply that sum by the basic multiplier, which shows what $1 would grow to. The table assumes that each investment is made at the start of each year.*

Plan Years Completed	Basic Multiplier ($1)	$1,000	$2,000 (Single IRA Maximum)	$4,000
			Examples	
1	1.160	$ 1,160	$ 2,320	$ 4,640
2	2.505	2,505	5,010	10,020
3	4.066	4,066	8,132	12,264
4	5.877	5,877	11,754	23,508
5	7.977	7,977	15,954	31,908
6	10.413	10,413	20,826	41,652
7	13.240	13,240	26,480	52,960
8	16.518	16,518	33,036	66,072
9	20.321	20,321	40,642	81,284
10	24.732	24,732	49,464	98,928
11	29.850	29,850	59,700	119,400
12	35.786	35,786	71,572	143,144
13	42.671	42,671	85,342	170,684
14	50.659	50,659	101,318	202,636
15	59.925	59,925	119,850	239,700
16	70.673	70,673	141,346	282,692
17	83.140	83,140	166,280	332,560
18	97.603	97,603	195,206	390,412
19	114.379	114,379	228,758	457,516
20	133.840	133,840	267,680	535,360
21	156.414	156,414	312,828	625,656
22	182.601	182,601	365,202	730,404
23	212.977	212,977	425,954	851,908
24	248.214	248,214	496,428	992,856
25	289.088	289,088	578,176	1,156,352
26	336.502	336,502	673,004	1,346,008
27	391.502	391,502	783,004	1,566,008
28	455.303	455,303	910,606	1,821,212
29	529.311	529,311	1,058,622	2,117,244
30	615.161	615,161	1,230,322	2,460,644
31	714.747	714,747	1,429,494	2,858,988
32	830.267	830,267	1,660,534	3,321,068
33	964.269	964,269	1,928,538	3,857,076
34	1119.712	1,119,712	2,239,434	4,478,848
35	1300.027	1,300,027	2,600,054	5,200,108
36	1509.191	1,509,191	3,018,382	6,036,764
37	1751.821	1,751,821	3,503,642	7,007,284
38	2033.273	2,033,273	4,066,546	8,133,092
39	2359.757	2,359,757	4,719,514	9,439,028
40	2638.478	2,638,478	5,276,956	10,553,912

■ 18% A: How IRA Would Grow at Constant 18 Percent

Return *To estimate what any sum invested regularly at this return would grow to for any period of from 1 to 40 years, multiply that sum by the basic multiplier, which shows what $1 would grow to. The table assumes that each investment is made at the start of each year.*

			Examples	
Plan Years Completed	Basic Multiplier ($1)	$1,000	$2,000 (Single IRA Maximum)	$4,000
1	1.180	$ 1,180	$ 2,360	$ 4,720
2	2.572	2,572	5,144	10,288
3	4.215	4,215	8,430	16,860
4	6.154	6,154	12,308	24,616
5	8.441	8,441	16,882	33,764
6	11.141	11,141	22,282	44,564
7	14.326	14,326	28,652	57,304
8	18.085	18,085	36,170	72,340
9	22.521	22,521	45,042	90,084
10	27.755	27,755	55,510	111,020
11	33.931	33,931	67,862	135,724
12	41.218	41,218	82,436	164,872
13	49.818	49,818	99,636	199,272
14	59.965	59,965	119,930	239,860
15	71.939	71,939	143,878	287,756
16	86.068	86,068	172,136	344,272
17	102.740	102,740	205,480	410,960
18	122.413	122,413	244,826	489,652
19	145.627	145,627	291,254	582,508
20	173.021	173,021	346,042	692,084
21	205.344	205,344	410,688	821,376
22	243.486	243,486	486,972	973,944
23	288.494	288,494	576,988	1,153,976
24	341.603	341,603	683,206	1,366,412
25	404.272	404,272	808,544	1,617,088
26	478.221	478,221	956,442	1,912,884
27	565.480	565,480	1,130,960	2,261,920
28	668.447	668,447	1,336,894	2,673,788
29	789.947	789,947	1,579,894	3,159,788
30	933.318	933,318	1,866,636	3,733,272
31	1102.495	1,102,495	2,204,990	4,409,980
32	1302.125	1,302,125	2,604,250	5,208,500
33	1537.687	1,537,687	3,075,374	6,150,748
34	1815.651	1,815,651	3,631,302	7,262,604
35	2143.648	2,143,648	4,287,296	8,574,592
36	2530.685	2,530,685	5,061,370	10,122,740
37	2987.389	2,987,389	5,974,778	11,949,556
38	3526.299	3,526,299	7,052,598	14,105,196
39	4162.213	4,162,213	8,324,426	16,648,852
40	4913.591	4,913,591	9,827,182	19,654,364

■ 20% A: How IRA Would Grow at Constant 20 Percent

Return *To estimate what any sum invested regularly at this return would grow to for any period of from 1 to 40 years, multiply that sum by the basic multiplier, which shows what $1 would grow to. The table assumes that each investment is made at the start of each year.*

			Examples	
Plan Years Completed	Basic Multiplier ($1)	$1,000	$2,000 (Single IRA Maximum)	$4,000
1	1.200	$ 1,200	$ 2,400	$ 4,800
2	2.640	2,640	5,280	10,560
3	4.368	4,368	8,736	17,472
4	6.441	6,441	12,882	25,764
5	8.929	8,929	17,858	35,716
6	11.915	11,915	23,830	47,660
7	15.499	15,499	30,998	61,996
8	19.798	19,798	35,596	79,192
9	24.958	24,958	49,916	99,832
10	31.150	31,150	62,300	124,600
11	38.580	38,580	77,160	154,320
12	47.496	47,496	94,992	189,984
13	58.195	58,195	116,390	232,780
14	71.035	71,035	142,070	284,140
15	86.442	86,442	172,884	345,768
16	104.930	104,930	209,860	419,720
17	127.116	127,116	254,232	508,464
18	153.739	153,739	307,478	614,956
19	185.687	185,687	371,374	742,748
20	224.025	224,025	448,050	896,100
21	270.030	270,030	540,060	1,080,120
22	325.236	325,236	650,472	1,300,944
23	391.484	391,484	782,968	1,565,936
24	470.981	470,981	941,962	1,883,924
25	566.377	566,377	1,132,754	2,265,508
26	680.852	680,852	1,361,704	2,723,408
27	818.223	818,223	1,636,446	3,272,892
28	983.067	983,067	1,966,134	3,932,268
29	1180.881	1,180,881	2,361,762	4,723,524
30	1418.257	1,418,257	2,836,514	5,673,028
31	1703.109	1,703,109	3,406,218	6,812,436
32	2044.931	2,044,931	4,089,862	8,179,724
33	2455.117	2,455,117	4,910,234	9,820,468
34	2947.341	2,947,341	5,894,682	11,789,364
35	3538.009	3,538,009	7,076,018	14,152,036
36	4246.811	4,246,811	8,493,622	16,987,244
37	5097.373	5,097,373	10,194,746	20,389,492
38	6118.048	6,118,048	12,236,096	24,472,192
39	7342.857	7,342,857	14,685,714	29,371,428
40	8812.629	8,812,629	17,625,258	35,250,516

■ B Tables: IRA Growth with No More Contributions IRA

growth at constant rates of return of 6 percent to 12 percent for basic $1 multiplier and for $1,000 if no more contributions are made.

To estimate what any sum would grow to at a constant rate of return if left untouched for from 1 to 40 years, multiply that sum by the basic multiplier, which is the growth of $1. (The table assumes that the original investment was made at the start of the first year.)

	6% B		8% B	
Plan Years Completed	Basic Multiplier ($1)	Example: $1,000	Basic Multiplier ($1)	Example: $1,000
1	1.060	$ 1,060	1.080	$ 1,080
2	1.123	1,123	1.166	1,166
3	1.191	1,191	1.259	1,259
4	1.262	1,262	1.360	1,360
5	1.338	1,338	1.469	1,469
6	1.418	1,418	1.586	1,586
7	1.503	1,503	1.713	1,713
8	1.593	1,593	1.850	1,850
9	1.689	1,689	1.999	1,999
10	1.790	1,790	2.158	2,158
11	1.898	1,898	2.331	2,331
12	2.012	2,012	2.518	2,518
13	2.132	2,132	2.719	2,719
14	2.260	2,260	2.937	2,937
15	2.396	2,396	3.172	3,172
16	2.540	2,540	3.425	3,425
17	2.692	2,692	3.700	3,700
18	2.854	2,854	3.996	3,996
19	3.025	3,025	4.315	4,315
20	3.207	3,207	4.660	4,660
21	3.399	3,399	5.033	5,033
22	3.603	3,603	5.436	5,436
23	3.819	3,819	5.871	5,871
24	4.048	4,048	6.341	6,341
25	4.291	4,291	6.848	6,848
26	4.549	4,549	7.396	7,396
27	4.822	4,822	7.988	7,988
28	5.111	5,111	8.627	8,627
29	5.418	5,418	9.317	9,317
30	5.743	5,743	10.062	10,062
31	6.088	6,088	10.867	10,867
32	6.453	6,453	11.737	11,737
33	6.840	6,840	12.676	12,676
34	7.251	7,251	13.690	13,690
35	7.686	7,686	14.785	14,785
36	8.147	8,147	15.968	15,968
37	8.636	8,636	17.245	17,245
38	9.154	9,154	18.625	18,625
39	9.703	9,703	20.115	20,115
40	10.285	10,285	21.724	21,724

■ B Tables (concluded)

Plan Years Completed	10% B Basic Multiplier ($1)	10% B Example: $1,000	12% B Basic Multiplier ($1)	12% B Example: $1,000
1	1.100	$ 1,100	1.120	$ 1,120
2	1.210	1,210	1.254	1,254
3	1.331	1,331	1.404	1,404
4	1.464	1,464	1.573	1,573
5	1.610	1,610	1.762	1,762
6	1.771	1,771	1.973	1,973
7	1.948	1,948	2.210	2,210
8	2.143	2,143	2.475	2,475
9	2.357	2,357	2.773	2,773
10	2.593	2,593	3.105	3,105
11	2.853	2,853	3.478	3,478
12	3.138	3,138	3.895	3,895
13	3.452	3,452	4.363	4,363
14	3.797	3,797	4.887	4,887
15	4.177	4,177	5.473	5,473
16	4.594	4,594	6.130	6,130
17	5.054	5,054	6.866	6,866
18	5.559	5,559	7.689	7,689
19	6.115	6,115	8.612	8,612
20	6.727	6,727	9.646	9,646
21	7.400	7,400	10.803	10,803
22	8.140	8,140	12.100	12,100
23	8.954	8,954	13.552	13,552
24	9.849	9,849	15.178	15,178
25	10.834	10,834	17.000	17,000
26	11.918	11,918	19.040	19,040
27	13.109	13,109	21.324	21,324
28	14.420	14,420	23.883	23,883
29	15.863	15,863	26.749	26,749
30	17.449	17,449	29.959	29,959
31	19.194	19,194	33.555	33,555
32	21.113	21,113	37.581	37,581
33	23.225	23,225	42.091	42,091
34	25.547	25,547	47.142	47,142
35	28.102	28,102	52.799	52,799
36	30.912	30,912	59.135	59,135
37	34.003	34,003	66.231	66,231
38	37.404	37,404	74.179	74,179
39	41.144	41,144	83.081	83,081
40	45.259	45,259	93.050	93,050

Appendix B:
IRS Life
Expectancy Tables

Following are the life expectancy tables to be used for calculating the minimum amounts that must be withdrawn from an IRA each year after mandatory distributions begin. The withdrawals must start by April 1 following the year in which you reach age 70½. Also, these are the tables IRA beneficiaries must use if they elect this method of distribution.

The first set of tables give the multiples for individuals; the second set, the joint multiples for the IRA owner and a designated beneficiary.

As explained in Chapter 11, to find the minimum amount that must be withdrawn each year to avoid a stiff IRS penalty, first find the appropriate multiple on the tables; then divide the money in the IRA at the start of the year by that multiple.

For instance, the multiple for a 71-year-old male who has designated a 65-year-old female as his beneficiary is 21.7. If there is $150,000 in the IRA at the start of the year, the minimum that would have to be withdrawn from the IRA by the end of the year to avoid a penalty would be $150,000 divided by 21.7, or $6,912.

A word of warning: At this writing, many questions related to the new mandatory distribution provisions (which as Chapter 11 explains permit the annual recalculation of life expectancies under many circumstances) remain to be answered by the IRS.

In addition, a 1985 technical corrections bill specifically states, for the first time, that distributions from IRAs are subject to what the IRS calls the "incidental death benefit rules." In effect, if the designated beneficiary is not the spouse of the IRA's owner, these rules place some constraints on how long payments can be stretched out if the beneficiary is substantially younger than the owner of the IRA. The rules require that the projected benefits payable to a beneficiary be *incidental* to distributions projected to be made to the account owner during his or her lifetime.

If all this sounds very complicated, it certainly is. IRS Revenue Ruling 72–241 (1972–1 C.B.108) states that one is within safe bounds if the "present value" of the projected lifetime payments to the IRA owner exceed 50 percent of the present value of the total payments to be made to the account owner and his or her beneficiaries. To make the calculations of present value, you would need the services of an actuary who specializes in this kind of work.

Moreover, professional tax practitioners are not in agreement on how to apply this complex rule in any single situation. There is a need for the IRS to clarify by specific language and examples how to precisely comply with this rule.

Consequently, competent professional advice is required if your designated beneficiary is much younger than you are or if your spouse and you wish a long payout period. Even though you make the calculation based on a multiple in the following tables, you could be subject to a stiff IRS penalty if you run afoul of the incidental death benefit rules.

ACTUARIAL TABLES

Table 1 (One Life) applies to all ages. The remaining tables apply to males age 35 to 90 and females age 40 to 95.

TABLE 1 ■ Ordinary Life Annuities—One Life—Expected Return Multiples

Ages Male	Ages Female	Multiples	Ages Male	Ages Female	Multiples	Ages Male	Ages Female	Multiples
6	11	65.0	41	46	33.0	76	81	9.1
7	12	64.1	42	47	32.1	77	82	8.7
8	13	63.2	43	48	31.2	78	83	8.3
9	14	62.3	44	49	30.4	79	84	7.8
10	15	61.4	45	50	29.6	80	85	7.5
11	16	60.4	46	51	28.7	81	86	7.1
12	17	59.5	47	52	27.9	82	87	6.7
13	18	58.6	48	53	27.1	83	88	6.3
14	19	57.7	49	54	26.3	84	89	6.0
15	20	56.7	50	55	25.5	85	90	5.7
16	21	55.8	51	56	24.7	86	91	5.4
17	22	54.9	52	57	24.0	87	92	5.1
18	23	53.9	53	58	23.2	88	93	4.8

TABLE 1 ■ (concluded)

Ages			Ages			Ages		
Male	Female	Multiples	Male	Female	Multiples	Male	Female	Multiples
19	24	53.0	54	59	22.4	89	94	4.5
20	25	52.1	55	60	21.7	90	95	4.2
21	26	51.1	56	61	21.0	91	96	4.0
22	27	50.2	57	62	20.3	92	97	3.7
23	28	49.3	58	63	19.6	93	98	3.5
24	29	48.3	59	64	18.9	94	99	3.3
25	30	47.4	60	65	18.2	95	100	3.1
26	31	46.5	61	66	17.5	96	101	2.9
27	32	45.6	62	67	16.9	97	102	2.7
28	33	44.6	63	68	16.2	98	103	2.5
29	34	43.7	64	69	15.6	99	104	2.3
30	35	42.8	65	70	15.0	100	105	2.1
31	36	41.9	66	71	14.4	101	106	1.9
32	37	41.0	67	72	13.8	102	107	1.7
33	38	40.0	68	73	13.2	103	108	1.5
34	39	39.1	69	74	12.6	104	109	1.3
35	40	38.2	70	75	12.1	105	110	1.2
36	41	37.3	71	76	11.6	106	111	1.0
37	42	36.5	72	77	11.0	107	112	.8
38	43	35.6	73	78	10.5	108	113	.7
39	44	34.7	74	79	10.1	109	114	.6
40	45	33.8	75	80	9.6	110	115	.5
						111	116	0

TABLE 2 ■ **Ordinary Joint Life and Last Survivor Annuities—Two Lives—Expected Return Multiples**

Ages												
Male	35	36	37	38	39	40	41	42	43	44	45	46	47
Female	40	41	42	43	44	45	46	47	48	49	50	51	52

Male	Female	35/40	36/41	37/42	38/43	39/44	40/45	41/46	42/47	43/48	44/49	45/50	46/51	47/52
35	40	46.2	45.7	45.3	44.8	44.4	44.0	43.6	43.3	43.0	42.6	42.3	42.0	41.8
36	41	45.7	45.2	44.8	44.3	43.9	43.5	43.1	42.7	42.3	42.0	41.7	41.4	41.1
37	42	45.3	44.8	44.3	43.8	43.4	42.9	42.5	42.1	41.8	41.4	41.1	40.7	40.4
38	43	44.8	44.3	43.8	43.3	42.9	42.4	42.0	41.6	41.2	40.8	40.5	40.1	39.8
39	44	44.4	43.9	43.4	42.9	42.4	41.9	41.5	41.0	40.6	40.2	39.9	39.5	39.2
40	45	44.0	43.5	42.9	42.4	41.9	41.4	41.0	40.5	40.1	39.7	39.3	38.9	38.6
41	46	43.6	43.1	42.5	42.0	41.5	41.0	40.5	40.0	39.6	39.2	38.8	38.4	38.0
42	47	43.3	42.7	42.1	41.6	41.0	40.5	40.0	39.6	39.1	38.7	38.2	37.8	37.5
43	48	43.0	42.3	41.8	41.2	40.6	40.1	39.6	39.1	38.6	38.2	37.7	37.3	36.9
44	49	42.6	42.0	41.4	40.8	40.2	39.7	39.2	38.7	38.2	37.7	37.2	36.8	36.4
45	50	42.3	41.7	41.1	40.5	39.9	39.3	38.8	38.2	37.7	37.2	36.8	36.3	35.9
46	51	42.0	41.4	40.7	40.1	39.5	38.9	38.4	37.8	37.3	36.8	36.3	35.9	35.4
47	52	41.8	41.1	40.4	39.8	39.2	38.6	38.0	37.5	36.9	36.4	35.9	35.4	35.0

TABLE 2 ■ (continued)

	Ages Male												
	48	49	50	51	52	53	54	55	56	57	58	59	60
Male \ Female	53	54	55	56	57	58	59	60	61	62	63	64	65
35 / 40	41.5	41.3	41.0	40.8	40.6	40.4	40.3	40.1	40.0	39.8	39.7	39.6	39.5
36 / 41	40.8	40.6	40.3	40.1	39.9	39.7	39.5	39.3	39.2	39.0	38.9	38.8	38.6
37 / 42	40.2	39.9	39.6	39.4	39.2	39.0	38.8	38.6	38.4	38.3	38.1	38.0	37.9
38 / 43	39.5	39.2	39.0	38.7	38.5	38.3	38.1	37.9	37.7	37.5	37.3	37.2	37.1
39 / 44	38.9	38.6	38.3	38.0	37.8	37.6	37.3	37.1	36.9	36.8	36.6	36.4	36.3
40 / 45	38.3	38.0	37.7	37.4	37.1	36.9	36.6	36.4	36.2	36.0	35.9	35.7	35.5
41 / 46	37.7	37.3	37.0	36.7	36.5	36.2	36.0	35.7	35.5	35.3	35.1	35.0	34.8
42 / 47	37.1	36.8	36.4	36.1	35.8	35.6	35.3	35.1	34.8	34.6	34.4	34.2	34.1
43 / 48	36.5	36.2	35.8	35.5	35.2	34.9	34.7	34.4	34.2	33.9	33.7	33.5	33.3
44 / 49	36.0	35.6	35.3	34.9	34.6	34.3	34.0	33.8	33.5	33.3	33.0	32.8	32.6
45 / 50	35.5	35.1	34.7	34.4	34.0	33.7	33.4	33.1	32.9	32.6	32.4	32.2	31.9
46 / 51	35.0	34.6	34.2	33.8	33.5	33.1	32.8	32.5	32.2	32.0	31.7	31.5	31.3
47 / 52	34.5	34.1	33.7	33.3	32.9	32.6	32.2	31.9	31.6	31.4	31.1	30.9	30.6
48 / 53	34.0	33.6	33.2	32.8	32.4	32.0	31.7	31.4	31.1	30.8	30.5	30.2	30.0
49 / 54	33.6	33.1	32.7	32.3	31.9	31.5	31.2	30.8	30.5	30.2	29.9	29.6	29.4
50 / 55	33.2	32.7	32.3	31.8	31.4	31.0	30.6	30.3	29.9	29.6	29.3	29.0	28.8
51 / 56	32.8	32.3	31.8	31.4	30.9	30.5	30.1	29.8	29.4	29.1	28.8	28.5	28.2
52 / 57	32.4	31.9	31.4	30.9	30.5	30.1	29.7	29.3	28.9	28.6	28.2	27.9	27.6
53 / 58	32.0	31.5	31.0	30.5	30.1	29.6	29.2	28.8	28.4	28.1	27.7	27.4	27.1
54 / 59	31.7	31.2	30.6	30.1	29.7	29.2	28.8	28.3	27.9	27.6	27.2	26.9	26.5
55 / 60	31.4	30.8	30.3	29.8	29.3	28.8	28.3	27.9	27.5	27.1	26.7	26.4	26.0
56 / 61	31.1	30.5	29.9	29.4	28.9	28.4	27.9	27.5	27.1	26.7	26.3	25.9	25.5
57 / 62	30.8	30.2	29.6	29.1	28.6	28.1	27.6	27.1	26.7	26.2	25.8	25.4	25.1
58 / 63	30.5	29.9	29.3	28.8	28.2	27.7	27.2	26.7	26.3	25.8	25.4	25.0	24.8
59 / 64	30.2	29.6	29.0	28.5	27.9	27.4	26.9	26.4	25.9	25.4	25.0	24.6	24.2
60 / 65	30.0	29.4	28.8	28.2	27.6	27.1	26.5	26.0	25.5	25.1	24.6	24.2	23.8

Male	Female	Male 73 / Female 78	72 / 77	71 / 76	70 / 75	69 / 74	68 / 73	67 / 72	66 / 71	65 / 70	64 / 69	63 / 68	62 / 67	61 / 66
35	40	38.6	38.6	38.7	38.7	38.8	38.8	38.9	38.9	39.0	39.1	39.2	39.3	39.4
36	41	37.7	37.8	37.8	37.9	37.9	38.0	38.0	38.1	38.2	38.2	38.3	38.4	38.5
37	42	36.9	36.9	36.9	37.0	37.1	37.1	37.2	37.3	37.3	37.4	37.5	37.6	37.7
38	43	36.0	36.0	36.1	36.2	36.2	36.3	36.4	36.4	36.5	36.6	36.7	36.8	36.9
39	44	35.2	35.2	35.3	35.3	35.4	35.5	35.5	35.6	35.7	35.8	35.9	36.0	36.2
40	45	34.3	34.4	34.4	34.5	34.6	34.6	34.7	34.8	34.9	35.0	35.1	35.3	35.4
41	46	33.5	33.5	33.6	33.7	33.8	33.8	33.9	34.0	34.1	34.2	34.4	34.5	34.6
42	47	32.7	32.7	32.8	32.9	33.0	33.0	33.1	33.2	33.4	33.5	33.6	33.7	33.9
43	48	31.9	31.9	32.0	32.1	32.2	32.3	32.4	32.5	32.6	32.7	32.9	33.0	33.2
44	49	31.1	31.1	31.2	31.3	31.4	31.5	31.6	31.7	31.8	32.0	32.1	32.3	32.5
45	50	30.3	30.4	30.4	30.5	30.6	30.7	30.8	31.0	31.1	31.3	31.4	31.6	31.8
46	51	29.5	29.6	29.7	29.8	29.9	30.0	30.1	30.2	30.4	30.5	30.7	30.9	31.1
47	52	28.7	28.8	28.9	29.0	29.1	29.3	29.4	29.5	29.7	29.8	30.0	30.2	30.4
48	53	28.0	28.1	28.2	28.3	28.4	28.5	28.7	28.8	29.0	29.2	29.3	29.5	29.8
49	54	27.3	27.4	27.5	27.6	27.7	27.8	28.0	28.1	28.3	28.5	28.7	28.9	29.1
50	55	26.5	26.6	26.7	26.9	27.0	27.1	27.3	27.5	27.6	27.8	28.1	28.3	28.5
51	56	25.8	25.9	26.0	26.2	26.3	26.5	26.6	26.8	27.0	27.2	27.4	27.7	27.9
52	57	25.1	25.2	25.4	25.5	25.7	25.8	26.0	26.2	26.4	26.6	26.8	27.1	27.3
53	58	24.4	24.6	24.7	24.8	25.0	25.2	25.4	25.6	25.8	26.0	26.2	26.5	26.8
54	59	23.8	23.9	24.0	24.2	24.4	24.6	24.7	25.0	25.2	25.4	25.7	25.9	26.2
55	60	23.1	23.3	23.4	23.6	23.8	23.9	24.1	24.4	24.6	24.9	25.1	25.4	25.7
56	61	22.5	22.6	22.8	23.0	23.2	23.4	23.6	23.8	24.1	24.3	24.6	24.9	25.2
57	62	21.9	22.0	22.2	22.4	22.6	22.8	23.0	23.3	23.5	23.8	24.1	24.4	24.7
58	63	21.3	21.4	21.6	21.8	22.0	22.2	22.5	22.7	23.0	23.3	23.6	23.9	24.3
59	64	20.7	20.9	21.0	21.2	21.5	21.7	21.9	22.2	22.5	22.8	23.1	23.5	23.8
60	65	20.1	20.3	20.5	20.7	20.9	21.2	21.4	21.7	22.0	22.3	22.7	23.0	23.4

TABLE 2 ■ (continued)

Ages			Male 61 / 66	62 / 67	63 / 68	64 / 69	65 / 70	66 / 71	67 / 72	68 / 73	69 / 74	70 / 75	71 / 76	72 / 77	73 / 78
Male	Female	Male													
66	66	61	23.0	22.6	22.2	21.9	21.6	21.3	21.0	20.7	20.4	20.2	20.0	19.8	19.6
67	67	62	22.6	22.2	21.8	21.5	21.1	20.8	20.5	20.2	19.9	19.7	19.5	19.2	19.0
68	68	63	22.2	21.8	21.4	21.1	20.7	20.4	20.1	19.8	19.5	19.2	19.0	18.7	18.5
69	69	64	21.9	21.5	21.1	20.7	20.3	20.0	19.6	19.3	19.0	18.7	18.5	18.2	18.0
70	70	65	21.6	21.1	20.7	20.3	19.9	19.6	19.2	18.9	18.6	18.3	18.0	17.8	17.5
71	71	66	21.3	20.8	20.4	20.0	19.6	19.2	18.8	18.5	18.2	17.9	17.6	17.3	17.1
72	72	67	21.0	20.5	20.1	19.6	19.2	18.8	18.5	18.1	17.8	17.5	17.2	16.9	16.7
73	73	68	20.7	20.2	19.8	19.3	18.9	18.5	18.1	17.8	17.4	17.1	16.8	16.5	16.2
74	74	69	20.4	19.9	19.5	19.0	18.6	18.2	17.8	17.4	17.4	16.7	16.4	16.1	15.8
75	75	70	20.2	19.7	19.2	18.7	18.3	17.9	17.5	17.1	16.7	16.4	16.1	15.8	15.5
76	76	71	20.0	19.5	19.0	18.5	18.0	17.6	17.2	16.8	16.4	16.1	15.7	15.4	15.1
77	77	72	19.8	19.2	18.7	18.2	17.8	17.3	16.9	16.5	16.1	15.8	15.4	15.1	14.8
78	78	73	19.6	19.0	18.5	18.0	17.5	17.1	16.7	16.2	15.8	15.5	15.1	14.8	14.4

Ages

		Male →	74	75	76	77	78	79	80	81	82	83	84	85
Male	**Female**	Female →	79	80	81	82	83	84	85	86	87	88	89	90
35	40		38.6	38.5	38.5	38.5	38.4	38.4	38.4	38.4	38.4	38.4	38.3	38.3
36	41		37.7	37.6	37.6	37.6	37.6	37.5	37.5	37.5	37.5	37.5	37.5	37.4
37	42		36.8	36.8	36.7	36.7	36.7	36.7	36.6	36.6	36.6	36.6	36.6	36.6
38	43		36.0	35.9	35.9	35.9	35.8	35.8	35.8	35.8	35.7	35.7	35.7	35.7
39	44		35.1	35.1	35.0	35.0	35.0	34.9	34.9	34.9	34.9	34.8	34.8	34.8
40	45		34.3	34.2	34.2	34.1	34.1	34.1	34.1	34.0	34.0	34.0	34.0	34.0
41	46		33.4	33.4	33.3	33.3	33.3	33.2	33.2	33.2	33.2	33.1	33.1	33.1
42	47		32.6	32.6	32.5	32.5	32.4	32.4	32.4	32.3	32.3	32.3	32.3	32.3
43	48		31.8	31.8	31.7	31.7	31.6	31.6	31.5	31.5	31.5	31.5	31.4	31.4
44	49		31.0	30.9	30.9	30.8	30.8	30.8	30.7	30.7	30.7	30.6	30.6	30.6
45	50		30.2	30.1	30.1	30.0	30.0	29.9	29.9	29.9	29.8	29.8	29.8	29.8
46	51		29.4	29.4	29.3	29.2	29.2	29.2	29.1	29.1	29.0	29.0	29.0	28.9
47	52		28.7	28.6	28.5	28.5	28.4	28.4	28.3	28.3	28.2	28.2	28.2	28.1
48	53		27.9	27.8	27.8	27.7	27.6	27.6	27.5	27.5	27.5	27.4	27.4	27.4
49	54		27.2	27.1	27.0	26.9	26.9	26.8	26.8	26.7	26.7	26.6	26.6	26.6
50	55		26.4	26.3	26.3	26.2	26.1	26.1	26.0	26.0	25.9	25.9	25.8	25.8
51	56		25.7	25.6	25.5	25.5	25.4	25.3	25.3	25.2	25.2	25.1	25.1	25.0
52	57		25.0	24.9	24.8	24.7	24.7	24.6	24.5	24.5	24.4	24.4	24.3	24.3
53	58		24.3	24.2	24.1	24.0	23.9	23.9	23.8	23.7	23.7	23.6	23.6	23.5
54	59		23.6	23.5	23.4	23.3	23.2	23.2	23.1	23.0	23.0	22.9	22.9	22.8
55	60		23.0	22.9	22.8	22.7	22.6	22.5	22.4	22.3	22.3	22.2	22.2	22.1
56	61		22.3	22.2	22.1	22.0	21.9	21.8	21.7	21.6	21.6	21.5	21.5	21.4
57	62		21.7	21.6	21.5	21.3	21.2	21.1	21.1	21.0	20.9	20.8	20.8	20.7
58	63		21.1	21.0	20.8	20.7	20.6	20.5	20.4	20.3	20.2	20.2	20.1	20.0
59	64		20.5	20.4	20.2	20.1	20.0	19.9	19.8	19.7	19.6	19.5	19.4	19.4
60	65		19.9	19.8	19.6	19.5	19.4	19.3	19.1	19.0	19.0	18.9	18.8	18.7

TABLE 2 ■ (continued)

	Ages											
	Male	74	75	76	77	78	79	80	81	82	83	84	85
	Female	79	80	81	82	83	84	85	86	87	88	89	90
Male	Female												
61	66	19.4	19.2	19.1	18.9	18.8	18.7	18.5	18.4	18.3	18.3	18.2	18.1
62	67	18.8	18.7	18.5	18.3	18.2	18.1	18.0	17.8	17.7	17.7	17.6	17.5
63	68	18.3	18.1	18.0	17.8	17.6	17.5	17.4	17.3	17.2	17.1	17.0	16.9
64	69	17.8	17.6	17.4	17.3	17.1	17.0	16.8	16.7	16.6	16.5	16.4	16.3
65	70	17.3	17.1	16.9	16.7	16.6	16.4	16.3	16.2	16.0	15.9	15.8	15.8
66	71	16.9	16.6	16.4	16.3	16.1	15.9	15.8	15.6	15.5	15.4	15.3	15.2
67	72	16.4	16.2	16.0	15.8	15.6	15.4	15.3	15.1	15.0	14.9	14.8	14.7
68	73	16.0	15.7	15.5	15.3	15.1	15.0	14.8	14.6	14.5	14.4	14.3	14.2
69	74	15.6	15.3	15.1	14.9	14.7	14.5	14.3	14.2	14.0	13.9	13.8	13.7
70	75	15.2	14.9	14.7	14.5	14.3	14.1	13.9	13.7	13.6	13.4	13.3	13.2
71	76	14.8	14.5	14.3	14.1	13.8	13.6	13.5	13.3	13.1	13.0	12.8	12.7
72	77	14.5	14.2	13.9	13.7	13.5	13.2	13.0	12.9	12.7	12.5	12.4	12.3
73	78	14.1	13.8	13.6	13.3	13.1	12.9	12.7	12.5	12.3	12.1	12.0	11.8
74	79	13.8	13.5	13.2	13.0	12.7	12.5	12.3	12.1	11.9	11.7	11.6	11.4
75	80	13.5	13.2	12.9	12.6	12.4	12.2	11.9	11.7	11.5	11.4	11.2	11.0
76	81	13.2	12.9	12.6	12.3	12.1	11.8	11.6	11.4	11.2	11.0	10.8	10.7
77	82	13.0	12.6	12.3	12.1	11.8	11.5	11.3	11.1	10.8	10.7	10.5	10.3
78	83	12.7	12.4	12.1	11.8	11.5	11.2	11.0	10.7	10.5	10.3	10.1	10.0
79	84	12.5	12.2	11.8	11.5	11.2	11.0	10.7	10.5	10.2	10.0	9.8	9.6
80	85	12.3	11.9	11.6	11.3	11.0	10.7	10.4	10.2	10.0	9.7	9.5	9.3
81	86	12.1	11.7	11.4	11.1	10.7	10.5	10.2	9.9	9.7	9.5	9.3	9.1
82	87	11.9	11.5	11.2	10.8	10.5	10.2	10.0	9.7	9.4	9.2	9.0	8.8
83	88	11.7	11.4	11.0	10.7	10.3	10.0	9.7	9.5	9.2	9.0	8.7	8.5
84	89	11.6	11.2	10.8	10.5	10.0	9.8	9.5	9.3	9.0	8.7	8.5	8.3
85	90	11.4	11.0	10.7	10.3	10.0	9.6	9.3	9.1	8.8	8.5	8.3	8.1

| Ages | | 86 | 87 | 88 | 89 | 90 |
Male	Female	91	92	93	94	95
35	40	38.3	38.3	38.3	38.3	38.3
36	41	37.4	37.4	37.4	37.4	37.4
37	42	36.5	36.5	36.5	36.5	36.5
38	43	35.7	35.7	35.6	35.6	35.6
39	44	34.8	34.8	34.8	34.8	34.8
40	45	33.9	33.9	33.9	33.9	33.9
41	46	33.1	33.1	33.1	33.0	33.0
42	47	32.2	32.2	32.2	32.2	32.2
43	48	31.4	31.4	31.4	31.3	31.3
44	49	30.6	30.5	30.5	30.5	30.5
45	50	29.7	29.7	29.7	29.7	29.7
46	51	28.9	28.9	28.9	28.9	28.9
47	52	28.1	28.1	28.1	28.1	28.0
48	53	27.3	27.3	27.3	27.3	27.2
49	54	26.5	26.5	26.5	26.5	26.5
50	55	25.8	25.7	25.7	25.7	25.7
51	56	25.0	25.0	24.9	24.9	24.9
52	57	24.3	24.2	24.2	24.2	24.1
53	58	23.5	23.5	23.4	23.4	23.4
54	59	22.8	22.7	22.7	22.7	22.7
55	60	22.1	22.0	22.0	22.0	21.9
56	61	21.4	21.3	21.3	21.3	21.2
57	62	20.7	20.6	20.6	20.6	20.5
58	63	20.0	19.9	19.9	19.9	19.8
59	64	19.3	19.3	19.2	19.2	19.2
60	65	18.7	18.6	18.6	18.5	18.5

TABLE 2 ■ *(continued)*

Ages						
Male	Male	86	87	88	89	90
Male	Female	91	92	93	94	95
61	66	18.1	18.0	17.9	17.9	17.9
62	67	17.4	17.4	17.3	17.3	17.2
63	68	16.8	16.8	16.7	16.7	16.6
64	69	16.2	16.2	16.1	16.1	16.0
65	70	15.7	15.6	15.5	15.5	15.4
66	71	15.1	15.0	15.0	14.9	14.8
67	72	14.6	14.5	14.4	14.4	14.3
68	73	14.1	14.0	13.9	13.8	13.8
69	74	13.6	13.5	13.4	13.3	13.2
70	75	13.1	13.0	12.9	12.8	12.7
71	76	12.6	12.5	12.4	12.3	12.2
72	77	12.1	12.0	11.9	11.8	11.8
73	78	11.7	11.6	11.5	11.4	11.3
74	79	11.3	11.2	11.1	11.0	10.9
75	80	10.9	10.8	10.7	10.5	10.5
76	81	10.5	10.4	10.3	10.2	10.1
77	82	10.2	10.0	9.9	9.8	9.7
78	83	9.8	9.7	9.5	9.4	9.3
79	84	9.5	9.3	9.2	9.1	8.9
80	85	9.2	9.0	8.9	8.7	8.6

TABLE 2 ■ *(concluded)*

Ages						
Male	Male	86	87	88	89	90
Male	Female	91	92	93	94	95
81	86	8.9	8.7	8.6	8.4	8.3
82	87	8.6	8.4	8.3	8.1	8.0
83	88	8.3	8.2	8.0	7.9	7.7
84	89	8.1	7.9	7.8	7.6	7.5
85	90	7.9	7.7	7.5	7.4	7.2
86	91	7.7	7.5	7.3	7.1	7.0
87	92	7.5	7.3	7.1	6.9	6.8
88	93	7.3	7.1	6.9	6.7	6.6
89	94	7.1	6.9	6.7	6.5	6.4
90	95	7.0	6.8	6.6	6.4	6.2

Index